Religion:
A Preface

SECOND EDITION

John F. Wilson
PEPPERDINE UNIVERSITY
W. Royce Clark
PEPPERDINE UNIVERSITY

90 -731

PRENTICE HALL, Englewood Cliffs, New Jersey 07632

LIBRARY OF CONGRESS
Library of Congress Cataloging-in-Publication Data

Wilson, John Francis.
  Religion : a preface / John Francis Wilson, W. Royce Clark. -- 2nd
ed.
      p.   cm.
  Includes bibliographical references and index.
  ISBN 0-13-771957-4
  1. Religion. 2. Religions. I. Clark, W. Royce. II. Title.
BL48.W494 1989
200--dc19   88-15602

> ## TO MY PARENTS
>
> Who were my own Preface to Religion

Biblical quotes are from the Revised Standard Version of the Bible, Copyright © 1946, 1952, 1971, 1973.
Quotations from *The Dhammapada*, translated from the Pali by P. Lal. Copyright © 1967 by P. Lal. Reprinted by permission of Farrar, Straus & Giroux, Inc.

Production supervision: Merrill Peterson
Cover design: Baldino Design
Manufacturing buyer: Peter Havens

© 1989, 1982 by Prentice-Hall, Inc.
A Division of Simon & Schuster
Englewood Cliffs, New Jersey 07632

Printed in the United States of America

10 9 8 7 6 5 4 3 2 1

ISBN 0-13-771957-4

Prentice-Hall International (UK) Limited, *London*
Prentice-Hall of Australia Pty. Limited, *Sydney*
Prentice-Hall Canada Inc., *Toronto*
Prentice-Hall Hispanoamericana, S.A., *Mexico*
Prentice-Hall of India Private Limited, *New Delhi*
Prentice-Hall of Japan, Inc., *Tokyo*
Simon & Schuster Asia Pte. Ltd., *Singapore*
Editora Prentice-Hall do Brasil, Ltda., *Rio de Janeiro*

Contents

Preface
to the First Edition

The ancient Hebrew Scriptures tell the story of Uzzah, who reached out and touched the sacred ark containing stone tablets inscribed with the Ten Commandments. Uzzah dropped dead. Not for any wickedness, mind you, but simply because he got too close to the Divine. Perhaps in the attempt to avoid repeating Uzzah's unfortunate mistake, some people have tended to cut a wide and respectful swath around religion. Others have felt that venturing too close to the sacred is folly, not because some mysterious wrath may consume them, but because up close the mystery would disappear like a highway mirage and leave them faithless and alone on the earth. Better, they opine, to remain in ignorance than to risk an unveiling of the Other and discover only emptiness.

This book is written for the rest of us—we who cannot help ourselves and despite the danger are drawn to the subject of religion like moths to streetlights, fluttering eagerly among the mysteries with an insatiable combination of expectation, fascination, and dread.

The book has modest goals. It is, after all, only a *preface* to the study of religion. It does not presume to provide more than a place to begin. If it is used as a text, it is an unpresumptuous one that must be supplemented with much additional reading, especially of primary religious documents, and with skilled lectures and discussion. If it is read by those who have set off on an individual search—intellectual or spiritual—or those who merely wish to see how religion fits into their own world of art or science or philosophy or auto mechanics, then such people can expect only a quick trip designed to help them get the lay of the territory—like a ten-minute helicopter ride over Disneyland.

Some will no doubt complain that the trip was unsatisfying or even unpleasant, that we were wanting in intellectual depth or even that we lacked proper piety. Others will find offense when they detect the author's bias peeking up here and there—as though anyone ever said much about religion and at the same time remained objective with any degree of purity. Sometimes complicated things will be made to seem too simple when the author's desire to communicate ran away with him.

Despite all this we have plunged ahead, guided by the principle and the hope that this book will help those who are merely beginning their journey and who should not be told more than they want to know. The direction this book takes was forged on the anvil of day-to-day classroom contact and private discussions with young adults. It is not the result of erudite discussions with fellow scholars—who will undoubtedly learn nothing by reading it.

The motif that ties the diverse subjects in the book together is religion and human culture. Or, to transpose the same thing into a question, "What has the human race *done* with religion?" Most of the classic academic categories are here somewhere (the philosophy of religion, the psychology of religion, comparative religions, Biblical studies, the sociology of religion, and so on). But because most beginners care little for the pigeonholes scholars use to organize themselves, not a great deal will be made of them.

The reader will probably be a product of Western culture, and the book's plan has such a reader in mind. It will alternately try to help that reader dig deeper into what is very close and familiar to him or her and then carry him or her as far afield as possible. Perhaps the reader will develop a taste for depth and breadth and want to go much farther than this book will take him or her. I certainly hope so.

Thanks are due to Dr. Gerrit tenZythoff for his consistent encouragement; JoAnne Brown, Kristin Engdahl, and Kristine Spurgeon for technical assistance; Dr. John B. Magee, for *Religion and Modern Man*, a book that blazes a trail and sets the standards for introductions to the study of religion and that provides much of the foundation for Chapters Two, Three, Nine, and Eleven of the present work; my friends and colleagues in the university and my family for providing the milieu in which books can grow; and the thousands of students whose facial expressions have said to me either "Please explain that one more time" or "Oh, now I see!"

JOHN F. WILSON
Pepperdine University

Preface
to the Second Edition

Response to *Religion: A Preface* has been gratifying. This second edition reflects suggestions from students and professors who have used the book. I am grateful to Fred Jappe of San Diego Mesa College and Fred Keck of Mercyhurst College who have provided helpful suggestions. The revision has been undertaken by Dr. W. Royce Clark whose careful and thoughtful contributions have sharpened and enhanced the work in numerous ways. I know the reader will share in my gratitude to him.

JOHN F. WILSON
Pepperdine University

1

Religion and Education

THE PLACE OF RELIGIOUS STUDIES

The universities have come to accept religious studies. More than 60 percent of the "secular" universities in the United States offer courses dealing with specifically religious questions. One might ask, "How can this be?" Is that not the responsibility of the churches rather than institutions of higher learning? What has religion to do with getting an education? Has not the Supreme Court banned religion in the schools?

Certainly the Court has found unconstitutional various state laws which mandated religious practices such as worship or the presence of religious symbols in the public classrooms. Religious indoctrination is of course illegal. But the Court has never settled the issue of whether an objective study of religion in public higher education is constitutional. In spite of this, after the famous Abington School Dist. v. Schempp, 374 U.S. 203 (1963), numerous state universities commenced religious studies programs on the assumption that the license had been granted. Only time will tell whether this interpretation was justified.

In any case, the Supreme Court has persistently underscored the importance of the inculcation of democratic values by public schools. In the degree to which these values involve mutual understanding and appreciation, tolerance, and morality, religious studies may play a vital role. In fact, there are quite a number of reasons why religious studies should be a part of one's education.[1]

Recent Revival of Religious Interest

Religions have acted in history much like camp fires. At times they recede and seem to have grown cold and dead. Then they suddenly flash into flame again, fed by a live coal here or there, hidden among the ashes. Then, after burning brightly a while, the flame is smothered in smoke and disappears once again.

This phenomenon can be seen in the history of the United States, which seems to experience sweeping revivals of religious interest every second or third generation, followed by a return to a more materialistic and secular way of thinking.

At this time we seem to be in a "hot" period. Religious movements are very much a part of the current scene. They are very visible. They include old forms revitalized and new forms flaming for the first time.

The United States is not the only place where this is true. Postwar Japan, for example, has seen a host of aggressive "new" religions (many having roots in older religious forms) arise. One of the most striking examples is Soka Gakkai, which has made millions of converts, including many Americans, and which, through its political activities, has become a significant force in Japanese life.[2]

In the United States, interest in the occult is another kind of flaming of fire in the ashes. Books about reincarnation, spirits, and the possibility of reaching beyond death, or of reaching people in the other world, sell by the millions. Astrology is a multimillion-dollar business. It dates its origin to thousands of years before the rise of science. Its world view is nonscientific, even antiscientific, yet millions of people are guided in their daily lives by their horoscope "readings."

On the streets of Dallas, Texas, one hears the tinkling of bells and the chant,

> Hare Krsna, Hare Krsna, Krsna Krsna, Hare, Hare
> Hare Rama, Hare Rama, Rama Rama, Hare, Hare.

There they stand, earnest, robe clad, their pale white shaved heads with a single tassel of hair remaining, their wives with children-on-hips, calling to passersby to accept the peace of Krishna. Dallas, Texas!

The Astrodome in Houston appeared to be an immense oriental tem-

---

[1]In this section, as elsewhere throughout this book, the work of John B. Magee, *Religion and Modern Man: A Study of the Religious Meaning of Being Human* (New York: Harper & Row, 1967) has been enormously helpful.

[2]See H. Byron Earhart, *Japanese Religion: Unity and Diversity*, 2nd ed. (Encino, Calif.: Dickenson, 1974), Part III, for a survey of the Japanese new religions.

ple when the teenaged Guru Maharaj Ji introduced his Divine Light Mission to thousands of young WASPS, crying out

Boyle Shri, Sat Gurudev, Maharaj KI JAI!
Boyle Shri, Sat Gurudev, Maharaj KI JAI!

At Madison Square Garden the Korean messiah figure Sun Moon has brought to the multitudes the new age and a new faith.

On Johnny Carson's *Tonight* show, the serene face of the Mahareshi Mahesh Yogi flickers on the screen, expounding the virtues of transcendental meditation.

How many religious personalities of our nation have made the front page in the 1980s, for better or worse! We heard of the Reverend Sun Moon's mass weddings—but also of his conviction for income tax evasion. Then there was Bhagwan Shree Rajneesh's prolonged silence, his Rolls Royce collection, and the debacle of the dissolution of his Oregon community when he returned to India. Oral Roberts' prayer tower and his alleged direct mandate from God to raise money or die found its way into cartoons for weeks, followed by a series of disclosures of sex scandals involving several of the more conservative television evangelists.

Meanwhile Andrew Greeley, Shirley MacLaine, and numerous others find their products on the bestseller lists, either because they are willing to explore the dark side of religious leaders and institutions, titillate the public by relating sex to religion, or fascinate readers with their own personal metaphysical potential. Whatever agenda these writers carry, they correctly read the market as having interest in hearing about religion—even if in heterodox or socially aberrant forms.

But the issues have not been confined to a mere continuation of exposure to Eastern religious ideas or to the human inability to measure up to the ideal. World-wide issues of religious import have been pervasive in the media because of such things as poverty and starvation in Africa, political upheaval in Central America, racism in South Africa, and a Pope whose travels correspond with his universal perspective.

So it would be difficult to understand the present state of the United States as well as the world without some acquaintance with and examination of the occurrences, personalities, and issues that have religious orientation. Even antireligious movements often carry symbols, practices, and mentalities that are traditionally associated with religions. Mao Tse-Tung attained almost divine status during his lifetime—his icons everywhere, his words collected into sacred scriptures. Thus the educated person needs to study the phenomenon we call "religion."

A Good Time for Religious Studies

This is a good time to study religion, because we have much more information available than we formerly had. There are several reasons for this. One is that we know much more about the original languages of the scriptures of various religions. This is important because often real understanding of a religion depends on reading its teachings in their original form. Today, many people in the West can study the Hindu scriptures in the Sanskrit language. Many others can read the Koran, the holy book of Islam, in Arabic, the Hebrew Scriptures in Hebrew, and the New Testament in Greek. These languages are taught in our universities; they are no longer exotic mysteries. So language study has been the prelude to better understanding.

There is a second reason why this is a good time to study religion: it is much easier to get objective information now. For most of history, the only reason anyone ever studied anyone else's religion was to prove that it was *wrong*. That was the purpose the "student" had in mind before he or she started. Small wonder that such a student ends up defining the other religion as being a series of superstitions, flaws in thinking, and corruptions of real truth! (In other words, one tends to find what one is looking for.)

Of course, the time comes when one must make up one's own mind—and that will mean choosing *for* some ideas and *against* others. But before deciding for or against, say, Buddhism, one's responsibility is first to look at Buddhism for what it *is*. In other words, one must gather as much objective information as possible.

It is much easier today to find such information. And the university is becoming a better and better place in which to find it.

Decoding Ancient Religious Texts. This stone tablet, found in 1881, provides a text to explain the religious ceremony depicted. The tablet was placed in an earthenware box by the Babylonian King Nabopolassar, evidently so that if the idol and temple depicted were destroyed, future generations would know how to reconstruct them. Modern decoding of such ancient documents has led to an explosion in knowledge of ancient religious beliefs. (British Museum)

Also, travel is relatively easy now. Travel means the mixing of ideas. It gives one a chance to observe and critique what one has read by means of firsthand experience. For many centuries the only way in which anyone could possibly learn anything about the Shinto religion in Japan was to read a book by some very daring soul who had gotten on a ship and sailed to Japan. There he or she had had many adventures and had observed many strange customs and had written them down for our entertainment and amazement. We read them as exotic things, far beyond the scope of our own lives.

But today multitudes of people visit Japan. For many people in our century the Far East became a practical reality when they were pressed into military service and sent off to war there. It no longer takes great wealth to walk among the ancient temples of India, to stand inside the fabled mosques of Arabia, to observe the tribal ceremonies of Africa. All it takes is a little determination and ingenuity.

In a slightly diluted form, one can confront these different cultures significantly even without leaving the United States because of the diversity in our larger cities.

Religious Studies as a Search for Clarity

Religious studies are popular now because interest in religion is on the upswing and because more objective information is available than ever before. A third reason grows out of the fact that college is, at least theoretically, the place where people clarify their thinking. Probably no other word is used so nebulously as the word "religion." It covers many different ideas; already, in the opening pages of this book, we have used the word in several different ways, to refer to several different things.

This situation makes it difficult to communicate. The word "religion" is perceived in dozens of ways, depending on the vantage point of the various hearers, their experiences, their feelings, the books they have read, the people they have met, and so on. So one of the things this book attempts to do is *clarify*. The word "religion" is much too complex for any one definition. We must begin to develop a thoughtful way in which to handle these definitions, however, and that is one of the main tasks of education.

Education and Freedom

Studying religion in college is an important part of the process of emancipation. People seek education for various reasons. A major goal for most is vocational training, learning so as to get a job. Many professors, particularly those in technical fields, tend to think that this is almost the exclusive purpose of education. Everything else must be sacrificed, if need be, to "make our graduates competitive in the job market." And an even higher percentage of students concurs. Their thinking runs something like this:

"I will study certain subjects to gain certain skills needed to get a certain job and make a certain amount of money. There is a nice straight, logical line between each of these items, connecting them tightly together. That connection is why I'm here. Courses that don't fit into this line are only endured. They are dirty tricks played on us by eggheads, obstacle courses designed by starry-eyed idealists who won't give us our license to go out and make money until we play their Mickey Mouse game."

Administratively, any course that cannot be shown to apply directly to getting a job is always in jeopardy. In times of financial crisis, it is likely to be the first to go. "We don't have time or money for that kind of peripheral material," the university seems to be saying. "We have to get these students trained so they can get the good jobs and make the good money."

Undeniably, education has some vocational goals. But an education with only vocational goals is a deficient and dangerous education. One of the reasons for studying religion, and other "impractical" subjects, is that true education involves not only training, but also autonomy of thought and emancipation.

The mastery of technological skills enables us to build remarkable machines. Our technological machine runs on the strength of our technological skills. But technology has not been able to replace the need for values. People who are oriented solely toward technical information and technical skill tend to suffer from a "value deficiency." Sadly, some people, very highly educated in highly technical ways, discover at a certain age that all that they really know is one very narrow field. They are unable to even carry on a reasonable conversation about anything else. They feel trapped. Listen to one medical specialist:

"If you want me to talk about the inner ear I'll do it. I'll tell you anything you want to know. But if you want me to make an informed, intelligent comment about politics, or art, or heaven forbid, religion, well, forget it. I'm just lost. I don't know where to start."

This comes from a person who sometimes has to make what are basically moral decisions, decisions that have to do with values. A physician may decide, for example, whether you will live or die. You do not want an intellectually narrow person there; you want someone who can move in many directions, one who is free and open and comfortable in the world. You want an emancipated human being.

Human values are caught, struggle, and die in the web of ignorance. Certain primitive tribes think that twins are dangerous. So they take them, newborn, and leave them in the forest to die of exposure or be carried away by animals. To learn that this is not necessary is to be emancipated. To respect the life in those twins is *freedom*—for them, for their mother, for the tribe.

In the eighteenth century, a really sick person was taken to a barber, who would slit the person's wrists and let him or her bleed a while. This, supposedly, got all the "poisons" out. At least one account of the death of George Washington says that he was bled to death by someone trying to cure him. When people learned more facts, they were freed from this deadly misunderstanding. They were emancipated.

And what is true of these is also true of human relationships, and true of ultimate questions, and true of "religious" questions—the more you know, the freer you become. Jesus put it succinctly:

> You will know the truth, and the truth will make you free.[3]
>
> (John 8:32)

So there is a connection between truth and freedom. And education can be not simply training, but a way to get oneself free, to open up one's life to all kinds of new possibilities, to become a person.

A college degree is no longer a ticket to financial success anyway. There are much quicker and less expensive ways to get a job—often one with more prestige and money than those available to a "merely" emancipated person.

Many college graduates do janitorial work and drive taxis and operate service stations and sell insurance. There is certainly no tragedy in that—no tragedy, that is, if these persons have been emancipated. Not a dollar or a day of it was wasted. They got exactly what they paid for—a kind of handle on life, a kind of freedom. It would be a tragedy only if they had spent all that time and money solely to train as a left-handed computer technician, and then could not find an opening for a left-handed computer technician, and then had to take a job as a cabbie. *That* would be a failure and a waste.

In modern times vocation has tended to become an eight-hour-a-day affair. The key questions are, "What about the other sixteen hours?" "How will I approach life?" "How will I approach other people?" "How will I read, and what will I read?" "How will I watch television, and what will I watch?" "How will I react to what is going on in my world?"

Religious studies is one very important area in which these questions are faced head on. It is part of the concept of education as emancipation.

Seeking Our Roots

Another reason for studying religion is to gain a better understanding of our culture. Our culture has numerous and pervasive religious presuppositions. They may be well hidden, but they are there. They can be detected even in families in which no one member has darkened a church door in seventy-five years. These presuppositions still operate in the way in which these families make decisions, in the things the parents tell the chil-

[3]Biblical quotations are from the Revised Standard Version unless otherwise noted.

dren, in the manner in which they live from day to day. There are some religious roots.

What is true of families is also true of society as a whole: religious presuppositions operate in the way in which we as a people make decisions, make laws, treat certain issues or certain people. Western Europe and America are obviously saturated with Judeo-Christian thought forms.

In some ways the university has always recognized this. Various disciplines there have been forced to deal with religious issues, because religious issues have so often exerted an influence on human behavior. Political science must deal with religious issues, for example, and education must, and business must.

In religious studies we meet the issues directly. We say, "If religion has always been so much a part of our culture, should we not study it? Perhaps in doing that we will come to understand our culture better." And so we do.

Religious studies, undertaken in the Western world, will try to understand the religious presuppositions of the West. But religious studies, undertaken anywhere, must deal with the subject of humanity—the universal human being. In religion people search for themselves and try to find out what they *mean*, not as Americans, or Englishmen, or Danes, or Italians, but as human beings.

One might even argue that religion is the primary discipline in the study of humanity. Biology, anthropology, sociology, and history all deal with important aspects of humanity's nature and activities. Religion asks the questions about *meaning* and *value*. What kind of judgment can be made on things-as-they-are? On human beings as they are? What do *I* mean? Do I mean *anything*? Am I going anywhere? If so, where? Do I have any present meaning, or any future purpose? Who *am* I, anyway?

These are the distinctly "religious" questions we must ask about humanity. We can, of course, search for answers among the test tubes and computers. But the problem is that the answers seem to come up in a totally unsatisfying way: What am I? "Well, you are a blob of protoplasm, . . . here by chance . . . and going nowhere." Not a very satisfying answer.

But maybe the answer gets no farther than that because we are asking it in the wrong place. On a once popular television space fantasy, a very friendly computer, when asked questions such as these, would always reply, "It does not compute." If the machine's answer is inadequate, it may not mean that no adequate answer exists. It may mean that the machine has none.

Religious studies is a search for the answers elsewhere.

Religion and Personal Values

Religious studies can also assist students in developing intelligent ways by which to judge whether a given religious or ethical claim has merit. Not all ideas are true. That is a basic axiom, as true in religious studies as in any other academic discipline. Somehow the idea exists that to believe that someone else's religious ideas are untrue is to be intolerant and bigoted and narrow minded. But we do not think similarly of other disciplines. When we hear the claim that one must bleed a patient to heal that person, we do not hesitate to say, "That is wrong!" When someone says that the Declaration of Independence was signed in 1492 we immediately reply, "That is incorrect!"

But when religious concepts are at issue, we become very hesitant. In many cases, this hesitancy is due to the realization that metaphysical issues cannot be resolved with the same approach as purely physical or scientific issues. Or it reflects the awareness of the difference between faith and reason. But this hesitancy may also betray our insecurity. When insecure persons are questioned about their convictions, they will probably respond by becoming angry. They regard the question to be a personal threat. That is why so many religious discussions turn into arguments—all heat and no light, all superficial prejudices and very few intelligent opinions.

Others, claiming tolerance, decline to discuss religion or make religious judgments, due to apathy. It is not really that they are so tolerant. They simply do not want to bother. So comes the rationalization: "Oh, I don't think I want to comment on that. I think everyone has a right to his or her own belief. I never discuss religion or politics. Who am I to say what's right and wrong?" After all, it is much easier to plead ignorance than to face the issues.

But the fact is that such people are making judgments; they cannot avoid it. They are simply choosing to make them without any intelligent investigation.

Such judgments usually crumble quickly under fire. Uninformed people tend either to get dogmatic and make fools of themselves or to sway in the wind like palm trees in a hurricane. When confronted with a new idea, especially if it sounds profound, they fall for it immediately. And then they fall for the next one, too. And the next one.

Religious studies will help us decide—perhaps *for*, perhaps *against*, but at least much more intelligently. This opportunity comes at an appropriate time.

Psychologists point out that at certain stages in a person's life each of us has certain specific developmental tasks. At one stage it may be "learning how to get our eyes focused." At another "getting our thumb and fingers to work together." Or "learning to share with others." The motor needs and psychological needs come, step by step, in the road to maturity.

One of the most pressing developmental needs of the college years is the need to acquire a *personal value system.* It is a time when one decides whether to keep what he or she has been taught or abandon it. It is a time when one draws one's own conclusions about what is real and what is fake, what is basic and what is secondary. Of course many students do this without consciously realizing that they are doing it. They do not reflect on the process; they just "let it happen." Others feel such a significant task is worth at least a few hours of sober thought.

Quite often this second group turns to religious studies for some help.

SOME PRACTICAL SUGGESTIONS
ABOUT STUDYING RELIGION

How does one proceed in attempting a mature, intelligent study of religion? Here are some basic suggestions.

Begin Where You Are

The French philosopher René Descartes claimed that to find truth one had to clear one's mind of all ideas which have rational grounds for doubt. To find absolute certainty, he felt it had to be a priori, that is, not dependent upon any experience outside the mind. Unfortunately, there are several reasons why this approach does not work very well in the study of religion. There is a *philosophical* reason, for example. Our minds have already developed certain categories and certain approaches toward data. It is too late to simply wipe everything out of our minds and pretend to know nothing at all. We do know some things. As bodily and not merely mental beings, we have developed a "world" through a certain language, for example. We think in forms compatible with that language. In this way objectivity is compromised at the very beginning of the thought process. We have to begin where we are.

Another reason this is true is a *psychological* one. It is psychologically damaging to say, "All the things I've always believed or been told are false. I will discard them all. I'm going to start all over again with nothing at all, and move up from there." Unfortunately, one of the worst places of all to be, psychologically, is nowhere at all. Even Descartes had to give himself ground rules psychologically and morally so he could continue to live in this interim stage of investigation.

Often people falling into severe psychosis are overwhelmed by a sense of not knowing anything, of not being sure of anything. Everything shifts like loose sand. There is nothing to hang on to anywhere.

So, begin where you are.

Here are three slightly different ways of saying the same thing.

Do Not Jump without Your Parachute

Think of what you believe now—the way in which you hold your life together, the way in which you keep things going—think of that as being a *parachute*. A parachute lets you down easily. When you are up in the rarified atmosphere of new ideas, bombarded on every side, it is not wise to jump without your parachute. Instead, hang on to those things that have always held you together and allow them to let you down gently.

Of course by the time you reach the ground you may have changed in all sorts of important ways. You may even decide to use a different parachute from now on. But in the meantime do not discard the one you have— not until you have the new one road tested. In other words, do not despise what you have received.

Sometimes people read a few books and take a few courses and decide, "Everything anybody ever told me before now is wrong. Now I know where the truth is. It resides with my fraternity brothers, and with one or two of my profs. Everything I ever heard before now is out."

There comes a kind of sinking feeling, or perhaps with others a kind of rebellious feeling, that says, "Some things I have always believed are obviously wrong. Therefore *everything* I have always believed is obviously wrong." Of course that kind of thinking is not very rational, but it happens nevertheless.

You see, some of the things that people have told you in the past may be true. Some may be false, of course, but some may be true. So do not count out the old family traditions altogether. New ideas are not always better than old ones.

One other way to say it is, Do not consider the exotic to be preferable. Of course it may or may not be preferable, but it is never preferable simply because it is exotic. Sometimes people begin to learn something about a religious system practiced far away in some storybook place. They see how people there deal with religious questions. It all sounds plausible, and it seems to have some strengths, and some answers they have never heard. So they quickly conclude, *they* are right and *we* are wrong!

Perhaps. But that conclusion may not have come from a sober reflection on the facts. It may have come from an approach that says, "Anything that is different must be right. Anything that sounds like what I have always heard must be wrong." Or it may have generated simply because the new data of the "other" came in a more intellectually sophisticated manner vis-à-vis the rather uncritical notions of one's childhood religion.

The exotic may turn out to be preferable. But the fact that something is exotic, and that you have never heard it before, does not automatically make it true. So, begin where you are.

Practice Creative Listening and Learning

Another basic suggestion is to *listen and then talk*. Be sure that you understand the new idea before you either accept it or try to refute it. It is amazing how superficial discussions about religion can be sometimes. Often that is because no one is paying attention to anyone else. Everyone is talking and no one is listening. All the other person wants to do is to make a point, and all you want to do is to make your point, and no one is learning anything. Neither of you is studying religion—you are just arguing. The first step toward real learning is to listen, and to listen very carefully. Ask questions. Be sure that you understand what the other person is saying or what his or her new idea really is.

And try to look at what is best in the other point of view. If you want to know how a religious system different from your own deals with things, do not start with a book written to refute that system. Read one written by someone who believes it. Allow the other person the benefit of the doubt. Let the other person represent the religion in the best possible light.

Then you are in a better position to say, "Now I've heard it at its best. I know the facts. And I've come to the conclusion that it is true here, and here, and here. But not here, and here, and here." But that kind of talk can come only after you have done a lot of hard listening.

There is another kind of nonlistener—the gullible one. This person does not really want an explanation. He or she is looking for a guru, to believe what the guru says to believe. This is a kind of emotional and intellectual escape method that says, "I'll accept that because I like you" or "because you are my teacher." That is really no better than saying, "I'm not going to believe you because I do not like you." Either way, you are not really listening. That means that no communication is taking place, and it probably also means that you are developing some distorted ideas about what the other person believes.

Sometimes statements are made about the tenets of a certain religion that are completely distorted and untrue. But the statements stay alive because no one bothers to ask the people involved whether they are true or not.

It is very important to listen. It minimizes sloppy thinking, sloppy statements, gross generalizations, and distortions of the other person's point of view. It results in clarification and real communication and learning.

You do not have to agree with someone to be able to listen to him or her. After all, it is really no threat to your personhood to listen to an idea different from your own. You do not have to get upset about it. You do not have to rant and rave and scream. Often it is not necessary to refute or agree with what you are hearing.

Of course there are times when a good, spirited discussion of differences is enjoyable and profitable—especially if all people involved are sure enough of themselves emotionally and can handle it. Nothing is quite as stimulating as a really good discussion about religious questions, about the basic questions of meaning. It can be a growing experience.

Some people say that it is never appropriate to discuss religious differences. On the contrary, religious differences are among the most important things to discuss. Of course if "discussion" means simply shouting the other person down without listening to that person, then the process is a waste of time. But if one is trying to understand, and not simply to refute, then it is an excellent activity.

The same principle applies to reading. Freud said that religion is a childish neurosis. Marx said it is an opium people are given to dull their sensitivity to their miserable conditions in the real world. Both leveled their major attack upon Christianity. Now a Christian reader might become very angry about this and throw the book down. Or he or she might look around a bit and discover that, sure enough, some people do use Christianity like opium, and some do treat religion merely as a form of wish fulfillment. People with serious mental difficulties are often religious, and their religion often reflects their neurotic approach to life. People in positions of power and wealth have often used religious teachings to hold the lower classes in poverty, telling them to look for their "pie in the sky by and by." So you see, Marx and Freud are not entirely wrong after all, are they?

When someone criticizes your religion, it is always a good idea to see whether the criticism is not directed toward a *misuse* of that religion. It may not be a valid attack upon the *essence* of what you believe at all. But you would not have noticed that if you had not taken time to listen.

Our next suggestion for studying religion is to *keep on learning*. Someone once described another person as "knowing too much for his own good." Such a thing is probably impossible. One might know too many wrong things for one's own good, but one will never have too many facts, or too much truth. More information is always helpful. Some people have very strong religious opinions that are precisely the same as those same people held fifty years ago. There has been absolutely no growth, no developing insight, no deepening understanding.

These people make frustrating conversationalists. They seem to have a bumper sticker taped to their foreheads that says, "My Mind Is Already Made Up; Don't Try to Confuse Me with Facts." They seem to be saying, "I don't want to hear anymore. I went through that whole thing a long time ago and I've made up my mind. I want no new evidence, pro or con. I just do not want to talk about it anymore."

People who do not keep learning about religion tend to resort to gross oversimplifications; they sound very narrow minded and bigoted, and they tend to make unintelligent comments. Sometimes they are very sophisticated in other areas, but when it comes to religion these usually suave and fluent types can say absolutely crazy things. They usually say them very confidently and have no idea how absurd they sound to anyone with a smattering of facts at his or her disposal.

Religious studies must not be thought of as the accumulation of a few convictions, followed by a lifetime of stubborn loyalty to those same convictions. Rather, it is a process that must keep happening to be of any use.

Study Religion Objectively

Our next suggestion is to *look at religion objectively*. It has not always been studied that way—not even in college. Some of the oldest private universities in the United States were founded primarily for the purpose of training ministers for the Christian church.

It was only natural then that the approach to religious studies in such a setting was not particularly objective. This approach to the study of religion we can call a "dogmatic" or a "theological" approach. That means that it is based on the teachings or position of a particular religious communion and that communion's definitions of the relation of the human to the divine.

Because religious conversion is usually experienced in an absolutistic fashion, a dogmatic approach for any particular religion has a legitimate place within that particular religious communion. But because of its narrow or even exclusive commitment, it cannot be followed in publicly funded higher education. Here a more detached or objective position is dictated by virtue of fairness to all taxpayers. We must be careful to realize, however, that such objectivity does not necessarily imply more truth.

The broadest area of the objective study of religion can be called the *history of religions*. It moved beyond the subjectivity and natural bias of commitments to particular religions that had preceded it in the eighteenth and nineteenth centuries. At that time, two extreme alternatives suggested themselves to this new discipline. One focused totally upon the description of phenomena that could be classed as "religious." This is often referred to as a "phenomenological" approach. The other emphasized the radical historical particularity of things people thought were "religious."

Both of these alternatives helped correct the former dogmatic approach. But the phenomenological approach suffered from its imposition of categories upon the material—often *a priori* categories or categories decided on without reference to the data. The historicist alternative correctly pointed to the historical rather than metaphysical nature of the data under examination. But it suffered from its inability to compare or make generalizations from a more holistic picture.

Today the history of religions approach attempts to stand between these extremes. Its relation to the data can be called "dialectical" or "dialogical." What this points to is the fact that its categories and definitions are intentionally defined only in continual *interdependence* with the actual historical materials themselves. The categories are therefore not *a priori*. And the method is inductive, not deductive nor reductionistic.

Further, the history of religions is theoretical or scientific in the sense that it utilizes theoretical methods recognized in other related disciplines such as anthropology, sociology, psychology, and history. And it is theoretical in the fact that it is continually self-correcting. That is, this approach to the study of religion not only recognizes the interdependence between data and interpretative categories by which to view the data, but it is genuinely open to new data, models, types, and methods.

This openness to the new enables this approach to use models and definitions without being absolutely committed to them. Or one could say that the models, types, categories, or definitions are viewed not as univocal but rather as analogical. By "analogical," we suggest that definitions or concepts such as suffering, monotheism, soul, sacrifice, the Holy, and so on will not be useful in comparing religions if we insist that only one definition of each must fit exactly all phenomena that claim any similarity.

For example, "monotheism," as the belief in a single god, is one thing in ancient Judaism and Islam but quite different if one looks to Zeus in the ancient Greek religion or to Purusa in Vedic Hinduism. That single god in Judaism and Islam is not infused with or identical with the cosmos in any sense but totally different, whereas Zeus and Purusa are both identical with and transcendent to the universe. Or "the Holy" as a category in ancient Israel or Egypt is not identical with "the Holy" in Christianity.

What we are saying is that, as in natural science, the models will serve only as analogies to move from the known to the unknown. Again, we hope that such an approach will not be reductionistic, that is, filtering out uniqueness or different nuances in other cultures' religions for the sake of finding a concept to be universal. Even our beginning definition of religion as "ultimate concern" *can* be reductionistic. This is the reason we will utilize *different* terms as *approximate equivalents* or as *analogical*—to open up more levels of comparison. Following this analogical route will also prevent the obvious diversities of language, historical particularity, or differences in meaning from simply bringing all analysis and comparison to a halt.

A further note or two about method. A history of religions approach focuses on both *belief* and *action* in a given historical community. It attempts to avoid the previous mistake of thinking that a religion was totally described when one had analyzed all its chief ideas or teachings. The actual practices or what the people did is just as important.

For example, to uncover what the people actually *did* in the ancient horse-sacrifice in India provides understanding of the religion not gained through a mere recitation of the fact that they believed in certain gods. Or to see the cremation of Indira Gandhi on television is surely as informative a disclosure of their religion as to say that Indians believe such-and-such about life, death, karma, or dharma. It is one thing to study that a Christian group in West Virginia *believes* that the "holy spirit" enables them to handle poisonous snakes; it is quite another dimension to see what they *do* in the snake handling. In many cases, we get a much truer picture of what people really believe only by watching their actions.

Also, a history of religions approach does not assume an evolutionary-evaluative stance. That is, it does not begin its examination of religious phenomena with the presupposition that earlier forms of religious phenomena are either inferior or superior to later forms.

Sometimes religious people have assumed that the primitive thought and activity of primitive religions can be classified only as superstition, animism, fetishism, and so on and are therefore inferior to the modern mentality. Hegel's classification of religions is a good example of this type of approach. Ironically, this is usually assumed by religious people only when they examine religions other than their own, for many religious people take somewhat the opposite view about *their* religion. They often assume that in its original formulation it was superior to all subsequent formulations.

On the other hand, the history of religions approach abstains from judging a religion's original form as either crude superstition or the definitive form for all time. Neither is it willing to assume that development in religion assumes the same form in different cultures. Cultures do not inevitably move from polytheism to henotheism to monotheism. The history of religions approach attempts to remain open to the *actual* forms religious ideas and actions have taken; it remains open to the "otherness" even in development.

This does not mean, however, that the history of religions dissolves into mere description with no normative or evaluative judgments. Although some professors have thought this, probably no study or teaching, either in or out of college, can assume such a sterile approach. But history of religions emphasizes openness to the data in their differences, with normative judgments being subordinated to and growing out of holistic, cross-cultural, or more globally encompassing understandings of the data in context.

Other approaches to religious study seem to go one of two ways. In some cases, the separate discipline itself, such as sociology or psychology, focuses on religion as a part of its objective study. Or, often religion will be studied in philosophy and theology. People usually think the philosophical study of religion would be more objective than the theological, and there may be a significant difference in commitment in these alternate approaches. Both *could* be objective to the degree that they follow the dialogical, dialectical, and analogical facets of the history of religions approach that we have described above. For example, the history of Jewish theology could be as objective as a sociological description of "rites of passage" in religions. But to the degree that *any* discipline approaches the religious phenomena from the conviction that the data *must fit* within their allegiance to a specific "final revelation," predefined ontology, language game, or "world-view," it is not so objective.

This issue of commitment or allegiance or final revelation raises the question of the "subjective" aspect of the religious experience, or of any Weltanschauung (world-view). That, in turn, tends to jeopardize its place in public schools to a degree. Yet to the degree that no study of *any* subject is possible without at least a temporary particular world-view, particular convictions about reality or the nature and tests of truth-claims or how knowledge is gained, the subjective element is never completely avoided.

Study Religion Subjectively

Another suggestion is: *do not neglect the subjective.* A purely scientific or objective study of religion is not sufficient to really understand it. In fact, the greatest strength of the scientific method becomes something of a limitation in studying religion, because simply analyzing religious ideas produces no evaluation of them. Analysis tells us what something is, that is, what *parts* make it up; but analysis cannot determine whether the thing is good or bad or mediocre.

An example might help to illustrate this problem. Every student in a university class was given a goldfish in a little glass bowl. The assignment was to take the goldfish home and in three weeks bring to class an essay entitled "What Is a Goldfish?"

People have different kinds of minds, and so the students went at this project in different kinds of ways. People who chose the scientific route immediately began with analysis, as you would expect. Pity the poor goldfish that belonged to these people! Its fate was set; it was headed for dissection, right? That, after all, is what one does to find out what a goldfish *is.* So they took their goldfish apart, categorized, weighed, and counted the parts. They came back to class with some highly technical analytical statistical studies on the goldfish. But they had hardly said everything that can be said about a goldfish!

Other students approached the problem from the viewpoint of wholeness, or evaluation. Many of their essays resorted to poetry because to them the goldfish was "the glint of gold when the sun shines through the delicate veins of the flowing fins." Or "quiet movement, serenity, untroubled gentleness." They were seeing the goldfish in a very different way—subjectively. They were reacting to a goldfish, to what it meant to them, to its *value.* Some students even gave their goldfish names and came to love them.

The things this latter group said were true. They were part of the reality of a goldfish. In some ways, they were the most important realities. For the subjective qualities of something may be more important "truths" than its objective qualities. For instance, think of your friends. They are so tall, so old, so this or that, statistically, analytically. But you will never know the truth about a friend when you insist on knowing him or her only in that way.

Of course subjective study can get a little frightening. It is very demanding. It is much easier to take a fact, lay it out, and count and measure it than it is to begin to ask, "Is this fact *important*? Is it important *to me*?"

Subjective study of religion can make one uncomfortable at times, but it is nevertheless very important.

Watch for Syncretism

Sometimes students accumulate information faster than they can assimilate it. The mass of data does not immediately fall into consistent order in their minds. They may, in fact, start jamming conflicting ideas into their "system" and end up with a hodgepodge. They pick up a book on Hinduism, grab an attractive idea or two, and glue them onto their system of thinking. Then they do the same with Islam, Zen, and so on.

The word we will use for the hodgepodge approach is *syncretism*. The student's mind is not moving fast enough to realize that it is picking up and accepting ideas that are mutually exclusive.

"But isn't it a good idea just to take the best from all religions, rather than settling on just one of them?"

This sounds good, but there are some serious problems in such an approach. It implies that the great world faiths have so little internal integrity that one can simply yank off a little here and pinch off a little there. On the contrary, these systems are usually made up of complex interwoven concepts. They are like a spider's web in which each strand depends on the tension of the other strands to hold itself together. One cannot simply detach and isolate an idea, because that idea may well have little meaning standing by itself; it becomes merely an isolated piece of data, supported by nothing.

The great religions have been considered "great" because there is a profound inner web of integrity in them. To study them properly, one must always watch for and appreciate that web.

2

Defining "Religion"

A WORD WITH NUMEROUS DEFINITIONS

"Religion" is one of those very common words that are often the hardest of all to define. Everyone uses it, but few people have a very well-developed idea of what they *mean* when they use it.

Definitions of religion often reveal the kinds of experiences their authors have had. For example, they may have encountered it oppressing science or depriving particular groups of people, and therefore they might be prevented from ever being able to consider possible benefits of religion. Or they may have found personal liberation or a group transcendence through a religious experience that has made it impossible for them ever to seriously consider the negative potential of religion. As Alfred North Whitehead wrote years ago, in a sentiment expressed by many insightful thinkers, religion is not an unambiguous good.

The nineteenth and early twentieth centuries furnished us with many profoundly influential definitions of religion. Some were sympathetic to religion, and others quite hostile. Any student of religion will need to struggle with these sooner or later. We list only a few from the Jewish-Christian tradition, in very simple terms, just to give the basic impact of their uniqueness.

Immanuel Kant (1724–1804) separated science from religion, showing that scientific proof required phenomenal and mental conditions that cannot be met by religious assertions and referents. Religion, however, as "practical knowledge," was socially necessary for humanity since it furnished symbols as well as communities that elicited morality. Religion, as morality, cannot be proven scientifically but must be postulated as other ideas basic to civilization such as "freedom." True religion, morality, he distinguished from "pseudoreligion." The latter was a disposition toward the transcendent that had little or no connection to morality.

Friedrich Schleiermacher (1768–1834), the "father of modern (Christian) theology," agreed basically with Kant's separation of religion and science. But he contended that Kant was wrong in equating religion with morality. It was more basic and more universal than any morality to which Kant could point. Rather, religion was a primal universal awareness, a consciousness of unity with the Whole, a sense of absolute dependence upon one's Source that precedes all cognition as well as moral action.

G. W. F. Hegel (1770–1831) felt Kant and Schleiermacher had gone too far, ripping religion from the cognitive or intellectual function of humanity. His solution was that religion was one of the primary forms of Absolute Spirit or God. But he was convinced that he could distinguish between cruder and more intellectually refined manifestations of religion. So he held that by the very power of the Spirit (Mind) in history, humanity would gradually evolve in its conceptions or understandings, moving away from the representations in religion that seemed so dependent upon phenomena. For example, the ancient polytheism which found a god or goddess for every power in the cosmos, such as the sun, moon, wind, water, and so on, would be left behind. Humans would eventually understand reality by reflecting upon concepts themselves rather than being driven by every natural force or phenomenon. With this evolution, religion would be realized in philosophy. Ethics and science, once separated by Kant, would be reunited as love or unity is emphasized rather than faith, and reflection would be restored to religion and to humanity.

Ludwig Feuerbach (1804–1872) turned Hegel's definition on its head. If Hegel had thought that human consciousness is simply a finite form of God's self-consciousness, Feuerbach argued, the truth is that God-consciousness is nothing more than human self- or species-consciousness. The infinite attributes humans traditionally assign to God—infinite will, power, and affection—are actually attributes of the human species. Of course, no single person possesses them in their infinite capacity. But Feuerbach believed that humanity as a whole was not limited. He saw religion as the mistake of unconsciously projecting this infinite capacity of the human species, thereby turning it into "God." If the masses could be brought to this scientific understanding of the nature of religion,

Feuerbach thought, religion could still be maintained. It would then be capable, as Hegel advocated, of leaving behind faith, superseding it with love.

Karl Marx (1818–1883) accepted Hegel's idea of the intellectual evolution of humanity. But its cause was socio-economic conditions rather than pure speculative thought or Absolute Spirit, as Hegel had maintained. Religion, therefore, had been useful to those on top in society. It had kept the exploited working class pacified. It served as an opiate, dulling their sensitivities to the misery and injustice of their exploitation. Thus scientifically explained, religion's other-worldliness was only a tool or symbol by which to propagate selfishness and injustice.

Søren Kierkegaard (1813–1855) distinguished between true religion and its state-sponsored perversion, between its subjective truth and its objective form, and between faith and reason. Christianity, the religion with which he was primarily concerned, was, he was convinced, not merely doctrine or ethics, inasmuch as these remain human formulations based upon reason. Instead, it was a relation with the Absolute. Such a relation demanded morality, but it might demand even more. A culture's definitions or morality might be suspended by this relation to the Absolute. So, for example, he argued against Hegel's interpretation of the story of Abraham's apparent willingness to sacrifice Isaac. To Hegel, the story proved the danger of faith being preferred to reason. To Kierkegaard, the story proved the possibility that if God is, God is not subject to or limited by particular cultural conceptions, either doctrinally or ethically. In fact, he was convinced that true faith is far above reason. It is demanded and created by the relation with the Absolute, but since it is not intelligible or communicable to others, it will appear absurd if not clearly irreligious. In this view, religion remains universal but, ironically, only in its subjective dimension.

Friedrich Nietzsche (1844–1900) opposed not only the alleged objectivity of religion and reason but also the ethics supported by such objectivity. He delighted in referring to himself as an "immoralist." By this he was objecting to all philosophical systems such as Hegel's. But even more so, he was challenging the primacy usually given in a religious culture to thinking over being, essence over existence, morality over instinct, democracy or equality over the will-to-power, ressentiment over tolerance and self-concern. His contention was that all religions, but particularly the Christian religion, carried on the priestly negative attitude toward everything natural in the world. Yet the religion's confessed ideals, such as celibacy and poverty, he found self-contradictory and self-defeating. Religion was imposed by priests to prevent others from enjoying a world which they felt incapable of enjoying themselves. And religion provided standards, incentive, and even God for humans who were too weak or cowardly to provide their own values and incentives or to realize that one has to live without any god.

Emile Durkheim (1858–1917) left his legacy in the relatively new study, the sociology of religion. He held that religious beliefs and doctrines are shaped and reshaped in times of intense collective effervescence. Although the content of these beliefs, which contain myths, magic, totemism, and so on, is not scientifically credible, their purpose or function is necessary. That is, they provide the group with its collective identity. As a part of that identity, they provide the ideals of the community, distinguishing between ideals outgrown and those that are relevant. Even their unscientific division of reality into "sacred" and "profane" spheres and their distinction between good and evil gods points to this sense of group identity that is quite realistic at root. Particularly important is the morality elicited by this identity, set within its particular belief system, and the dramatizing and continual reshaping of this ideal and identity. Durkheim believed that this scientific understanding of the roots and functions of religion could make the human community more responsible toward itself and the world as a whole.

Sigmund Freud (1856–1939) found religion an unscientific, authoritarian, and immature wish-fulfillment approach to the world. Religion was an "illusion," that is, built upon a wish or need, which, though not utterly out of touch with reality as a "delusion," is nevertheless quite unlikely. One could see this in religion's prayers, myths, and general practices, whether ancient sacrifices or modern morality. Religion's inability to admit its own change or evolution, Freud contended, made it an inferior approach to reality. Science's willingness to admit its own fallibility and continual process was in fact its great claim for supremacy as a method of ascertaining the truth of reality in the world. Freud was convinced that no amount of authoritarianism would eventually restrain people within the antiquated illusions of religion. They would mature and leave it behind. And no amount of postulating, as Kant did, would suffice to spare an ethic once religion is dislodged by science.

From the turn of the century, the history of religions has provided us with many more intellectual giants who have defined religion even more precisely. The above are simply representative of how religion, as a unique Western category, has begun to be explored. Obviously the particular communal settings and the unique experiences of each individual affect his or her definitions of religion. But just admitting that does not exhaust the possible claims to truth in each definition nor release us from the obligation of examining each very closely. Yet we must also be aware of how "Western" the whole idea of religion is, and thus be careful not to force particular definitions upon "Eastern" data just because we are convinced that religion, or our definitions of religion, must be universal.

It is possible to gain a little more clarity if we can distinguish between different kinds of definitions. That is, one can look at any phenomenon such as religion from several different angles. They need not be mutually exclusive. But it may improve our discussion of religion with others if we can clarify how we are defining it. We suggest that there are at least four different types of definitions.

A *descriptive* definition is simply whatever a given person or group chooses to *call* religion.

> "What is your religion?"
> "I'm a Baptist."
> "I'm a Buddhist."
> "I'm a Druid."
> "I'm a Sun Worshipper."

Whatever you call your religion is, descriptively, your religion. Whenever I describe you as an adherent of that religion ("You are a Unitarian"), I am giving a descriptive definition. I am making no judgments; I am simply stating the case descriptively.

A *normative* definition has an "ought to" or a "should" in it. It occurs whenever someone defines religion according to what he or she feels it should be. This definition introduces the concept of judgment. It implies rightness or wrongness. It implies that certain systems that call themselves religions are not. For example,

> Religion should meet man's emotional needs.
> Religion should deal with living a better life.

An *essential* definition tries to be comprehensive. It tries to define religion in such a way that all religious expressions fit the definition. It seeks the essence that is the root of all religion. For example,

> Religion is man's way of relating to the transcendent.
> Religion is a state of being grasped by an ultimate concern.

As you can see, these are very broad definitions that try to deal with every instance of religion.

Often beginning students, asked to define religion essentially, say that "religion is the means by which man relates to God." But there are religions that make no reference to "God." Some forms of Buddhism, for example, are basically atheistic, or at least divine beings play no part in the practice of these faiths. So an essential definition would have to be broader than that.

A *functional* definition describes religion in terms of what it does or what its effect is. Marx's definition ("Religion is the opium of the people") falls into this category. He defines religion as he sees it working. He sees it as a stultifying phenomenon. It so distracts people that they do not worry about their real problems. That is a functional definition. Here is another example of a functional definition: "Religion is the power that frees humanity from sin." This example sees religion working in a very different way, but it is the same kind of definition—a functional one.

For us to talk to each other intelligently, we need to come to some agreement on which face of religion we want to discuss. If I insist on talking about what religion *should* be, but you will only talk about what it *is*, we can argue at length and never communicate with each other. I say, "Religion should make people love one another." You reply, "Religion has resulted in many people having been burned at the stake." We are not communicating because we are trying to compare apples with oranges. You are talking about religion descriptively, and I am talking about it normatively. We will have to agree on which face of religion we wish to discuss before there will be any progress. On the other hand, it is possible for an essential definition to be general enough to encompass a functional and normative definition, thereby elucidating the descriptive definition of any particular religion.

RELIGION AS ULTIMATE CONCERN

The essential definition of religion that we will use as a "working definition" is short and concise: *religion is ultimate concern*. This may or may not be the best essential definition. It is certainly not the only one. We borrow the phrase "ultimate concern" from *Paul Tillich* (1886–1965). Religion, he notes, is the state of being grasped by something unconditional, holy, absolute. If this definition is accepted, then a person is acting "religiously," even if one does not recognize it or admit it, when one

1. Struggles with the ultimate *meaning* of life.
2. Feels an ultimate *obligation*, something that must be done, no matter what.
3. Relates oneself, by action or devotion, to what one believes is ultimately *real*.

"Ultimate" designates both the object of our concern and the passion of concern. It affects not merely our existence, but rather our whole being. As Tillich put it, it is the question "to be or not to be," or less abstractly, "Will I be?" Ultimate concern is, then, something that would cause one to sacrifice everything else. It is the ruler by which one measures everything. It is that which is ultimate—really real. There is not the slightest touch of illusion in it. It is at the root of everything, and everything grows out of and depends on it.

When we are grasped by what is really *real*, what we must really *do*, and what existence really *means*, then we are religious, regardless of our denominational commitment or theological commitment or lack of it. These questions belong to everybody.

Here are some examples of essentially religious questions: "Is there anything so dear to me that I would allow myself to be put against the wall and shot, rather than compromise?" "Are there things that I would do, even if I knew I would be shot for doing them?" "Are there things that I would refuse to do, even if refusal meant certain death?" "What is the last thing among my possessions (material and nonmaterial) that I would be willing to give up?"

Ultimate Concern and Atheism

From the perspective of this definition, no one is really a pure atheist. Atheism is not the lack of ultimate concern. Ultimate concern is a universal human experience, even if it is not always acknowledged. Atheism is then only a rejection of an objectifiable being called "God," or it is a disbelief in some particular god. There are, therefore, various varieties of atheists. There are some who do not believe in the Judeo-Christian god. There are some who do not believe in the Hindu god or gods. There are some who do not believe in the African gods or the "gods" of scientific humanism. Atheism, in this context, implies a negative judgment toward someone else's definition of ultimate.

The atheist is religious, that is, has ultimate concern. He is atheistic only with reference to certain gods, say, Yahweh, or Krishna, or Marduk. And, of course, all of us are atheists with reference to some gods. No one believes in all of them: the very act of believing in one god usually necessitates disbelief in many others.

Everyone has "god"—if we use the word to mean "ultimate concern," something that is of ultimate meaning in his or her life, something that means more than anything else. When one commits oneself to particular symbols which represent the ultimate, then of course that person becomes an "atheist" with reference to claims of ultimacy by other particular symbols or traditions.

So, when religion is defined in this way, everyone is in some sense an atheist and in some sense a believer.

Crypto, Pseudo, and False Religions

The term *crypto* means "hidden." Cryptoreligion is the word we will use to describe ultimate concern that wears a secular mask. It does not think of itself as a religion. It avoids using religious terms such as "god" or "holy spirit" or "church." But it is ultimate concern; it matters more than anything else to the person who possesses it.

Patriotism is the cryptoreligion of some people. Their love for and commitment to their country is absolutely the highest of their concerns. They will willingly die to protect it or serve it. They sense an immense, all-comprising obligation toward it. They may say, "I'm not a religious person; I'm a patriot." But according to our working definition they *are* religious. Patriotism is their cryptoreligion.

The term *pseudo* means "false." A pseudoreligion is one that claims to be, or outwardly appears to be, dealing with the ultimate, but actually is not. Its adherents claim that it guides all their thinking and actions, and they claim to base their lives upon its teachings, but actually they do not.

On any given Sunday in the United States, hundreds of people sit through various rituals that purport to deal with ultimate concerns. They say words and sing hymns that speak of ultimate commitments. They hear sermons saying, "What's really real is this. What one must die for is *this*." The people listen, and appear to agree, but they would not really die for those things at all. They do not believe those are ultimate at all.

They adhere to the rituals and use the vocabulary of ultimate concern, but the result is a pseudoreligion. Their real commitments are hidden behind the façade. Sometimes they cannot even admit to themselves what they really believe, what is really basic to them, what really guides their actions and decisions. In other words, their real religion is hidden behind the pseudo one. So what one says, or even superficially believes is ultimate for him or her, may not really be ultimate at all.

Even though our working definition makes everyone "religious" in the essential sense, it does not follow that all religions are equally true. People can truly, sincerely, and totally commit themselves to something as ultimate when it is not ultimate. They may believe with all their hearts that it is true and real and basic, when actually it is none of those things.

When Mount Vesuvius began to pour ashes and lava over the ancient Roman city of Pompeii (A.D. 79), there was time to escape. But in the face of immense danger, some people lingered long enough to run back into their houses to rescue what was ultimately important to them. As they rushed back into the streets the ash poured down upon them and covered them, snuffing out their lives. Their bodies disintegrated, but left a perfect mold or impression in the hardening volcanic ash.

Centuries later the archaeologists began to excavate the city. Whenever they discovered one of the human molds, they would make a small hole and fill the cavity full of a liquid substance that would then harden. Next they carefully removed the ash, leaving a perfect model of the ancient citizen of Pompeii just as he or she looked at the moment of death.

Do you know what those people had run back to get, causing them to lose their lives? The ancient hands still clutched them:

Bags of gold!

Here were people who had taken an ultimate stand; they had risked everything for what they thought most important. From our perspective, two thousand years later, it seems pathetic and tragic to trade life for a bag of gold, especially since, being dead, one could hardly use it. These people had paid the ultimate price for something that was unworthy of it. They had worshipped a false god.

And, indeed, when anyone exalts the penultimate to the place of the ultimate, one worships a false god and follows a false religion. Of course we might disagree about what *is* ultimate—people always have. Still, sad as it may be, the fact remains that in these disagreements some people may turn out to be wrong.

Death and the Ultimate

The people of Pompeii died in their struggle to grasp the ultimate. Death has always been intimately associated with the ultimate, because as the final and irreversible suffering of life, it raises the question of meaning and the question of reality more directly than does any other human experience. Why? Because it is final and it is certain. One can avoid almost anything—love, sensitivity, responsibility, relationships—but one cannot avoid dying.

Of course people can employ a kind of mental maneuver that avoids the *issue* of dying (but not the reality of it). I call it the *invincibility syndrome.* I experienced it myself, in my closest brush with death.

It happened not six blocks from my home. I was driving along rather absentmindedly, engaged in some obscure errand. Suddenly I was conscious of a white flash to the right rear of my car. I had been hit broadside by a big station wagon. My car went out of control and took off, sailing through the air. When I looked out the front window I found myself confronted with two choices: hit a telephone pole or hit the back end of a paint truck.

Actually, I had no choice at all, since my car was careening out of control. Rather, I had the role of a very interested observer, wondering which object I was going to slam into.

Well, there I was, sailing toward an inevitable head-on collision. But do you think I was scared? Not a bit. Now I have been frightened half to death a time or two when I almost hit a dog running in front of my car. That really made my heart pump. But this time—no fear at all. I felt completely invincible. I *knew* this kind of thing could not happen to me.

But of course it did. As it happened I hit the paint truck instead of the telephone pole. I remember seeing the equipment in the back of the truck explode into the air. The front end of the station wagon was resting partially in my lap, headlight and all; the front end of my car had simply disintegrated. Pieces of vehicles were lying everywhere.

My first thought was, "Oh, no. My eyes! I can't see anything." Then I realized that my glasses had been knocked off. I was conscious of having little bits of glass in my hair. But I just sat there calmly, still feeling invincible.

A police officer came up, looked in the window and asked, "Are you all right?"

"Well, I don't feel anything. Maybe I'm paralyzed from the neck down. Or maybe I'm dead—never having been dead I don't know what *that* feels like."

The look on the patrolman's face said, "Boy, have I ever gotten hold of a live one here!"

The whole adventure was very instructive to me—because I will never forget that sense of invincibility. You would think at least at a time like that you would admit that you are mortal—that it is possible for you to be killed. But, no, I still felt that that happens only to other people.

Nevertheless, the statistics are overwhelmingly against living forever. Still many people have treated death more like an obscenity than a reality. Someone has said that all the obscenities in the last generation were sexual but that all the obscenities of this generation deal with death. We can accept it in movies. We have a morbid curiosity to see blood spurting on the screen. But we do not want to deal with death as a real, personal kind of issue.

We seem unwilling to look at it calmly and say, "In view of the fact that I am not immortal, what does today mean? What does tomorrow mean? What does existence mean?"

Once I was conducting a class discussion on death and various theories were being bandied about. In that class, one student, fifth row back, fourth person over, was four hours from his death. He did not know it, of course. No one did. He had a number of things to say on the subject. He left school that afternoon, and drove toward his home a few miles away. As he crossed a railroad track a fast-moving train struck his car broadside and killed him.

I have often thought about the difference between our theorizing that afternoon and the *reality* of the thing. I have wondered how he would have treated that discussion if he had known that before the next day dawned he would be dead.

Fyodor Dostoyevsky, in his novel *The Idiot*, describes a man who had this opportunity. He was condemned for a political offense to be shot by firing squad. Soon he found himself with only five more minutes.

> He told me that those five minutes seemed to him an infinite time, a vast wealth; he felt that he had so many lives left in those five minutes that there was no need yet to think of the last moment, so much so that he divided his time up. He set aside time to take leave of his comrades, two minutes for that; then he kept another two minutes to think for the last time; and then a minute to look about him for the last time. He remembered very well having divided his time like that. He was dying at twenty-seven, strong and healthy. As he took leave of his comrades, he remembered asking one of them a somewhat irrelevant question and being particularly interested in the answer. Then when he said good-bye, the two minutes came that he had set apart for *thinking* to himself. He knew beforehand what he would think about. He wanted to realize as quickly and clearly as possible how it could be that now he existed and was living and in three minutes he would be *something*—someone

or something. But what? Where? He meant to decide all that in those two minutes![1]

The sentence was changed at the last moment, so the man lived to share his "final" thoughts. But the questions he grappled with are real questions for every human being—and should be dealt with openly and calmly—not as whispered obscenities.

To deal with such basic questions is one of the important parts of reflecting on religion's claims and functions.

RELIGION AND HUMAN EXISTENTIAL NEED

Now we turn to defining religion *functionally*, that is, defining it in terms of what it *does*. What purpose does it have? How does it function? What are its results? The working functional definition for religion that we will propose is this:

> Religion is the means by which a person fulfills existential or ontological needs or ultimate concern.

The word "existential" can mean many things. We simply use it to point to that which is basic to the whole person. It includes every aspect of one's being, so it is "ontological." This distinguishes it from needs that could be defined if one considers a human being as primarily, if not only, a thinking being. It also distinguishes it from needs unique to particular cultures or eras. So it is the need or concern of one's whole existence within the whole of the cosmos and history. Even the most radical existentialist philosophers have had to assume something that humans have had in common. And that is all we are claiming at the outset: a universal human need that involves the totality of each person.

Technology does not function well to fulfill this kind of need. If anything, human existential needs have a way of becoming even more pressing in technosocieties because physical needs are not so much of a problem in such societies. People in technosocieties are fairly safe from invasion, starvation, and diseases. There are more opportunities to get inside oneself. The needs that grow out of *existence* begin to surface. Ironically, the more progress people have made toward meeting external needs, the more conscious they often become of unmet internal needs.

Many examples of this phenomenon can be seen in the children of upper-middle-class families. Their parents worked very hard. They had struggled through the Great Depression. They had somehow overcome,

[1]Fyodor Dostoevsky, *The Idiot*, trans. Constance Garnett (New York: Macmillan, 1913), p. 57. Emphasis added. Reprinted by permission of William Heinemann Limited.

gotten themselves a good bank account, a couple of nice cars, a vacation home, maybe even a boat. The children always had the confidence that funds were available for whatever they wanted to do. If they wanted to take ballet lessons they could do so. If they wanted to go to Europe they could do that too.

But in numerous cases the reaction of the children has been rebellion—a total rejection of the life-style that brought them such comfort. Sometimes they have become leaders of the "prophetic minority"—the counterculture critics of their parents' life-style. They find the world of their parents abhorrent—even shocking. By the thousands, they turn their backs on such a world and drop out.

In other words, the very people who have had their physical and financial needs most consistently and completely met have often become the most unhappy with life itself and have gone off on a desperate search for something with more and deeper meaning.

"Religion" is whatever these or any other human beings have used to meet these existential needs. And while many different religions have functioned in this way, they have all functioned to meet the *same* needs. That is, their symbols, rituals, and doctrines have been experienced as "answering" their needs by pointing to the ultimate or the ground of their being.

We will look at some of the most significant of these needs and some of the religious responses to them.

Precariousness

The first human existential need (the following are not listed in order of importance, necessarily), is

The need to overcome the sense of precariousness.

People of ancient and modern times share the sense of shakiness, the feeling that nothing is solid, that things are unstable, that there is no really unmovable place to stand. You have undoubtedly felt it yourself. There seems to be nothing to hang onto very well. Everything seems to be flowing, shifting like desert sand. You feel that you are about to plunge into some great emotional or psychological chasm. You dream of falling through space, grabbing for trees along the side of the cliff, feeling them slip out of your hands. You just keep falling and falling.

Religion has responded by attempting to provide some sense of personal stability, some sense of cosmological stability, some sense of wholeness. It has tried to supply the conviction that there are some solid places, some solid foundations, unmoved and unmovable. It expresses itself in such statements as this one, from Max Ehrmann's poem "Desiderata":

You are a child of the Universe;
You have a right to be here.

Or in dozens of hymns that speak of solid rocks and safe harbors:

On Christ the solid rock I stand,
All other ground is sinking sand.

Loneliness

Another existential need is to *escape from loneliness*. This is not the loneliness that results from not having friends or from being physically alone. It is an existential loneliness. "Alienation" and "separation" are synonyms. It is much deeper than physical loneliness. It can occur in the middle of 50,000 people at a football game. It can happen to you when you are looking into the eyes of the person you love most, somebody you know would gladly die for you.

It is a kind of ache that says, "When all is said and done, the truth is that I am alone."

In college I used to feel it most right after supper. It is beginning to get dark. You have been to supper and return to your room. It is dark there, too, and you do not know if you even want to turn the light on. You feel very alone. It is not homesickness—you were home last weekend. It is not a lack of friends—you have plenty.

No, it has something to do with your whole existence, with the act of being. You begin to think, "Here is this infinite universe—billions of stars and millions of light-years. And here am I—tiny speck of existence and all alone."

There it is: existential loneliness.

This experience can take various forms. Sometimes it is a sense of alienation from the whole universe. You ask "What's going on here? Who am I? Where is this place? Where am I? Where else could I go?" You feel trapped. You feel alone. You feel separated from what is ultimately real. You wonder where the real center of things may be, where the real action is taking place. Am I at the center, you ask, or am I out on the edge somewhere?

Or it may take the form of alienation from other people. The question keeps pursuing you: "Who *are* all these people?" It can happen as well at the family dinner table as in a crowd of strangers. You can be married twenty years and this loneliness can hit you and you can look across the table at the person you have eaten with, lived with, slept with, shared tragedy and joy with—you can look him or her right in the eyes and think, "I have no idea who you are."

Or it can come to you as self-alienation. You can look in the mirror and say, "I have no idea who I am. I cannot get hold of what this is—what this body is, what this mind is. I am looking at a stranger."

Most religions incorporate both human and divine powers to overcome this alienation. One communion or branch of a particular religion may emphasize the human effort needed, usually speaking in terms of moral effort or meditation; other branches within that same religion will de-emphasize the human while laying great weight on what God does. In any case, alienation, whether it comes from ignorance or basic perverseness, must be overcome, as most religions assess the human predicament.

Meaning

A third universal human need is the need to *find meaning*. From the most ancient songs, poems, and books, to the most modern, these themes appear over and over again: What does suffering mean? Why do I suffer? Why do you suffer? What do joy and beauty mean? Where do they come from, and why?

Human beings have found as much mystery in joy as in suffering, although the latter gets most of the attention. How could I deserve this? Why do I feel so good? Why are things so nice? And, what does death mean? And, in view of death, what does life mean?

Religion attempts to deal with the question of meaning by suggesting the reordering of perception. It says, in one way or another, that reality is not what it appears to be on the surface. Reality lies deep; it lies behind what a human being superficially experiences. Religion calls, in one way or another, for *faith in the unseen*. It maintains, in fact, that the unseen is more real than the outward and obvious. One must cut through the obvious; one must dig deeper, below the surface, to reach reality and meaning.

Religions may disagree as to what this reality and meaning are, but they agree that they are not what the superficial and casual observer believes them to be. Religion would argue that there is some kind of meaning in suffering, joy, and death. This meaning might be hidden; one might never really get hold of it. But one has the assurance that somehow, behind all seeming chaos and lack of meaning, there is order, that the universe is not an accident, that things fit together, even though they do not fit together in our perception. To return to the words in "Desiderata,"

> And whether or not it is clear to you, no doubt the universe is unfolding as it should.

Our perception sees these mysteries as parallel lines, permanently separated from each other. But a master physicist, using the most highly sophisticated equipment, may find that seemingly parallel lines lack one billionth of a degree of being truly parallel and are moving imperceptibly toward each other. He may then confidently predict that somewhere out in space, millions of light-years away, those lines will come together at a point of perfect harmony.

In the same way, the religious masters have seen imperceptible movements among the seemingly incongruous and contradictory events of life. They have therefore predicted confidently that out there, far beyond human capacity to perceive, the mysteries are resolved into perfect harmony. Truth, then, is not what may first *appear* to be true.

The way in which one searches for and finds truth differs from one religious system to another.

In any case, when one finds the truth, one finds that it is not what it had first seemed to be. One discovers that one has reordered one's perception.

Holiness

Another existential need is to find a way to deal with the Holy. The word "holy" is used here in a specialized way. We are not using the word as in the sentence, "I can't stand Harvey; he has such a holier-than-thou attitude." We are using the word in the special way Rudolf Otto used it—to designate the experience of the "numinous." Its otherness is terrifying, awe-inspiring. If one does not approach the "Holy" properly, there will be irremedial suffering.

This experience is expressed in various ways. Primitive peoples speak of taboos:

"Don't go under that tree!"
"Why not?"
"Because it is a holy place."

When Moses saw a burning bush in the desert of Sinai he heard a voice commanding him,

"Take off your shoes!"
"Why?"
"You are standing on holy ground."

(Exodus 3)

Humans have always experienced this brush with "the Other" and have always tried to deal with it. And religion has always offered some way for people to cope with the Holy. One of the functions of religion, then, is to provide devotees, through myth and cult, ways in which to relate to the otherness that they sense in their world.

Religions have approached the Holy in a variety of ways. One approach is through the cultus we will call *ritual*. It provides special actions that one performs to show his or her reverence for the Other, or at least to keep from angering It. Elaborate systems of sacred places, sacred objects,

Religious Ritual. One way human beings have attempted to relate to the "other world" is through ritual ceremonies such as sacrifice. In this scene on an ancient Greek vase, two youths offer a goat as a burnt offering to the god Hermes. One youth roasts part of the goat on a spit. Other parts of the corpse lie on the table and floor and are suspended from the ceiling. By offering the life of the animal, they hope either to placate the god's anger or to gain his favor. (British Museum)

sacred names, sacred actions, sacred persons, and sacred writings have been developed. Through these, people try to become safely involved with the Other—to be able to live with It without being constantly in terror.

The second approach is by way of *morality*. Most religions give an ethical content to the Holy. They claim that what this Other wants is, primarily, for one to live with a certain life-style that is pleasing to or conforms to It. And if one will live in this way, one will have peace with the Other. So, in these religious systems, there is more emphasis on the kind of person one is than on the kind of rituals he or she performs. That does not mean there are no rituals, of course, but it does mean that the emphasis is on ethics or life-style.

The difference between these two approaches to the Holy has been distinguished as *priestly* and *prophetic*. The prophetic demands morality, and this is central to every religion. But by itself, the moral demand ultimately buries people beneath guilt. The priestly element is necessary when people realize that perhaps no matter how hard they try, they may never really be more moral. The prophetic or moral demands, however, remain necessary. Hopefully they will not be cheapened or relegated to meaninglessness by virtue of the rituals by which one obtains forgiveness. But by the forgiveness or reunion with the Ultimate obtained in the priestly route, one senses an acceptance of himself or herself that is much different from simply self-acceptance. And this changes one's whole attitude toward the moral demands, as one realizes that his or her will is in fact consonant with the moral demand rather than at odds with it. Here sheer autonomy as well as offensive heteronomy are superseded by what could be called "theonomy," that is, where God's will is discovered as also being one's own will.

Suffering and Joy

A religious community also fulfills one's need for a group with which to share meaningfully the deep moments of suffering and joy. The dramatic moments in life as well as the traumatic moments have to be shared. People without particular religious affiliation often find substitute groups to carry somewhat the same function. But many people express the frustration we have spoken of earlier—of loneliness. In such situations, suffering can often become greater than a person can bear. And joy fades immediately without a concerned community to support the person.

Whether one thinks of joy as happiness or the mere relief from pain and suffering, humans have always seen it as one of the primary worthy goals in life. Yet realistically, religious people have acknowledged that even their beliefs and community did not enable them to become immunized to pain or suffering. But they provided a method for controlling the pain or controlling their reactions to the suffering. By spreading the pain or suffering through the group, its effect on the individual was minimized if not transcended. The rituals, myths, and stories by which the religious community is provided its identity tend to blunt or dissipate by familiarity the "otherness" of life's experiences. This is the case whether the otherness originates with the Holy or not. The most traumatic experiences can be accommodated by virtue of ritual and mythical familiarity. Obviously, by *myth* and *ritual* then, we are not referring to something that is untrue, contrived, or dispensable. Rather, these are parts of the individual and group identity of the religious person, etched on the unconscious self.

When one gives birth, or is baptized, or is accepted into the adult community, or is married, or dies, the rituals, myths, stories, traditions shared by the community provide an answer that goes beyond mere cognition or intellect. They connect one subconsciously with the ideal, with the Source of being. So most religions have admitted sooner or later that the Answer is beyond words or concepts, beyond the intellect, found in the deeper recesses of humanity. It can be found in a suffering or joy beyond words. But it will be realized only in community as that suffering or joy is shared.

3

The Many Forms
of Religion

RELIGION: A DESCRIPTIVE DEFINITION

If you were to ask, "What is the major religion in India?" and I answered, "Hinduism," we would both be talking about religion descriptively. When one observes and records what people call "religion" and then states his or her findings objectively, that person is dealing with religion descriptively. Religion is, in this sense, whatever an individual or a group calls religion. Of course, there may be problems if the "outsider" wants to call it religion and thinks that it can be described, while the adherent to the religion either does not think of it as a religion or rejects the idea that it can be described.

Religion, defined descriptively, has appeared in thousands of forms. To study it in this way is like walking through a huge art gallery observing paintings in the style of hundreds of great artists. Because there is so much, and because the forms seem so diverse, it is easy to become confused. We will try to simplify the process a bit by putting the religions of the world into three major categories:

> Primitive religions
> Cultural religions
> Supracultural religions

No evolutionary order is implied here. Primitive religion does not necessarily evolve into cultural religion and then into supracultural religion. At any moment in history it is possible to find all three types of religion existing side by side.

PRIMITIVE RELIGION

Use of the word "primitive" may be misleading. Primitive religions are not necessarily crude, nor are those who belong to such religions necessarily ignorant and simple minded. As scholars learn more about primitive religions, they find them to be dealing in sensitive and often complicated ways with the human existential needs we have discussed.

Unfortunately, Western colonialists often entered a primitive or underdeveloped country, made some superficial observations, and pronounced what they saw to be simple minded. The people were thought of as savages, hardly superior to the "other animals" of the jungle.

Fortunately, more careful study has now been done. The result is a more sympathetic verdict upon these cultures. Rather than regarding primitive religions as a sort of primeval form out of which other religions have evolved, we now may appreciate these forms in their own right. They are remarkably stable religious systems, often changing little over thousands of years.

They only thrive in isolation, however. While the primitive community is bound together tightly and shielded from outside ideas, the primitive religion is strong. But when it is forced to cope with new cultures and new ideas, the primitive religion begins to crumble.

It may *not* evolve into a "higher" form. At least, it is difficult to find examples of such an evolution in historic times. Rather, changes have more often come dramatically, and usually through the influence of the tremendous religious genius of one person or group of persons. It was this idea of some rather uniform historical evolution of religion articulated by Hegel that Schleiermacher opposed with his "positive-individual" explanation. He insisted that a new impulse lay at the root of each religion rather than a new religion simply evolving out of its predecessor. So the history of religion is in large part a story of great religious geniuses, gurus, saints, and prophets. What these people have said and done has always been tied to the past, of course, but it has had something unique, ingenious, and new in it.

Furthermore, the followers of these geniuses seldom reach the spiritual heights of their teachers. The normal movement in religion is as likely to be degeneration as upward evolution. Compare, for example, the richness of the *Tao Te Ching*, the sacred book of Taoism, with the set of superstitions and rituals that later carried the same name. Or compare the richness of the teachings of Jesus and Paul with many of the ideas called Christian during the Dark Ages.

Religions may start at their apex. What comes afterward is a constant struggle to prevent degeneration and the loss of the spark of genius that created them. Disciples' attempts to be faithful to the founder may lack insight or tolerance or other qualities that were part of the founder's character. But on the other hand, the continued reflection usually provides greater profundity to the original teachings.

In any case, primitive religion is not dead. It is still a thriving force in the twentieth century. In fact, some 10 percent of all living persons practice some form of primitive religion. Most of these are in Africa, with Asia coming next. In South America there are one million such worshippers, and in the United States they number in the tens of thousands.

Perhaps this last fact is surprising. But consider the "native religion" of America—that of the Indians. It is primitive religion in its classic form. And, far from dying, it is now experiencing a kind of revival. This is especially true among some of the youngest and best educated Indians, who see the old faith as an alternative to the one they feel has been forced upon their fathers and grandfathers by white oppressors.

And then, of course, there are various forms of primitive religion among the aboriginal populations of Australia.

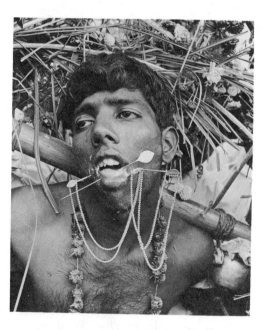

Scene from a festival in Mauritius, the Indian Ocean nation. (Christian Zuber, Rapho/Photo Researchers, Inc.)

The following are some of the characteristics usually common to the many types of primitive religions.

Primitive Religion's Omissions

Primitive religions are characterized by the lack of certain things. They lack, first, an *organized system of thought*. They consist of many more or less disconnected ideas with no particular attempt to fit these ideas into a "theology." There is no attempt to create a rational progression of thought or overarching set of concepts.

Second, they lack *theological development*. In a religion such as Christianity, we find the development of various dogmas or concepts that were only in germ form in the New Testament. An example is the doctrine of the Trinity, which spelled out the relationship between the Father, Son, and Holy Spirit. For hundreds of years Christian theologians struggled to develop a way of stating this relationship that would integrate all the various data in the New Testament. Eventually they came up with various creedal statements that were not found in the New Testament but, rather, it was maintained, developed the ideas found there.

In primitive religions such theological development is lacking. Belief and practice remain constant; primitive "theologians" seldom convene conferences to work out new responses to new situations.

Third, primitive religions lack *sacred writings*. There is nothing in them comparable to the Bible or the Koran. Most primitive religions exist in preliterate or nonliterate cultures—among people who have no written language. Thus the past must be retained in other ways. Usually the traditions are kept and guarded by an old holy man or by shamans or groups of priests. They have been passed down by former generations, all the way back to the ancestors who knew how it was at the beginning, or who knew how the gods created it all. In addition to this oral tradition there is the use of artistic symbols. In the caves of France, for example, are found hundreds of ancient pictures painted on the walls. While their mysteries are not solved entirely, they seem to have served in religious ceremonies thousands of years ago. And as the generations passed, they provided guidance and help in retaining the beliefs of the people and in passing them along.

Fourth, primitive religions lack *literature*. Because they have no written history, the remembrances of the past eventually take on the qualities of myth. Primitive people realize that they are, and must be, tied to their forebears. But they do not remember them by name, or date, as we think of remembering history. Rather, they remember them through symbols and myths. Great persons of the past may become animals; they may be thought of as living in a misty netherworld, where they slay monsters that threaten their descendants. In these myths lie the essence of the past, and its *real* truth, as far as primitive people are concerned.

The High God and the World of Spirits

Even the simplest and most remote jungle tribes seem to believe in the existence of a "high god" or "mother-goddess." He or she is identified as the creator of everything, the generative force from which everything has come.

He usually is thought to have little to do with people's everyday life, however. He is far away; although he is responsible for everything and has authority over everything, he chooses to stay out of the picture. People's mundane needs were therefore usually met by their entreating other gods, who by their association with more immediate aspects of the natural world, appeared more approachable as well as more effective.

In addition to their recognizing many different gods, most primitive religions also believed in other powers we could call "spirits." Primitive religions recognize, and relate themselves to, two categories of spirits. There are, first, the spirits of the dead. This includes the spirits of ancestors, and particularly recent ancestors—fathers, grandfathers, and so on. These are thought of as lingering on earth after their bodies have died. They will, in fact, continue to remain in the area so long as anyone is alive who can remember their names and continue to keep in contact with them through prayer.

It is very important to have children who can remember and reverence one after his or her death. It is also very important to retain these ceremonies and prayers because if they are neglected the ancestors fade away.

This concept is one of the hardest for primitive people to relinquish, even when they are converted to other religious forms. They become very concerned that if the ceremonies end their forefathers will lose their identities—that they will have "killed" them.

The spirit of a recently dead person is believed to be very close to the corpse, especially for the first few hours after death. It is very important to convince the deceased that the survivors are stricken with grief, lest he become angry and cause them trouble. So some tribes have the custom, for example, of requiring young girls, sisters of a dead older brother, to hack off two or three fingers at the first joint. Other types of disfigurement are also practiced. These are to convince the deceased that life is not just going on as usual, but that he is highly respected and sorely missed.

A friend of mine who lived for years in a primitive village tells an interesting story that illustrates how vividly and concretely the spirit world is believed to interact with the physical world. The village in which my friend lived had not had rain for several months and the situation was getting desperate. So the village council met and decided to ask for help from the previous chief, who had been dead several years. They wanted to urge him to make some contacts for them in the spirit world to see if the rain could be started again.

The contact began with two old women who had known the chief personally. They went to his grave, which was unmarked but carefully remembered, and danced on it. Since my friend was trusted and respected, he was allowed to watch and even take photographs.

The women danced and called out the chief's name. They sang songs about the good old days. "Do you remember the time we had a great feast and how we all drank beer until sunrise?" they asked in song.

Then the old man's son went to the grave. He carried with him a pot of beer (a favorite drink of the old chief), which he poured onto the grave. Then he turned the pot over and sat down on it. He leaned forward with his ear close to the ground and said, "Now, Father, first I want to explain this white man with the little black box. Don't worry about it. He has had it all along and it doesn't seem to hurt anybody. He has lived here a long time and is our friend, so he can hear what we talk about."

Then the son and the women carried on a long conversation with the grave about the rain situation. My friend said that it was perfectly obvious to everyone there that a real conversation was occurring.

I do not know whether it rained, but obviously there was a vivid sense of communication with the spirit world.

The second kind of spirits are not of people, but *are spirits of mountains, rivers, animals, and other natural elements.* Every stream, every tree, every valley has a certain spiritual power that controls it. If one wants to cross the stream or climb the tree or hunt in the valley, one must make peace with the controlling spirit. The old fairy tale about Billygoat Gruff, who guarded the bridge, may well be a dim memory of some ancient European form of primitive religion.

In primitive religion, there is a strong sense of being one with nature. Nature has a mind of its own, and one must learn to deal with it. Humans are only one part of nature and must be very careful how they deal with the other parts. If a tree is cut down, certain things must be said and done to convince the spirit of the tree that there is no intention to harm him or usurp his powers. An American Navaho Indian pointed out that his people have a respect for the world in which they live far greater than does the white man. The white man is an exploiter of nature, whereas the Navaho is a partner to nature. This is because the Navaho does not see the world as simply matter, a mere combination of molecules; he sees the world as being animated, alive, having will, having mind, having soul. This statement introduces the next characteristic of primitive religion: *animism.*

An animist believes that material objects and nonhuman creatures have mind, will, passion, feeling, and so on. They have *mana*. Mana is the soul or life that inhabits and animates such things. Some objects have a special power and are called fetishes, amulets, or talismans. These might be feathers from an eagle, the tooth of some ferocious animal, or the scalp of an enemy. They may be kept in a special pouch and brought out on special occasions when their owners need some contact with the spiritual world.

Power in Primitive Religion

Another aspect of primitive religion is the use of *magic*. In magic an attempt is made to use the forces of the invisible world through various occult rituals. The magician knows secret words and ceremonies. He must be very careful to get all the words right; he must stand in precisely the right spot; he must proceed correctly at every point to get in touch with this other world.

There are two kinds of magic: natural and supernatural. For *natural magic* one uses charms, omens, and divinations. For example, one might look at the entrails of a chicken or throw an object into the air and watch the direction in which it falls. The result will give a clue as to how to solve a problem at hand.

Supernatural magic, however, is a much more sober matter. It is often used for evil purposes by witches or sorcerers. You probably remember the witch doctors in the Tarzan movies who were always putting a hex on someone. But actually a witch doctor is just what the name implies. He is the one who can combat what an evil witch has done. A witch doctor is not a witch. Such a person is sometimes called a medicine man or, more precisely, a *shaman*. He knows how to reverse the spells cast by evil witches. He is able to contact and at times even control the powers of the other world.

Because the primitive religionist senses such an intimacy with the other world, he tends to conclude that almost everything that happens is influenced from over on the other side. If a family's house burns down, for example, its members immediately begin to search for an evil witch—because there must have been a witch somewhere using supernatural powers to make such a thing happen.

A friend of mine, living in a village in Zambia, had a rather frightening experience of this kind. He and his family had lived in the village for several years. One day he was cooking over an open fire. Somehow the fire got out of control and caught his hut on fire. Soon the fire spread and the whole village was in flames. He was very concerned, not only because of the loss, but because he knew that the people would begin to look for a witch who had caused such a terrible thing to happen. And, of course, *he* was a likely candidate!

Fortunately, he did not come under suspicion. There was, however, a great deal of discussion about who the witch might be and why he would do such a thing.

Even more ominous is the use of the death hex by a witch. Often persons who are hexed actually die (the power of suggestion?). Even in a "supracultural" religion's earlier forms, such as in ancient Israel, one can see this idea of a death hex. For example, witches were outlawed, and any child found to pronounce a curse on its parents was to be immediately put to death. The "curse" was surely regarded as real.

We can see that the other world, the Holy as we called it earlier, is very real in the primitive religions. Coping with this other world takes a great deal of time. The material world is constantly being influenced by what is happening in the other world, by powers in the *other* reality. By the primitive religion's view, if human beings are going to survive in this world, they must always keep good contact and good relations with the other world.

While the primitive world view is usually associated with tribal societies, it can sometimes be found directly in the middle of the most modern technological societies too. I was once invited to attend the spring rites of a rather large group of people who described themselves as "followers of the old religion," "neopagans," or simply "witches" (but not evildoers, as with the "witches" mentioned). The gathering took place in Kansas City, Missouri, almost within sight of a huge modern medical complex. Participants were from all age groups and educational levels. The ceremonies were dedicated to "the Goddess" who, said the worshippers, has been variously called Diana, Venus, Ishtar, Anath, Isis, and so on throughout history. The names of the goddess derive from the great ancient culture religions (discussed in the next section), but the world view of the group corresponds closely to that of the primitive nature worship that predates the ancient empires.

Indeed, said the worshippers, this is the "natural" religion of the human race, followed everywhere by those who have not been "corrupted." They have been worshipping as I saw them, they claim, throughout the ages—a faithful few who have retained the "old ways."

Prayers are offered to the four winds as a sacred circle is drawn within the modern apartment living room. Participants are crowded together in the room. The air is heavy with incense (and marijuana). The atmosphere is reverent. The liturgy proceeds as a black woman and a Hawaiian man in white robes chant praises to the Goddess. A priestess with long golden hair moves through the crowd dispensing blessings and serving the ceremonial wine. Four priests recite the long ceremony. Cries of joy go up as another priestess, representing the Goddess, sweeps into the room, her hair adorned with spring flowers and her sheer blue gown and veils flowing. The worshippers shout in joy at the arrival of the fertile powers of the earth and the meeting dissolves into wild dancing, drinking, and unrestrained celebration.

Kansas City, Missouri!

CULTURAL RELIGION

A second group of religions in our gallery is the cultural religions. They are tied closely to the concept of civilization; each one has an intimate relationship to a particular civilization—rising when it rises, falling when it falls. By definition, then, a cultural religion is one that lasts only until the culture or civilization that practices it passes away.

There are many ancient examples of this. The first great cultural religions date from the rise of civilization—somewhere between 4000 B.C. and 3000 B.C. When Egypt was a great power, gods such as Amon and Re and goddesses such as Isis were widely known and worshipped—but no more. They died when the culture that supported them died. The same can be said for the great god Marduk and the great goddess Ishtar, who fell with the powerful cultures of ancient Mesopotamia. And the gods of ancient Greece, the gods of the poems of Homer, disappeared with that civiliza-

Cultural Religion and Polytheism. Cultural religions, unlike supracultural ones, usually pay homage to many gods. The seal from which this impression was made belonged to an Akkadian scribe named Adda about 2300 B.C. Depicted is the sun god rising from between two mountains, holding aloft his emblem, the saw. To his right stands the god of the deep with fish-laden waters flowing behind him and a bird in his hand. His attendant, Janus-headed Usmu, stands behind him. Ishtar, the winged goddess of war, rises from the mountain on the left, quivers of arrows on her back, while another god, perhaps Ninurta, advances with his bow. (British Mution, except, of course, for those that were adopted by the Romans. While Rome ruled the world the cultural religion of Rome flourished. When Rome disintegrated, so did her gods.

The explanation for this phenomenon can be found in the two major characteristics of the cultural religions: their relationship with *tradition* and their relationship with the *power structure*.

Cultural religion has a vital connection with tradition. It serves as the *conveyor* of tradition, being the vehicle by which tradition passes from one generation to another. It goes further: it also serves as the *sanctifier* of tradition. It pronounces this benediction:

The Blessings of God, may they rest on the way *we* do things.

Priests of the cultural religion appear at every important cultural event, pronouncing it holy and good, tying it to the will of the deity.

Not only does cultural religion convey and sanctify tradition, it also seeks to *protect* tradition. It responds intensely, sometimes even violently, when tradition seems threatened.

Cultural religion always has a vital connection with the power structure. This, no doubt, is the reason why it resists all kinds of innovation. It enjoys a good relationship with those who hold power. And it is always to the advantage of those in power to maintain the status quo. Change may well result in a shift in power, and this becomes disastrous for both the power structure and the religion it supports.

In fact, one of the surest tests in classifying religions is to observe what happens when a given culture is threatened with a new cultural idea. The priests of the cultural religion will be the first to object. This will be true whether the new idea is overtly "religious" or not. One would expect such a reaction to a new religious idea. But the cultural religion will also feel threatened if it is an idea about wearing clothes differently, or wearing hair in a different style, or living in a different kind of housing, or rearranging the family structure in some way, or getting paid in a different manner, or changing the ownership of businesses and factories.

The cultural religion's representatives will immediately perceive some connection between the proposed change and the will and the *law of God*. They will begin to crusade against the change in the *name of God*.

The story has been repeated thousands of times in history. It is a perfectly predictable form of behavior. Once the bond between theology and culture is fixed, everything else follows.

Modern examples might include such religious forms as the prerevolutionary Russian Orthodox Church or, even more recently, the Church of Ethiopia. These very ancient forms of Christianity had so completely tied themselves to the status quo that each came to depend almost entirely on the emperor and the power structure he represented. In each case, when the emperor was overthrown, the church found itself in great trouble. It had fought every change, but change had won in spite of its opposition. Now, without the emperor to protect it, its future became very dim.

The modern totalitarian states, right wing and left wing, have had their cultural religions, though they have often been cryptoreligions. In Nazi Germany, as in other fascist states, there has been the worship of "the people," of "the spirit of the Fatherland," and so on. In communist states, as we have seen already, the same process exists, although overtly religious language is seldom used to describe it.

Some have detected the same process at work in the custom of some American Protestant churches of placing side by side, at the front of the house of worship, two flags, one bearing the cross and the other the Stars and Stripes.

SUPRACULTURAL RELIGION

The third major section in our gallery of religious types consists of the supracultural faiths. A supracultural religion may be defined as one that *transcends cultural bounds.* It is "over" or "above" culture, thus, supra. It is able to move from one culture into another one. It is able to survive the death of its host culture (the one in which it first appeared). The religion of Ishtar and Marduk died with the Babylonian empire—no Babylon, no Marduk. A supracultural religion would have been able to survive in such a case.

Certain characteristics help us to identify supracultural religions. First, they serve a *prophetic* role as well as a *priestly* one. These two words are used in special ways: a priest sanctifies, a prophet judges. A priest says, "God forgive what we are doing" or "God bless what we are doing"; a prophet says, "God is appalled by what we are doing." A priest speaks the blessings of deity on the way in which a culture is presently conducting itself, whereas a prophet speaks to evaluate culture in the name of a higher law.

Supracultural religions are not entirely prophetic. All religions serve a priestly function to some extent. But the prophetic element is present and active to a greater extent in supracultural religions.

Since they criticize, and do not simply sanctify, supracultural religions are often at odds with the power structure. A cultural religion gets into trouble when its host culture collapses. But a supracultural religion tends to be in trouble all the time. The power structure sees it as a threat and often opposes it—sometimes even physically.

This aspect of supracultural religion is called "prophetic" because it is illustrated by the "prophets" of the Hebrew Scriptures. These men fearlessly approached the kings of their day, saying, "If you do not change your policies, then, in the name of God, you will be punished for your deeds!"

Of course, that sort of talk does not make one very popular at the palace. Prophets are seldom invited to gala evenings there. Kings much prefer to be surrounded by priests rather than by prophets. On one occasion the eighth-century B.C. prophet Amos went up to speak out against the false altar at Bethel. On the way he was met by a representative of the king who said, "Why don't you go back down South where you came from and prophesy there? We have all the prophets we need up here!" That is the way supracultural religion is often treated.

A second characteristic of supracultural religion is its *interest in human existential needs*. It is more concerned to serve these needs (which were discussed at length in Chapter Two) than in cultural preservation. People need a sense of joy, they need to find meaning in the things that happen to them, and they need freedom from the feelings of alienation and precariousness that plague them. Supracultural religions focus on these questions rather than bemoan changes in society or in "our way of life."

This helps us to see why such religions can survive the death of the culture that hosts them. They are not overly concerned about such things. They are much more interested in the needs of *human beings* than of any particular *group* of human beings. They can therefore adapt to another culture, because the basic human needs are the same everywhere and at all times. It is the human predicament, as well as unique problems of a given political or cultural predicament, that occupies their energies.

A third characteristic of supracultural religions is their emphasis on the *internal* aspects of religion. There is a movement, for example, from magic to morality. Other religious types, at various levels of sophistication, attempt to control the powers of the other world with secret or sacred words and rituals. The supracultural religion, on the other hand, is more apt to emphasize the *kind of person* one is and the kind of *personal decisions* he or she makes (morality) and the theoretical basis on which these actions are based (ethics) than the ceremonies or sorceries he or she may know.

Put another way, there is a movement from ritual to correct attitude. Other religious forms place great importance on using the correct forms and ceremonies. Every step, every word, must be precisely executed. Of course supracultural religions have ceremonies, too. But the difference is in emphasis. In them, the emphasis lies on what a person is, in his or her heart, more than on what he or she is doing outwardly.

The ancient prophet Amos, whom we have mentioned, furnishes a classic example of this emphasis. Speaking for God, he says,

> I hate, I spurn your pilgrim-feasts;
> I will not delight in your sacred ceremonies

When you present your sacrifices and offerings
I will not accept them,
nor look on the buffaloes of your shared-offerings.
Spare me the sound of your songs;
I cannot endure the music of your lutes.
Let Justice roll on like a river
and righteousness like an ever-flowing stream.
(Amos 5:21-24 NEB)[1]

The whole concept of sacrifice is transformed in the supracultural religion from propitiatory sacrifice to self-sacrifice through morality. Propitiatory sacrifice emphasizes the offering of something external to oneself, such as the killing of the best of one's animals or the burning of the finest grain of the harvest. Self-sacrifice involves giving one's own life in service to ultimate causes. "Present your bodies as a living sacrifice," says the Christian Apostle Paul, "for this is your proper ritual." The same emphasis is found in the Upanishads as they see the Vedic system of sacrifices as inadequate.

A fourth characteristic of supracultural religions is their conception of ultimate reality as being either *monotheistic* or *monistic* rather than polytheistic. Culture religions can be characterized by many gods. The adherents are pulled in many ways. They owe their allegiance to many things. Their loyalties are divided. They are polytheistic.

In the supracultural religions, reality is thought of as *one* thing. Thus, the adherent is committed to and subservient to only one thing. Supracultural religions differ in that some of them are monotheistic and some are monistic. *Monotheism* is the belief that there is one God, one ultimate personal reality. But it often carries with it the idea that human beings are separate from that one God and must relate themselves to God. God creates a separate, distinct world and then places human beings in that external world.

Monism is distinguishable from monotheism in the sense of not asserting that the One is or is conceivable as personal. Monism differs from dualism in holding that Ultimate Reality is not two or more. Monism, like pantheism, has often been the butt of jokes or caricatures, implying that its adherents believed that they or their fishing rod or their motorcycle were "God." But it is doubtful that anyone has ever held those crude ideas.

Usually when monism is found, it is embedded within a deep mysticism. It will assert that God is the fire over which we cook, the fire in the sky, and the fire in the heart, but God is none of these or none of these is God. God is not what we see or hear but the power by which we see or hear. Thus God, as in the Hindu Upanishads, is, as true reality, beyond all hu-

---

[1]From *The New English Bible.* Copyright © 1961, 1970 by the Delegates of the Oxford University Press and the Syndices of the Cambridge University Press. Reprinted by permission.

man description, beyond all attributes. One can only say that God is "not this, not that." That is, no matter what one says about God, God is more. This realization that God cannot be described with positive attributes is not simply present in Hinduism. It was articulated in Judaism by Moses Maimonides, and in Christianity by St. Anselm, that is, in religions that are "monotheistic." So monotheism and monism finally are often distinguished only by the question of how personal this "God" is. And even monotheistic thinkers have often asserted that as necessary as the idea of "person" is for "God," it too must be a symbol.

The Sources of Supracultural Religion

The term "supracultural" should not be taken to imply that such religions are completely detached from culture, of course. Historically, the supracultural religions were born within culture. They borrowed profusely from the thought forms and vocabularies of the culture religions around them. But they also showed the ability vastly to expand these concepts and words and to universalize them—making them apply to people of very different cultures and vocabularies. For the most part, supracultural religions were rocked in the cradle of some cultural religion.

Usually, the spark that ignited the supracultural explosion of a new religious form can be traced to one person or one small group of persons. The supracultural dimensions derive from some genius who appears, seemingly out of nowhere, using the language and ideas of his or her culture and his or her people, but developing them in ingeniously broad and universal ways. Sometimes a few others share in this process with the genius, but more often he or she works alone. A supracultural religion is born!

The result is the initiation of a struggle between the new religion and its host culture. The two exist together in a state of constant tension. The culture tries very hard to "recapture" the supracultural religion and pull it back, to smother it within its cultural origins. Often a religion slips back and forth between the cultural and supracultural as it alternately loses and wins in this struggle.

Christianity serves as an example. The history of Christianity is, in one sense, the history of a supracultural religion trying to escape from the various cultures in which it has existed. Each of these cultures has tried to maintain that "Christianity belongs to *us*. It is part and parcel of *our way of doing things*. We are a *Christian* culture. To be Christian is to be culturally like *us*."

Thus, early Christian missionaries who went from England and the United States into Africa often made no noticeable distinction between Western culture and the Christian religion. They insisted not only that the people in that different culture accept the universal concepts of Christianity about universal human needs, but also that they take baths more regularly and dress more "modestly"—practices having little or no connection with the universal insights of Jesus.

When the "Christians" of medieval Western Europe went off on the Crusades, they came in contact with the "Christians" of Byzantium, who had a very different culture and language. After a period of puzzlement, the Westerners began slaughtering the Easterners right along with the "unbelievers." Evidently they were not able to conceive of Christians who were not culturally like themselves. Their actions proved that their type of Christianity was indistinguishable in their minds from Western European culture. Of course, the same sort of thing has happened to other supracultural religions like Buddhism and Islam.

So you can see that a religion may exist in two forms at the same time. In some places, and by some people, it may be practiced as a supracultural religion; in other places it may function as a classic cultural religion.

Examples of Supracultural Religions

We will divide the major religious systems that have proved their ability to cross cultural lines into three groups. The first group appeared during the centuries between 1000 B.C. and 500 B.C. It is one of the amazing facts of history that many of the most persistent religious ideas of humanity, including those most prevalent today, appeared during these centuries. It was a very creative period for religious ideas. The following are some specific examples.

Greece entered the period with a classic polytheistic cultural religion. Then there arose people who struggled intensely with the ultimate questions about existence—people like Socrates, Plato, and Aristotle. In their quest for reality they developed a truly supracultural way of looking at things. Within the philosophies of these men, and others like them, can be found almost every possible direction of rationalistic philosophical thinking about the meaning of human existence. The philosophical alternatives they proposed have influenced and guided men and women in numerous succeeding cultures.

Meanwhile, during the same period, something dramatic was happening in the tiny country of Israel, a relatively short distance to the southeast of Greece. The religion of Israel had, prior to this time, followed rather classic culture-religion lines. It was a religion of the children of Israel, wandering in the desert, on their way to the promised land. It was a religion for them and for them alone. It contained a strong emphasis on propitiatory sacrifice and ritual and priestly ties to the power structure. Then during the years from 1000 B.C. to 500 B.C. a group of prophets arose, one at a time, here and there (this was no committee!), with an amazingly similar message.

The God of Israel is the God of the Nations, they began to say. He desires mercy and not sacrifice. It is His will to pull the human race together. He operates among and above the empires of humanity, bringing about His purposes in history. He seeks people who will make a covenant with Him in their hearts. Speaking as the mouthpieces of Yahweh, the God of Israel, men such as Amos and Jeremiah and Isaiah, though still conceiving of God in nationalistic terms, began to open up the door to a supracultural conception of religion and "God" which would eventually come in Judaism with the final destruction of its temple and its adaption to dispersion and study of the Torah.

And in Iran (ancient Persia) a remarkable religious genius named Zoroaster was bringing about a similar change in the old Aryan culture religion. The remarkable coincidences continued in India, where Gautama, the founder of Buddhism, was developing insights that allowed a new faith to emerge from the old Hindu culture religion—a faith that eventually spread far from its Indian homeland to become a world religion. Within Hinduism itself there were genuinely creative stirrings at the same time. During these centuries were produced profound documents of Hinduism, documents that reflect many of the most basic supracultural characteristics. These include a collection known as the Upanishads and then, somewhat later, the Ramayana and the Mahabharata, the latter of which eventually included the famous Bhagavad Gita.

The first century A.D. is a pivotal one in the history of supracultural religion. Three of the major religions of the world arose around this same hundred years. None were entirely new; all were built on earlier foundations.

This was, of course, the founding century of Christianity. Christianity had two host cultures—a sort of grandmother and grandfather, you might say. The first was Israel, particularly the Israel of the great prophets just mentioned. The second was the Graeco-Roman world into which Christianity came. When the early Christians spoke of their faith they used not only the language of the sacred books of Israel, but also the Greek language, the language that had formed the thinking of the Roman Empire. As noted already, Judaism also underwent another major change during this century. The Jewish state had been severely damaged by the Romans around A.D. 70. A religion of the rabbis replaced the old forms—blood sacrifices, the priesthood, the divinely anointed kingship—all disappeared entirely. While Judaism is perhaps still tied to a given culture more than the other religions we are discussing in this section, it is also very resilient and has been able to survive in diverse cultural situations for many centuries. Thus it is included here.

The third of the first-century developments took place within Buddhism and resulted in what is called Mahayana Buddhism, a religion that has spread into many parts of the earth and has become truly a world religion.

There are a number of significant supracultural movements of a later date, also. In the heart of the culture religion of Arabia there arose, in the seventh century A.D. another remarkable religious thinker—Muhammad. Out of the raw materials of his culture, he expounded universal concepts about the nature of God, the nature of reality, and the meaning of existence. The new faith, Islam, eventually conquered the far-flung cultures of North Africa, Central Africa, the Middle East, Iran, and Turkey.

Hinduism has finally transcended the Indian culture through the Vedanta, and through the bhaktimarga that centers on Krisna and Rama. Buddhism became supracultural very early on as it moved into other Eastern countries. Zen Buddhism and the Pure Land Buddhism have spread to Western lands as well.

Several of the religions mentioned in this chapter will be investigated in detail in the following chapters. For now, it is important to remember that in the gallery of religious forms there are three major sections: primitive religions, cultural religions, and supracultural religions. In each section there are hundreds of individual pictures of faith, ready for viewing by the student of religion.

4

The Spiritual World of Eastern Religion

THE EASTERN WORLD VIEW

Scientific humanism is a Western phenomenon, which, as we shall see, grew out of the secularization of the Medieval Man. But most of the world is *not* Western. Most of the world's population resides on the side of the world we call "the East," in nations such as China, India, Japan, and Indochina.

The scientific humanist, whose viewpoint will be discussed at length in Chapter Ten, says that reality could be found only in the material world. But in the East, even those who do not believe in the existence of a personal God (and thus are atheists from a Western point of view), do not believe that only matter is real. In other words, they might be atheistic, but never materialistic.

Many Hindus would say that the real world is not the material world at all. The real world is not obvious like the material world. It is, rather, a spiritual world that lies behind and beyond the world of the eyes and ears of human beings. This means that the physical world around us and the events that occur in that world (historical events) are no more than what some Hindus call *Maya*, or "illusion," and *Lila*, or "the play of the gods."

The Westerner tries to become rich, to become famous, to gain physical comfort. Ambition drives him or her toward the "top"—materially. Once on top, the Westerner is pronounced a "success." Desire and ambition are the stuff of life. Without them people are doomed to mediocrity and failure. Of course, we are not implying that these are the ideals of Western religions.

According to many of the holy men of the East, however, desire and ambition create nothing but problems. In fact, our troubles are caused by our desires. So to feed one's ambition is sure to bring nothing but more misery. It will only result in pain.

Furthermore, say some traditions of the East, you move closer to truth and reality not by striving and great effort, but by being very quiet—by not doing anything. Taoism, for example, one of the ancient religions of China, speaks of the great Tao as the spiritual eternal reality, the thing behind and beyond everything else. But the Tao can never be found with test tubes and laboratory experiments. Rather, says the Taoist, you find it by doing nothing at all, by allowing yourself to flow with the true spiritual nature of things. It is a process called Wu-Wei. By doing this (or, rather, by not doing it!) one quietly gets oneself on the track of the Tao or the "way," thereby gaining access to things as they really are.

Of course, this is a completely different way to search for truth than that of the Western scientific humanist, who studies hard, works hard, experiments, struggles, and strives.

The Taoist, instead, may retreat to the countryside and seek a sense of oneness with all things. He or she seeks an end to striving. Unless one calms oneself, says the Taoist, one will never know the truth.

Another Eastern religion, Hinduism, offers the practice of yoga as one of its answers. Here the approach to truth lies in self-denial, in pulling in one's senses like a tortoise pulls its legs and head into its shell. By closing out the outside world of illusion and looking deep into oneself, one moves toward truth. The yogi, sitting in the lotus position, eyes closed, cuts off all stimulation from outside. The physical world disappears. The *truth* appears. The yogi would have little use for a laboratory filled with electronic devices, as they would show only more and more sophisticated views of illusion.

Even one's own body partakes of illusion. The Hindu holy man says that the real *you* is not your physical body at all. It is rather the *Atman* or the Self, according to the Hindu Upanishads. There is something in you which is the infinite, ultimate reality. And by reaching inward, by shaking off everything not connected with the Atman, one is lost in the wonder of the absolute—in the true.

So, if you want to find truth, you search, not out there somewhere, in the physical world, but within. Only by excluding what is outside can you attain the depths of what is inside.

THE INTERACTION OF EASTERN AND WESTERN IDEAS

Modern China is a striking battleground between the Eastern and Western ways to search for truth. This huge country, home of one third of human-kind, has operated historically on the basis of the Eastern view of truth. The major religions of China—Taoism, Buddhism, Confucianism—all shared some of the ideas we have been discussing.

But then, suddenly, revolution came to China in the 1940s and 1950s. It was a communist revolution. No one adheres more completely to the Western technophilosophy of materialism than does the communist. He represents the pinnacle in the evolution of the Autonomous Human, a way of being human discussed in Chapter Nine.

And so a group of Chinese began restructuring Chinese society on the basis of ideas learned from Westerners such as Karl Marx. These ideas were almost completely opposite to all the ancient ideas of Chinese society. The basic concept behind the new ideas was "dialectic materialism." It held that the motivating force of life is but matter—matter clashing with matter and creating new forms of matter. Taoism had found reality in the Tao, or the way, which, it said, was more basic than matter. But Maoism (the Chi-nese form of communism), said that humans should be concerned only with the material world. Confucianism had said that ethics grow out of the "will of Heaven." Confucius did not exactly mean "God" in the Western sense, but he did mean that there was some kind of higher plan that people were supposed to follow on earth. It was a spiritual kind of ethic. But Maoism looked to this earth alone for rules of behavior.

China, then, became a battleground between two very different ideas: the ancient idea that only the spiritual world is ultimately real and the com-munist idea that only the material world is ultimately real. No wonder that the friction that resulted caused the death of millions of people.

Some people believe that the old ideas in China will eventually smother the new ones, since the latter are, after all, imported into China from a foreign and hostile world.

There are few Buddhists in India, not entirely because Hinduism fought Buddhism but because Buddhism failed to retain its original dis-tinction from Hinduism. Will the old ideas in China do the same thing to communism? The communist leaders recognized the danger. That is why they have developed elaborate systems to separate children from their nat-ural families, putting them in places where they will hear only the new ideas, hoping to raise them as new people without any sense of the reality of the spiritual world.

In the meantime, the Chinese leaders have to carry on a continuous "revolution." Periodically it is necessary to stir up the young against the old. Thus, during the famous Red Guard period, students were encouraged to kidnap their professors in the universities, put dunce caps on them, and march them around in humiliation. This was punishment meted out because the professors were not yet free of the old ideas.

From time to time great campaigns are mounted in China against Confucius. Although dead for hundreds of years, he is attacked in the press as though he were about to take over the country! This can only mean that the old ideas are still around and are strong enough to be considered a threat to the materialists. Post-Mao China continues to struggle to find its place between the two worlds of spiritualism and materialism. Mao himself is treated less and less like a divine being, but the tension he introduced into Chinese culture is sure to have its effect for generations to come. The new capitalistic interests of China show how pervasive and appealing the Western measure of "success" can be.

In the West, the clash of ideas seems to be moving in exactly the opposite direction. Is it not curious that, while China took over scientific humanism and is trying to build a society on it, many elements in the West have decided that scientific humanism will not work and are beginning to look with favor toward the old Eastern religions! The interest in transcendental meditation, the Hare Krishna sect, the popularity of Zen Buddhism, the practice of drug-induced meditative techniques—all these represent a "looking Eastward" by the children of Western technology.

HUMAN EXISTENTIAL NEEDS: A REVIEW

Earlier we saw that the supracultural religions, the "higher religions," existed to try to meet human existential needs—the needs that all people everywhere have always had. In beginning to study the writings of Eastern religions, this fact should constantly be kept in mind. One should keep asking the question, "How does this particular religious concept seek to answer the basic problems of human existence?"

A review of some of these basic problems might help.

1. *The sense of precariousness*—religion tries to provide a sense of wholeness and stability.
2. *The experience of alienation, separation, and loneliness*—religion tries to provide a sense of kinship with the Ultimate. As we have seen, the Eastern religions often speak of looking into one's own soul to discover in it the great oneness and to commune with that oneness.
3. *The demand for meaning*—religion seeks to fulfill this need by reordering perception, helping one to see that things are not what they seem to be. The Eastern religions teach that through meditation one learns what is illusion and what is real.
4. *The right relationship with the "Holy"*—in the supracultural religions, this need is fulfilled through ethics, or rules of behavior, as well as through ceremonies and rites.

5. *The need to share suffering and joy*—religion seeks to supply emotional and intellectual peace. As you read the Eastern holy writings, you can see many suggestions and guidelines, often calling for the use of exercises and meditative techniques, to attain this goal.

There are many excellent books on each of the Eastern religions. It is not necessary to repeat what has been done so well elsewhere. We will limit ourselves to a brief glance at two major religions of the East—Hinduism and Buddhism—to gain some additional "feel" for the Eastern way.

A HINDU ANSWER

Here is a basic list of Hindu words:

Bhagavad Gita
Krishna
Arjuna
Caste
Dharma
Atman
Brahman
Karma
Moksha
Maya
Lila

The Bhagavad Gita is one of the most famous Hindu holy writings. In it, the god Krishna appears to the warrior Arjuna. In Krishna's conversation with Arjuna we have one of the clearest and most concise explanations of one Hindu "path of salvation"—the bhakti marga, or path of devotion to a god. Arjuna is upset by the prospect of killing people in war. Krishna explains to him that people are divided into *castes*. Certain people are born warriors, certain others merchants, certain others priests, and so on. The castes are firmly set; there is no movement from one to the other. One does not simply decide what to major in, go off to school, and then get a job. One must fulfill the duties of the caste in which he or she was born. Those duties are called one's *dharma*.

If, then, one is in the warrior caste, one's dharma is to fight and kill. If one is in the merchant class, one's dharma is to sell; if a priest, it is to pray and offer sacrifices, for example.

By the time the Bhagavad Gita was well known, many Hindus believed that the *Atman* or the "Self" is the indestructable reality that is the real person. It is never dying and travels through several bodies, not just the one in which it dwells now. Finally, after a long, long struggle and pilgrimage, it manages to reunite itself with *brahman*, or the "Ultimate." Brah-

Arjuna and Krishna on a chariot. South Indian painting, ca. 1800 A.D.
(British Museum)

man is the eternal oneness in its purity. Brahman is God—but we must not
think of the Western meaning of "God."

The Self, or the Atman, goes through body after body, both animal
and human, in a continual search. Finally, it is fused with The Brahman
entirely, so that it no longer exists as a separate entity in any way.

The principle of *karma* is, as someone has said, the belief that "the universe keeps books." That is, when you do good things, you generate good
karma and move forward in your search for The Brahman. When you do
bad things, you generate bad karma and slip backward. "Moving forward"

means progressing through a series of reincarnations, with each body being a bit higher up the scale than the last. By doing well in a given reincarnation, that is, by performing one's dharma well, one accumulates good karma. And good karma sends one higher up the ladder in his or her next reincarnation.

So, if a man like Arjuna does well as a warrior, he may progress upward, finally becoming a brahman (the highest caste). There, as a priest, he will enable himself to spend all his time in spiritual exercises. This will increase his chances of going into the final stage where he is not reincarnated at all, but becomes fully one with the Ultimate.

For men of the upper caste, the last state is *moksha*. It is a state of having transcended one's individuality, being fused with the oneness. The holy men say that it is like a drop of rain water falling into the sea. It no longer has any of the experiences peculiarly connected with being a drop of water, because it has become one with the infinite ocean. So humanity hopes to free itself from being reincarnated over and over again. Human beings hope to cease to exist as distinguishable, finite beings. They aim to realize the eternal.

One of the ways in which one achieves this state is by coming to know what it means to say "I am The Brahman." To say this is to say that what is real in me is the ultimate realness, the ultimate oneness. And so the holy man may sit motionless for days saying, over and over, "I am The Brahman." He will say this thousands of times, until he gradually begins to catch hold of what that means. In this way, he frees himself from ignorance.

In Hindu thinking ignorance is anything that keeps one from true reality, true self-awareness, anything that keeps one from seeing what really is. And in the monistic strand of Hinduism (there are also dualist Hindu schools of thought), one of the worst forms of ignorance is the "illusion of multiplicity"—the idea that there are lots of things. One who has really realized the truth will know that there are *not* lots of things—there is only *one* thing. Everything is illusion except that one thing, and one must come into complete union with that one thing to be free from all ignorance.

Maya is illusion. It is seeing things wrongly, perceiving incorrectly. Maya is the curtain that hides the truth from us. When this curtain is pulled back we meet the truth face to face. And when this is done, we see and know that the world and history are nothing but *lila*—the play of Brahman or OM.

The sannyasin or liberated person will observe what is going on around him like a spectator at a play. He will never get involved in what happens on the stage, beyond simply watching it in a detached way. He may be slightly interested in the plot, but he realizes that what he sees is not of ultimate importance. What is of ultimate concern is to realize one's unity with the Unmanifest, the Ground of Being, which dwells even in the "lotus of the heart."

Twice in my life I have seen someone lose his sense of perspective at a dramatic production. The first was a college play. One of the actors, whom I knew, was an unstable and very disturbed person. By some fluke, he was given a part in the play that almost exactly paralleled his own life. According to the plot, this character gradually falls deeper and deeper into despair and at the end of the play he is left prostrate on the stage, hopelessly lost.

The curtain closed and the audience began to applaud. Suddenly this fellow appeared at one of the wings and rushed to center stage. The audience thought the play had simply been provided with a brief epilogue and became quiet to hear the final lines.

But as the actor began to talk the mood changed to shock. "You just do not understand," he said. "I've got to have help. HELP ME!"

We gradually came to the terrible realization that these were not lines in the play. The actor had lost his identity in that of the character he had played. He was that person. The plot had been real. The real world had slipped away, and the stage had taken its place. The poor fellow had to be carried away, sobbing and calling for help.

The second incident occurred in a movie theater where the film *Easy Rider* was being shown. This film builds up in the last few moments, carefully manipulating the audience into a frenzy of hate. When the climax occurred a young man behind me jumped to his feet and began to curse and flail his arms at the screen. He had forgotten that he was only watching a movie.

The Hindu holy man would say that the young man's mistake is a common one made by all who do not realize the difference between the transient and eternal. People are foolish when they treat the material things around them as though they are ultimate. People are wise when they learn to be witnesses and not players, spectators and not actors, or at least when they learn that only by first renouncing the world can they enjoy it.

Hinduism's attitude of tolerance is well known. So, although the path through devotion (bhakti) is the most popular, Hinduism knew of two other paths of salvation even prior to bhakti. Karma marga had offered salvation through one's work, whatever it was, as long as it was performed with no thought to the results. And jnana marga was the path through knowledge that arose particularly by the impetus of the Upanishads. These paths are also called "yogas" since one binds oneself spiritually.

A basic yoga underlying spirituality in general is raja yoga. It is a highly developed series of physical and psychological exercises designed to help one shut out the unreal outer world and get into oneself. It is truly amazing what the master yogi can do with his body and mind. He can control muscles that we ordinarily think of as involuntary. He may gain so much control over his stomach muscles, for example, that he may form a perfect letter "J" by simply tensing certain muscles and relaxing others. He can cause them to move up and down, back and forth, even round and round. There are also the psychological exercises, which develop the ability to control the mind's activities.

Most of us have very little mental control. This fact can be illustrated by the following little test: For the next thirty seconds, do *not* think of a *white bear*.

Were you able to do it? I doubt it. Even though you had not thought of one in ages, just being told not to think of one makes it very hard to keep a white bear from popping into the mind, no matter how hard we try.

The yogi, on the other hand, can cast all thoughts from his mind, bringing it to perfect rest. There is spiritual value in this, say the holy men, for by learning to control one's body and mind, one finds the real or attains Nirvana, in which the self is united with The Brahman.

Before we move on to look at Buddhism, remember that, just as there are over four hundred kinds of Christianity, there are also hundreds of kinds of Hinduism. We have generalized, and any serious student of this religion, or any other, must dig much deeper to really understand.

A BUDDHIST ANSWER

Buddhism begins with the story of its founder, Siddhartha Gautama. Siddhartha was born about 563 B.C. in India. He began life with every material advantage. Born into a very wealthy family of royal blood, he married a beautiful girl, they had a beautiful child, and, according to legends, lived in three beautiful palaces.

Siddhartha was purposely shielded from anything unpleasant or evil. He never saw anyone sick, anyone suffering, anyone old, anyone poor, anyone dead. One day, however, he ventured out into the streets. There he saw a very old man, then someone suffering, and then a corpse.

He was stunned. For days he struggled with this revelation of evil. Finally he decided that he must go out in search of answers. He took a final look at his beautiful wife and family, lying asleep, left them a note and slipped away to seek for what is real and true.

Siddhartha tried several things to find the answer. He studied with brahman philosophers. Later, he joined several ascetics. He took self-mortification to such an extreme that he almost died while fasting. Finally, down to skin and bones, he decided that, while such men knew a great deal about bringing their bodies into subjection, they really know no more about the truth than anyone else.

Then one day he sat down beneath the bo tree. There his own inner struggle took place. Before he arose again he had received Enlightenment. He understood now the nature of the world and the answer to the question of how to live.

Painting on the core pillar of the pagoda at the Daigoji Monastery. (New York Public Library)

Buddhism is the religion that developed from Siddhartha Gautama's teachings following his Enlightenment. It arose in India and flourished there for a thousand years. In many ways the Hindu roots of Buddhism are obvious. Eventually Indian Buddhism disappeared as a separate religion, but by that time the faith had spread widely into other countries and cultures. Today the major concentration of Buddhism is Southeast Asia (Cambodia, Vietnam, Thailand), Japan, and China.

Buddhism exists in two major branches: Theravada Buddhism, more prevalent in the southern countries, and Mahayana Buddhism, more prevalent in the northern countries. To taste the flavor of Buddhism we will look at one of the sacred books of Theravada Buddhism called the Dhammapada.[1]

Siddhartha Gautama the Buddha was not interested in metaphysical speculation. He was interested in life and in getting some hold on it. So he says to a disciple,

[1] Quotations from *The Dhammapada*, trans. P. Lal (New York: Farrar, Straus & Giroux, 1967).

Therefore, consider carefully, Malunkyaputta, the things that I have taught and the things that I have not taught. What are things I have not taught?

I have not taught that the world is eternal. I have not taught that the world is not eternal. I have not taught that the world is finite. I have not taught that the world is infinite. I have not taught that the soul and the body are the same. I have not taught that the soul and the body are different. I have not taught that the liberated person exists after death. I have not taught that he does not exist after death. I have not taught that he both exists and does not exist after death; that he neither exists nor does not exist after death.

Why, Malunkyaputta, have I not taught all this? Because all this is useless, it has nothing to do with real Dhamma, it does not lead to cessation of passion, to peace, to supreme wisdom, and the holy life, to Nirvana. That is why I have not taught all this.

And what have I taught, Malunkyaputta? I have taught that suffering exists, that suffering has an origin, that suffering can be ended, that there is a way to end suffering.

Why, Malunkyaputta, have I taught this? Because this is useful, it has to do with real Dhamma, it leads to the cessation of passion, it brings peace, supreme wisdom, the holy life, and Nirvana. That is why I have taught all this.

Therefore, Malunkyaputta, consider carefully what I have taught and what I have not taught.[2]

To make the same point, the Buddha tells a story. People who always want to deal with philosophical questions are like the man who was shot with a poison arrow. When people came to aid him he would not let them touch his wound. Instead, he wanted them to explain to him what kind of arrow it was, where it came from, what kind of poison was on it, the motivation of the person who shot him, and dozens of other similar questions.

None of those questions is important, says the Buddha. The important question is, how can I remove the arrow and stop the suffering it causes? Those who seek Enlightenment will deal only with that question.

The right path, he says, is the middle one between sensuality, the indulgence of the body, and extreme asceticism, the torture of the body. To his followers he says,

Avoid these two extremes, monks. Which two? On the one hand, low, vulgar, ignoble, and useless indulgence in passion and luxury; on the other, painful, ignoble, and useless practice of self-torture and mortification. Take the Middle Path advised by the Buddha, for it leads to insight and peace, wisdom and enlightenment, and to Nirvana.[3]

Nirvana is the goal of the Buddhist. The Theravada Buddhist describes it as a state in which all the flame of desire has been blown out. The Mahayana Buddhist calls it a state of being so full of the infinite that the

[2]Quotations from *The Dhammapada*, p. 20.
[3]Ibid., p. 22.

loss of the finite is of no consequence. Nirvana lies beyond all concrete states of existence.

> But where is the Buddha? Here or There?
> Neither here nor there, sire.
> What do you mean, respected Nagasena?
> Supposing, sire, the flames of a great fire are extinguished,
> where do they go? Here or there? Where?
> Neither here or there. They disappear.

> So, when the Buddha achieved Nirvana, sire, he became neither here or there. But you may know him by the Dhamma, for he taught the Dhamma, and left it behind.[4]

So we see that the Buddha is beyond existence now and has left behind only his teachings as a guide for others to follow him. The Buddhist holy man, says the Dhammapada, is

> Like a bird invisibly flying in the sky,
> He lives without possessions
> knowledge his food, freedom his world,
> while others wonder.

> Like a bird flying invisibly in the sky
> while others wonder, he lives, the saint
> Without passions, indifferent to food,
> aware of the meaning of freedom.[5]

In this poem we can see clearly the detachment so common to Eastern spirituality. The key to the Buddhist life-style is mental self-possession:

> We are what we think
> Having become what we thought . . .[6]

> Clear thinking leads to Nirvana . . .

> [The Wise Man] meditates, he preserves,
> He works hard for the incomparable freedom
> and the bliss of Nirvana . . .[7]

> A disciplined mind is the road to Nirvana . . .[8]

For the Theravada Buddhist, we can see that the rewards of Buddhism come from what one does for himself. Siddhartha Gautama the

[4]Ibid., p. 34.
[5]Ibid., p. 71.
[6]Ibid., p. 39.
[7]Quotations from *The Dhammapada*, p. 45.
[8]Ibid., p. 49

Buddha has left good advice and enlightened teaching, but the believer will gain nirvana only through his *own* efforts.

To think wrong thoughts is to remain separated from nirvana. The kinds of thoughts that are wrong are those that agitate the mind, that prevent the mind from being quiet and calm, like a bird flying invisibly in the sky. In particular, there are four kinds of thoughts that must be purged from the mind: *possessiveness, anger, hatred,* and *lust.*

Right thoughts, those that contribute to gaining nirvana, include *detachment* and *compassion.* It is best to love other people and to never return evil for evil. This ensures mental tranquility.

And as for the world around, one must simply think to oneself,

> The world is a bubble,
> the world is a shadow . . .

Buddhism seeks to relieve men of suffering. And before this can be done the believer must come to understand the truths that Siddhartha himself received under the bo tree: the four noble truths.

The *first noble truth* concerns suffering:

> For there is suffering, and this is the noble truth of suffering—birth is painful, old age is painful, sickness is painful, death is painful; lamentation, dejection, and despair are painful. Contact with the unpleasant is painful, not getting what you want is painful.[10]

One must, then, first recognize the condition of human beings, that they are in anguish.

The *second noble truth* concerns the origin of suffering:

> Suffering has an origin, and this is the noble truth of the origin of suffering—desire creates sorrow, desire mixed with pleasure and lust, quick pleasure, desire for life, and desire even for non-life.[11]

Why do people suffer? They suffer because they *desire.* It is desire that creates sorrow—even the desire for life, even the desire to not live.

The *third noble truth* concerns the end of suffering:

> Suffering has an end, and this is the noble truth of the end of suffering—nothing remains of desire, Nirvana is attained, all is given up, renounced, detached, and abandoned.[12]

[9]Ibid., p. 97.
[10]Ibid., p. 23.
[11]Ibid.
[12]Ibid.

We want something but cannot get it. We are miserable. We blow out the flame of desire. We are no longer miserable.

Suppose that you see a very attractive member of the opposite sex and immediately fall deeply in love. But the love you feel is not returned. You become miserable, caught in the web of an unfulfilled and unfillable desire. Either you must end the desire, and gain peace, or resort to force, and bring even more unhappiness on yourself.

Some years ago a student told me about a bizarre incident in which the second alternative was used. Deciding that her relationship with her boyfriend had no future, she broke up with him. He was grief stricken. Determined to have her, he came to her apartment with a pistol and forced her to come with him to an adjoining state. There he kept the gun in her ribs while a judge, unaware of what was happening, married them.

She did not dare let the judge know what was happening, so she said her vows with a forced smile. But as soon as the ceremony was over and the couple got back to the groom's apartment, she forcefully administered a lamp to his head and called the police before he regained consciousness.

Now she is happily married to someone else and, unless her violent suitor has blown out the flame of his desire, he presumably still lives in misery!

But the real misery, says the Buddha, is not that we do not get what we desire; it is the desire *itself* that makes us miserable. The only sure escape comes when all desire is given up, renounced, detached, and abandoned. And when desire is gone, so will suffering disappear.

The *fourth noble truth* provides the practical plan for attaining nirvana:

> And this is the noble truth that leads to Nirvana—it is the Eightfold Way of right views, right intentions, right speech, right action, right profession, right watchfulness, and right concentration.[13]

It all boils down to this: one must free oneself from craving. Only in this way comes peace.

> Craving is like a creeper,
> it strangles the fool.
> He bounds like a monkey, from one birth to another,
> looking for fruit.
>
> When craving, like poison,
> takes hold of a man,
> his sorrows increase
> like wild grass.
>
> This is my advice:
> "Root out craving! Root it out,

[13]Ibid. The eighth, right effort, is not listed in this quote.

like wild grass is rooted out.
Do not let death destroy you
As river waters destroy reeds."[14]

DIVERSITY OF EASTERN ANSWERS

The preceding brief descriptions show *one* way that both Hinduism and Buddhism have addressed the existential or ontological question, the question of one's being, or one's "ultimate concern." But these were not comprehensive in scope. They were only illustrative.

The same must necessarily be true when we look at the Western answers in the following chapters. We simply cannot cover the *diversity* of views even within any *single* religion with some overarching concept. That is extremely difficult. About all we can do is sketch a few examples of answers that have been given by particular groups within those religions at certain times and places.

In the study of religion, a student needs to be very careful of accepting gross generalizations or characterizations of any given religion. This is particularly true when the generalizations are being utilized more in a "normative" way than in a merely "descriptive" one. For example, the Indian mentality has seemingly been tolerant of other religions. So this tolerance or inclusiveness is quite often cited as one of the most fundamental features of the Hindu mentality.

But if we suggest that tolerance or inclusiveness is one of the chief characteristics of Hinduism, we would do so only by ignoring a huge amount of data. While it might help explain how Buddha was simply absorbed into the recognized avataras of Visnu, Indian history also shows considerable conflict and strain during the centuries between Hinduism and Buddhism. And the conflict did not all come merely from the Buddhists. Further, the idea of inclusivism would hardly describe the ancient Vedic religion. And it certainly fails to acknowledge the strong sectarian division so basic to Hinduism between the worship of Siva and Visnu.

Another characteristic so often assigned to Eastern religions is that they are largely monistic. This too is not a useful nor accurate description. Certainly the Upanishads are monistic, and Sankara used them around 800 C.E. to expound a nondualistic school of Vedanta thought.

But this is not the whole story of Hinduism. The bhakti path to salvation is the most pervasive form of Hinduism today, and it emphasizes a faith in the very personal gods of Siva and Visnu, which can in no way be called "monism." Certainly "monism" does not describe Buddhism at all. In Theravada or Hinayana teachings, Buddha is only a mortal who has found the truth; while in forms of Mahayana, Buddha has become a savior, and in

[14]Ibid., p. 157.

the True Pure Land school, for example, he provides all the power of salvation by his grace and vow to save. So we see various degrees of the process of divinization in Buddhism. But there is no monism here.

Often the Eastern religions are considered to be "world-denying." Renunciation is cited as the key, the sannyasi as the only ideal. But the majority of Hindus have never striven for the goal of "liberation" or moksa. In fact, that goal was not open except to men of the upper castes. Most Hindus remain very much involved in this world. Dharma has continued to be vitally important. And for some schools, such as the Mimamsa, any talk of "salvation" was considered an unresponsible shirking of one's duty or dharma. Even when the paths of salvation became fully accepted in Hinduism, however, the majority did not seek salvation by ascetic practices or world-denial as much as by devotion to a particular god. The "middle path" of Buddha certainly did not originally sound like world-denial, though certain monastic and contemplative trends later did try to sever their connection with the "world."

If by "world-denying" one is contrasting some alleged Eastern position with the Western mentality, one finds the same sort of mix in a typical Western religion, Christianity. That is, it has spawned strong monastic movements and so developed an ideal that is quite world-denying. Yet the majority of its adherents, as was the case in India, were not able to totally leave the world behind, but rather sought salvation while being vitally connected to the world. And despite strong attachments to family, nation, and the material world that we find as a part of one's duty in Judaism and Islam, the ideal of both of these religions is *non*material. That is, the focus is on finding salvation in God, Who is spiritual.

Yet that salvation implies, in both Eastern and Western religions, living responsibly by God's law in this world. So any kind of dichotomy set up between "world-denying" and "world-affirming" never really does justice to the whole picture of any single religion.

Sometimes, ancient religious people were considered to believe that time was cyclical. In fact, Mircea Eliade felt that was one of the most obvious characteristics of being "religious" rather than "secular" or profane. And people often suggest that this also distinguishes the "Eastern" from the "Western" mentalities, the Eastern believing in repetitious cycles vis-à-vis the Western, which sees time as linear. While it may be that a rather thorough linear consciousness of history or time became explicit first in the Jewish religion, both linear and cyclical elements are present in most religions, Eastern and Western.

The West *seems* more linear oriented. Yet the "end" is simply the recapturing of the paradise lost at the "beginning," so there is just one big cycle, or the whole of history is viewed as sacred. But even in the West, the rituals done periodically, particularly yearly, show that a natural-seasonal or cyclical view of time was always part of the larger scheme. Especially is this true when we see those adherents protesting that their ritual is not just a "remembering" of a past event, but the *actualizing* or re-presentation of it in the present. The Roman Catholic "sacrifice of the mass" and "transubstantiation" are good examples. But, on the other hand, the very idea of transcending or breaking the "chain of causality" found in both Hinduism and Buddhism shows a *linear* progress. That is, things do not and must not simply repeat themselves indefinitely. Nirvana is a goal to be achieved once and for all, whether it is defined as the "void" or whatever.

What we *can* say, however, on the basis of these brief words about Hinduism and Buddhism (which we will find confirmed in the three Western traditions to which we turn next), is that the "answer" always comes ultimately from *beyond* the person, although there may be things one can do to make oneself more prepared to receive the answer. The answer is usually received as *absolute* or final. And the answer always has to be *believed* by the adherent and then *acted upon*. So faith and morality become central as responses to the moment or encounters with the Ultimate.

We now turn briefly to sketch a few particulars about Judaism, Christianity, and Islam. But, again, we are limiting these descriptions rather than attempting to incorporate all the centuries of diversity. And we are intentionally not approaching any religion in exactly the same way. This is to encourage the student to go further into these particular religions before feeling the necessity to make binding normative judgments.

Finally, by way of reminder, we must be fair in comparisons as well as tolerant of the weakness of humanity. There is always a difference between a religion's ideal and its actuality. Fairness demands that we never compare or contrast the ideal of one religion with the actuality of another. That would prejudice the results from the outset, no matter what the two religions are that are being compared. For the actuality of any given religion, consisting of frail and selfish human beings, is always far less noble than the religion's ideal. But the actuality, no matter how bad, should not deter us from examining the ideals of each religion, for all life is spent trying to attain the ideal, however it may be defined from culture to culture.

5

The Religion of Israel

THE ACTS OF GOD IN HISTORY

The scholar Edmond Jacob summarizes very well the essence of biblical religion in this brief statement:

> The special characteristic of biblical revelation is that God binds Himself to historical events to make them the vehicle of the manifestation of his purpose.[1]

The Infinite, the Transcendent, the Other, has come down and become involved in the imminent, the now, the historical, the material world.

The Bible begins with a story that maintains that the human race in its present state is fallen.[2] By "fallen" we simply mean that, due to disobedience, self-assertiveness, and unwillingness to live according to the created order of things, people have created an enormous gulf between themselves

---

[1]Edmond Jacob, *Theology of the Old Testament* (New York: Harper & Row, 1958), p. 188. Another excellent introduction to the thinking of the Hebrew Scriptures is Otto J. Baab, *The Theology of the Old Testament* (New York: Abingdon, 1949).

[2]Read Genesis 1–3. This account underwent considerable interpretation by Christian theologians. Our use of the term "fallen" should not necessarily be identified directly with traditional Christian doctrines of the depravity of the human race. Judaism does not see this story as a "fall" in the Christian sense at all.

and the Ultimate Reality—a gulf for which they have only themselves to blame.

Because this gulf exists, people are plagued with certain feelings, feelings we described earlier as "human existential needs." They feel guilt. They sense that the universe is not friendly toward them, that they are separated from what is real, that they are not measuring up to standards. They feel alienated. They are somehow alone. They are cut off from their roots. And they sense a lack of meaning: they are here, but they do not know why. They do not know where they came from. They do not know where they are going.

All these problems come, according to the first few chapters of the Bible, from the human race's rejection of the One who made it, from its disobedience to that One, and from its assertion of its own will above the will of that One. The Biblical story has two parts. The first is "prehistoric"; that is, it deals with the beginning of the world and humanity, painted in broad and poetic strokes. The second interprets a period of history heavily documented by archaeology and surviving records.

In the beginning, Adam and Eve passed their time in a beautiful garden, trimming the trees, the Bible says, living in harmony with nature. Although there were almost no rules or restraints, nevertheless Adam and Eve lost their place in Eden.

To vary the analogy somewhat, it is as though the race began its existence on a high mountain, surrounded by steep cliffs. On top of this mountain is a beautiful garden filled with flowers, fruits, and cool streams of clear water. Then humanity is told, "This lovely place is yours; but never go beyond its boundaries."

The people, however, do step outside the limits of the garden. They lose their footing and slip down the steep cliff. They find themselves unable to climb back up again. They are mired down in a horrible swamp. They can look up and catch only fleeting glances of the beautiful place where they used to live. But they cannot return to it, no matter how they struggle.

This is humanity's condition. People can conceive of a place so much more beautiful than where they are now. They sense themselves to be separated from the real life that is potentially theirs. They are frustrated because they cannot climb to the heights of their dreams and expectations. Unable to climb, they can only look up and dream, or hope, or even sometimes *remember* the paradise from which they came. The human race has fallen farther than it can climb; that is the condition of humankind pictured in the early chapters of Genesis.

However, the Bible continues, this God who made the beautiful garden and put people in it pities their plight and stretches out His arm to restore them. The intimate relationship of Eden, where God walked with Adam in the cool of the evening, is gone. But God will now, through the march of historical events, reach out to humanity and offer to heal the wounds of the past.

He will, moreover, do this in such a way that the human race is not robbed of its own free will. This has always been God's most precious gift to humanity. He could have made it in such a way that it *could* not have fallen. Then it would have lived forever in the garden and there would be no need for religion at all. But it would not live in the garden as *human*. It would live there like a plant or an animal, acting out of instinct instead of through moral choice.

But humanity is made, so says the book of Genesis, in the image of God. Humanity has been created with its own personhood and its own will. God is not willing to interfere with that. He chooses to open Himself up to humanity in such a way that the human race can respond to Him openly and freely, without any compulsion.

Such a procedure is, of course, very complicated. Thus the method by which God acts is also a bit complicated. According to the Bible, what God does is to select a tiny group of people who live in the Near East and make a special covenant with them. Then He begins to work out a revelation of Himself in their history. They are to become a "light to the nations," He says.

And by involving Himself with them and acting within their history, He will gradually work out His plan to reconcile the human race to Himself and to restore His people to Eden. This little community is called *Israel*.

The history of Israel, says the Bible, is not ordinary history. It is history with the acts of God mixed in—"holy history," as it were. The events of this history are not just normal events, explainable by the normal theories of cause and effect of the objective scientific historian. Rather, they are events into which God has inserted Himself, making them "vehicles for the manifestation of His purpose."

Of course one can study the events recorded in the Bible as an objective historian. The Biblical writers might not object to such a study. But they would be quick to point out that the acts that they recorded have another dimension beyond the mere objective recounting of them. So, one might maintain that the Red Sea had parted on numerous occasions. One might even furnish scientific explanations. But that it parted at one particular time, just at the moment when the children of Israel could cross and escape the Egyptians, and thereby flee the bondage of Egypt and become a people—that was for the Biblical writers a mighty act filled with the presence of God. In acts such as this, they claimed, God was manifesting Himself and working out His purpose.

It is this point of view that explains why so much of the Hebrew Scripture is an account of the history of Israel. In this history the writers perceived God coming to the human race to redeem it.

Here, very briefly, is how the story continues: God selects a motley group of slaves living in Egypt as the people through whom He will work. They will be a light to the nations. He sends them a leader named Moses who leads them out of Egyptian servitude and into the desert of Sinai. There, on Mount Sinai (presumably somewhere in the region we call the Sinai Peninsula), God presents Moses with a covenant for the people. It contains the Ten Commandments and, by extension, the codes and law by which these slaves will become His people. On His part, God promises to work with and through them and to be their God.

For many years the people of Israel wander in the wilderness, in the land that is today populated by Bedouin tribespeople and oil sheiks. Finally they enter the land of Canaan (modern Israel and Jordan) and, after a number of centuries of struggle, gradually dominate the local population and build a nation.

First they are organized into semi-independent tribes, and then, eventually, into a monarchy ruled over by kings such as David and Solomon. The monarchy and the nation itself split in two, resulting in a northern kingdom (Israel) and a southern kingdom (Judah). Through stormy centuries these little kingdoms gradually become caught in the great power struggles of the day, caught between the mighty empires to the north, south, and west of them. They are battered around constantly until finally, in 722 B.C., the northern kingdom is destroyed by a massive Assyrian invasion. The people are carried away into exile and lose their identity. History knows them as the ten lost tribes. In a few more generations' time the southern kingdom also falls to the Babylonians and the temple of God is destroyed (587 B.C.).

Some of the southerners (who became known as Jews) are taken into Babylonian exile, there to remain for seventy years. While in exile they firmly retain their cultural identity and their worship of the God who had so many centuries ago revealed Himself to them. Their understanding of the nature of this God was immeasurably strengthened during this time; so much so that when they returned from exile they were ready to present to the world the documents that are often called the Old Testament—documents that have formed the basis for all Western religions.

THE HEBREW PROPHETS:
THE RIGHTEOUS REMNANT

Several times the people of Israel almost disrupt the whole plan. Even though God is working in them, they are perfectly capable of rejecting His work or even working at cross-purposes with Him. Sometimes the light almost goes out entirely. But somehow always a few people remain faithful to the covenant. The Biblical writers call them the *remnant*.

In particular there were the group of persons we call the prophets.[3] These were, says the Old Testament, God's people, His special spokespersons, who observed and recorded and interpreted the acts of God in history, who learned what God was like and what His will was, and who passed this information to those who wrote it down in the holy books.

As time passed it became more and more clear to these prophets that the full purposes of God were never going to be completed in the normal course of history. There would never be a perfect society, or a restoration to the perfect life of Eden, in the regular process of events. The prophets began to talk more and more about the futility of the way secular human beings were trying to build their kingdoms—military might, politics, and social reform. They began to predict more and more insistently that God would eventually act in a most decisive way, that He would intervene as He had never done before, in a crowning act in which He would bear Himself as fully as the human mind and senses can comprehend. In that intervention would come the restoration to Eden.

The flavor of these dreams can be well illustrated from one of the most profound of the books of the prophets, the Book of Isaiah:

> It shall come to pass in the latter days
>> that the mountain of the house of the LORD
> shall be established as the highest of the
>> mountains,
>> and shall be raised above the hills;
> and all the nations shall flow to it
>> and many peoples shall come, and say:
> "Come, let us go up to the mountain of the LORD,
>> to the house of the God of Jacob;
> that he may teach us his ways
>> and that we may walk in his paths."
> For out of Zion shall go forth the law,
>> and the word of the LORD from Jerusalem.
> He shall judge between the nations,
>> and shall decide for many peoples;
> and they shall beat their swords into plowshares,
>> and their spears into pruning hooks;
> nation shall not lift up sword against nation,
>> neither shall they learn war any more.[4]

This beautiful quotation is inscribed on the front of the United Nations building in New York (where the extent of its influence seems doubtful).

[3]For further study, see Stephen Winward, *A Guide to the Prophets* (Richmond, Va.: John Knox, 1968), or Emil G. Kroeling, *The Prophets* (Chicago: Rand McNally, 1969).
[4]Isa. 2:2–4.

Behold, the Lord, the LORD of hosts will lop
   the boughs with terrifying power;
the great in height will be hewn down,
   and the lofty will be brought low.
He will cut down the thickets of the forest with an axe,
   and Lebanon with its majestic trees will fall.
There shall come forth a shoot from the stump of Jesse,
   and a branch shall grow out of his roots.
And the spirit of the LORD shall rest upon him,
   the spirit of wisdom and understanding,
   the spirit of counsel and might,
   the spirit of knowledge and the fear of the LORD.
And his delight shall be in the fear of the LORD.

He shall not judge by what his eyes see,
   or decide by what his ears hear;
but with righteousness he shall judge the poor,
   and decide with equity for the meek of the earth;
and he shall smite the earth with the rod of his mouth,
   and with the breath of his lips he shall slay the
      wicked.
Righteousness shall be the girdle of his waist,
   and faithfulness the girdle of his loins.

The wolf shall dwell with the lamb,
   and the leopard shall lie down with the kid,
and the calf and the lion and the fatling together,
   and the little child shall lead them.
The cow and the bear shall feed;
   their young shall lie down together;
   and the lion shall eat straw like the ox.
The sucking child shall play over the hold of the asp,
   and the weaned child shall put his hand on the
      adder's den.
They shall not hurt or destroy in all my holy mountain;
for the earth shall be full of the knowledge of the LORD
   as the waters cover the sea.[5]

    The themes of this dramatic poem are striking: God acts in a very decisive way, like a mighty ax laying the forest of human culture and human attainments low. All these were but frustrating failures, unable to bring human beings to Eden. Then, among the ruins, a tiny shoot springs up from an old stump, promising new life. It is the "stump of Jesse" (Jesse was the father of King David). This "anointed one" or Messiah will institute a truly just social order, where even poor and weak are treated fairly. What results

[5]Isa. 10:33–11:9.

is a paradise void of all violence and death, where every person enjoys a perfect relationship with God.

Here was a truly glorious dream, a dream of God's intervening, of God's ruling, of God's Kingdom, of the coming of the Kingdom of God to humanity. This is the dream of the Hebrew Scriptures. It is the dream, as we have said, that becomes the basis for the Western religions, though the precise understanding of the Messianic motif has been differently understood in each of them.

It is an unfinished dream. And out of its unfinishedness has come the religion we call Judaism.[6] Out of the ancient stories and prophecies comes the amazing hope and strength of the Jewish people throughout the ages, feeding on those events and those dreams.

Yet the fond dreams of the prophets have an unfinished character about them. It is as though someone had shot an arrow into the air toward a goal. It is well aimed and well shot. It is sure to land in its intended place. It is moving swiftly and surely toward its goal. But as we see the arrow go by, we cannot predict where it will land. We do not know its target, for it lies beyond our view, over the horizon. Only the One who shot it knows its destination.

In that simple analogy lies the essence of the Biblical view of history. The accompanying chart helps us to visualize this view. God reaches down and touches history at various points, represented in the chart by arrows. History itself is pictured as an arrow, plunging toward its goal; The Day of Yahweh.

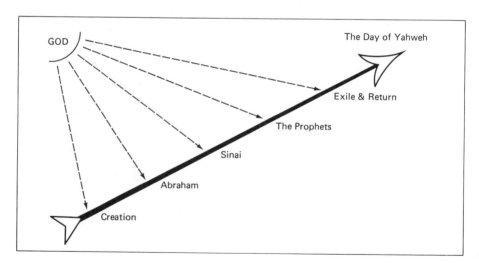

[6]To trace the development of this religion from Biblical times to the present, see Leo Trepp, *Judaism: Development and Life* (Belmont, Calif.: Dickenson, 1966).

TEMPLE AND TORAH

As important as it may have been, the prophetic movement was not the only religious expression among the ancient Jews. Alongside this movement, existing in dynamic tension with it, was the religion of the temple and the Torah, administered by the priests and scribes.

The temple in Jerusalem, built originally by King Solomon around 950 B.C. and magnificently rebuilt by King Herod in the first century B.C., was the center of a massive cultus involving thousands of priests. The entire economy of Israel during the second temple period (approximately 400 B.C. to A.D. 70) was dependent on this cultus that attempted to carry out the elaborate sacrificial system outlined in the Torah (the first five books in the Hebrew Scriptures).[7]

With the fall of the Jewish state and the destruction of Jerusalem and the temple by the Romans in A.D. 70, however, the sacrifices were abruptly halted, since the Torah allowed them to be performed nowhere else. For several previous centuries, Jews had settled in many lands throughout the eastern Mediterranean, forming the *diaspora* (or scattering). In combination with the Pharisees, the only Jewish sect substantially surviving the destruction in Judea, the diaspora communities developed a faith tied not to temple and Torah, but to the Torah alone. The Pharisees did not understand the Torah to be an absolute, unchangeable document of God's final word to humanity. Rather, it was a living document to be interpreted in the light of changing conditions. The study of the Torah, then, never ended. It was in fact to be one of the major responsibilities of religious leaders from that point until the present day.

The temple, on the other hand, declined in significance, replaced by the synagogue as the center of religious expression. In diaspora centers the synagogue was not only a place of worship, but a center in which to keep Jewish culture and aspirations intact. In the place of the animal sacrifices, the Pharisaic leaders elevated prayer and the proper applications of dietary and Sabbath day prohibitions. Thus, noted Jacob Neusner, "The Temple cult is to be replaced by study of Torah, the priest by the rabbi [scribe]; and the center of piety was shifted from cult and sacrifice entirely."[8]

Thus the major characteristics of Judaism, which were to determine the nature of that religion, were in place. The impact of the modern world on this ancient faith will be discussed in Chapters 10 and 11.

---

[7]For a full account of this period, see Joachim Jeremias, *Jerusalem in the Time of Jesus* (Philadelphia: Fortress, 1969).

[8]Jacob Neusner, " 'Pharisaic-Rabbinic' Judaism: A Clarification," *History of Religions*, vol. 12, no. 3 (Chicago: University of Chicago, 1973), p. 265.

THE GOD OF THE HEBREWS

The major presupposition of the Hebrew Scriptures, the one upon which everything else rests, is the existence of God. He is always understood to be the first reality in sequence (He is the first ever to exist) and the basic reality in existence (He is the foundation and origin of everything that exists).

The cantor blows the shofar or ram's horn during the Jewish High Holy Days. (Al Kaplan, dpi)

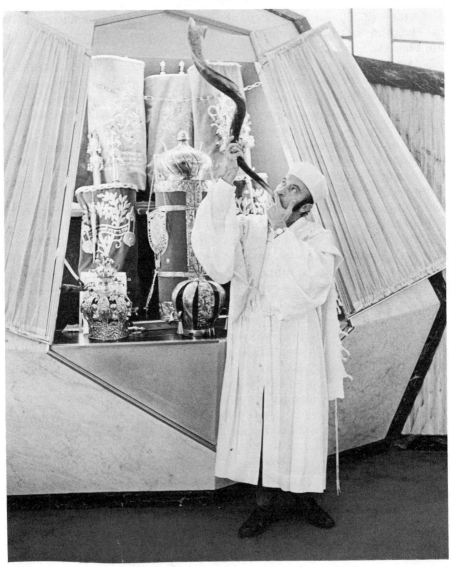

This God is called by various names in the Hebrew Scriptures. Often he is called "El." This is the name given to the father-god or high god in a number of ancient religions, including the polytheistic ones, where El is the most basic god.

But the name that distinguishes the god of the Hebrews from all others is the mysterious word YHWH. We are not sure how to pronounce this four-letter word. For many centuries the Jews did not speak this name aloud in order not to show irreverence to its holiness. For this reason the original pronunciation was eventually forgotten. The most common scholarly guess is to pronounce the word "Yahweh" (Yah-way).

Whereas the word "El" simply means God, the word "YHWH" serves as a personal name for the Ultimate. Just as, say, a physician might be called doctor, but also, John Brown. When the prophet Moses was first confronted by God, he was told,

> You must tell the Israelites this, that it is YHWH, the God of their forefathers, the God of Abraham, the God of Isaac, the God of Jacob, who has sent you to them. For this is my name for ever; this is my title in every generation.[9]

So far, archaeologists and ancient historians have never found this word used to refer to any other god or in any other culture.[10] It was the distinctively Israelite way of referring to the Ultimate. The God of the Bible, then, is Yahweh.

As we have said, the Hebrew Scriptures presuppose Yahweh's existence. But *how* does he live? In three basic ways:

Life
Holiness
Oneness

First, Yahweh lives. He exists, says the Bible, not like an idea exists, but like a person exists. He exists by doing things. There is a difference between merely existing and living. Concepts have existence, but they do not do anything. They are abstractions that have reality only when some intelligence thinks about them. But when the Hebrew says that "Yahweh lives," he does not simply mean that He exists as a philosophical abstraction; rather, he means that He is someone who does things. That is the way in which persons exist. That is the way in which you exist. You exist not simply by being here, but by doing things. And so it is with Yahweh.

For this reason, The Bible tends to describe God with verbs rather than with abstract nouns. In other words, it talks about what God does.

This approach is in strong contrast to the Greek way of talking about God. For the great Greek philosophers God was a philosophical abstrac-

[9]Exodus 3:15 (*NEB*).
[10]Jacob, *Old Testament*, p. 49.

tion—the Unmoved Mover, the Ultimate Essence, and so on. The same thing is true of Eastern metaphysical thinking, as we saw in the last chapter: the ultimate reality is not personal, it does not do anything—it is a state. It stands majestically still in a state of ultimateness. Yahweh, on the other hand, is very active in His ultimateness.

The Hebrew prophets claim that the idols of the nations around them, and the speculative gods like those of the Greek philosophers, are man-made gods. Such gods, they claim, are dependent upon human beings for their existence.

Remember the puzzle about the tree that fell in the forest? If there were no one there to hear it, would there have been any sound of falling timber? Some would say, "No." Likewise, the Hebrew writers say that some gods have no existence unless there is someone around to worship them. Their existence depends entirely on the people who developed a religion around them.

Take Marduk, for example. Marduk was a major Middle Eastern deity at one time. But no one worships Marduk anymore. For the most part, modern people would claim that Marduk no longer exists. His existence depended on having someone around to cry out "Oh, Holy Marduk!" When people stopped doing that, no more Marduk.

All the speculative gods and all the idols, say the prophets, are eventually shown to be empty ideas, dependent on the human minds that conceived them.

In the book of Isaiah, the prophet pictures what he regards as the folly of worshipping such gods in a delightfully satirical passage:

> The carpenter stretches a line, he marks it out with a pencil; he fashions it with planes, and marks it with a compass; he shapes it into the figure of a man, with the beauty of a man, to dwell in a house. He cuts down cedars; or he chooses a holm tree or an oak and lets it grow strong among the trees of a forest; he plants a cedar and the rain nourishes it. Then it becomes fuel for a man. He takes a part of it and warms himself; he kindles a fire and bakes bread; also he makes a god and worships it, he makes it a graven image and falls down before it. Half of it he burns in the fire; over the half he eats flesh, he roasts meat and is satisfied; also he warms himself and says, "Aha, I am warm, I have seen the fire!" And the rest of it he makes into a god, his idol; and falls down to it and worships it; he prays to it and says, "Deliver me, for thou art my god!"
>
> They know not, nor do they discern; for he has shut their eyes, so that they cannot see, and their minds, so that they cannot understand. No one considers, nor is there knowledge or discernment to say, "Half of it I burned in the fire, I also baked bread on its coals, I roasted flesh and have eaten; and shall I make the residue of it an abomination? Shall I fall down before a block of wood?" He feeds on ashes; a deluded mind has led him astray, and he cannot deliver himself or say, "Is there not a lie in my right hand?"[11]

[11]Isa. 44:13–20.

In contrast, the prophet quotes Yahweh as saying,

Remember these things, O Jacob and Israel,
for you are my servant;
I formed you; you are my servant . . .[12]

You did not fashion me, says the God of the Hebrew prophets; rather I fashioned you. Here is a God who is not discovered by the human race but who takes the initiative and Himself discovers humanity.

Thus says YHWH, your ransomer,
who fashioned you from birth:
I am YHWH who made all things,
by myself I stretched out the skies,
alone I hammered out the floor of the earth.[13]

Most modern religious systems join the ancient Eastern faiths in maintaining that the human being reaches out for God—that it is the human being who must climb up to the heavens. But the Hebrew prophets say that the process is exactly reversed: it is God who climbs down to humanity. It is God who discovers humanity, not humanity who discovers God. It is interesting that the prophets were not philosophers, theologians, or meditating saints. They were much more likely to be, like Amos the prophet, herders or "dressers of sycamore trees,"[14] rather than members of the professional clergy.

Often they showed great reluctance to accept their call from Yahweh. The classic example is the dour prophet Jeremiah, who constantly complains of his lot:

O YHWH, thou hast deceived me,
and I was deceived;
thou art stronger than I,
and thou hast prevailed.
I have become a laughingstock all the day;
everyone mocks me.
For whenever I speak, I cry out,
I shout, "Violence and Destruction!"
For the word of YHWH has become for me
a reproach and derision all day long.
If I say, "I will not mention him,
or speak any more in his name,"
there is in my heart as it were a burning fire
shut up in my bones,
and I am weary with holding it in,
and I cannot.[15]

[12]Isa. 44:21a. Emphasis added.
[13]Isa. 44:24 (*NEB*).
[14]Amos 7:14.
[15]Jeremiah 20:7–9.

The "fire" in Jeremiah's bones is a far cry from the quiet enlightenment of the philosopher or the Hindu holy man. He is dragged into the arena of life to prophesy, kicking and screaming. He has been chosen. He himself has had no choice. He wishes someone else had been selected!

Since Yahweh lives, and does not merely exist, He can be thought of as having *personality*. As a person, I, too, live and do not merely exist. I have experienced personhood. I can, therefore, since I share this experience with God, work back from my own experience of existing to some understanding of God. I have a vocabulary to talk about God; it is the vocabulary of *personhood*. Thus, the Hebrew prophets use very "human" language in describing the acts of God. This is not because they can in that way make God to be like them; it is because they believe that God has made *them* like *Him*.

The technical term for this kind of talk is *anthropomorphism. Anthropos* means "pertaining to man, human" and *morphe* means "form, shape." Thus, to describe something anthropomorphically is to describe it as though it were a human being. To say, for example, that a tree "cradles the nests of birds in its gentle arms" is to describe that tree anthropomorphically. The Hebrew Scriptures constantly describe God in this way.

Some have thought that this procedure is quaint and that phrases such as "God's eyes are on the righteous" betray primitive ideas. But it is important to note that the Israelites ordinarily did not make images of YHWH or draw pictures of Him. They might, in periods of apostasy, worship images of others' gods, but not of YHWH. This indicates that they conceived of Him as a god not to be drawn or sculpted. The word pictures they used (His eyes, His arms, His back, etc.) were not meant to describe some white-bearded old fellow sitting high upon a throne of clouds. Rather, such descriptions were attempts to communicate the personhood of God. The anthropomorphic language, then, grew out of a profound conviction that Yahweh *lives*.

Now since this Yahweh is the Ultimate Person, He acts without any models or rules. The Taoist holy writings describe the Tao or "the way" as a "preface to God." For the Hebrew prophet there is no preface to God. Rather, God is the preface to everything else. He looks nowhere else to determine what a person ought to be. He is completely self-initiating. He is what He desires to be. Nothing exists that guides or limits His behavior except His own will.

Because of these things, Yahweh often acts contrary to human reason. It is very interesting that some of the greatest heroes of the Old Testament are people who are constantly disagreeing with God. Jeremiah often argued with God. So did Moses. From their point of view, much of what He was doing made no sense at all. But of all the Old Testament characters it is Job who takes God to task the most vehemently. For chapter after chapter in the book bearing his name, Job complains bitterly about the things God does and the way He does them. And God's response is that He refuses to be drawn into picky arguments with human beings! To all who would judge Him on the basis of human reason, Yahweh says,

> For my thoughts are not your thoughts,
> and your ways not my ways.
>
> For as the heavens are higher than the earth,
> So are my ways higher than your ways
> and my thoughts than your thoughts . . .[16]

The practical result of this is that the knowledge of God cannot come from human philosophical speculation. There is nothing within the human mind or human rationality that can teach one about God or in any way predict what He will do. This is because He acts without any reference to human rationality. So, say the prophets, if one expects to know about the nature of God, one must simply wait until God reveals what He is and what He wants.

The second basic characteristic of Yahweh is His holiness. In an earlier chapter we defined holiness as "otherness," as that reality that exists apart from this world. So when the Hebrew writers say that "God is holy," they are saying He is not a part of this world, that He does not originate in this world. And therefore anyone who comes in contact with Yahweh, either directly or indirectly, experiences what Rudolf Otto called the "numinous," the other. Two examples illustrate this.

The first is the initial encounter that Moses had with Yahweh:

> Now Moses was keeping the flock of his father-in-law, Jethro, the priest of Midian; and he led his flock to the west side of the wilderness, and came to Horeb, the mountain of God. And the angel of YHWH appeared to him in a flame of fire out of the midst of a bush; and he looked, and lo, the bush was burning, yet it was not consumed. And Moses said, "I will turn aside and see this great sight, why the bush is not burnt." When YHWH saw that he turned aside to see, God called to him out of the bush, "Moses, Moses!" And he said, "Here am I." Then he said, "Do not come near; put off your shoes from your feet, for the place on which you are standing is holy ground."[17]

The second is the prophet Isaiah's account of his call to be a spokesperson for Yahweh:

> In the year that King Uzziah died I saw the Lord sitting upon a throne, high and lifted up; and his train filled the temple. Above him stood the seraphim; each had six wings; with two he covered his face, and with two he covered his feet, and with two he flew. And one called to another and said:

[16]Isa. 55:8–9 (*NEB*).
[17]Exodus 3:1–5.

"Holy, holy, holy is YHWH of hosts;
The whole earth is full of his glory."

And the foundations of the thresholds shook
at the voice of him who called, and the house
was filled with smoke. And I said:

"Woe is me! For I am lost; for I am a man of
unclean lips, and I dwell in the midst of a
people of unclean lips; for my eyes have seen
the King, YHWH of hosts!"[18]

Some Old Testament scholars believe that this encounter took place in the temple dedicated to Yahweh in Jerusalem. One day Isaiah, evidently a priest, sees the symbolic items in the "holy place" become reality. Instead of a representation of the spot where YHWH touches the world (the room in the temple called the Holy of Holies), Isaiah sees God Himself. The veil over the entrance to the room becomes a long robe. The temple begins to shake. The winged beasts inside the room come alive and fly through the air crying out "Holy, Holy, Holy is YHWH of Hosts!" Isaiah is terrified but nevertheless offers himself as a spokesperson for the Holy God who called him.

"Idolatry," so roundly condemned by the prophets, is a human attempt to make the secular into the sacred, to claim the this-worldly to be other-worldly. It is carving a cedar tree and falling down to worship it. It is creating a culture and then claiming that culture is a product of the divine.

On the contrary, say the prophets, it is Yahweh who decides what will be holy and what will not. Humanity cannot build an altar and expect God to meet them there. (They never tire of crying out against such "false altars" that are, they say, "abominations.") God Himself will decide where and when the people will meet Him. Idolatry, then, is a human attempt to create holiness.

Because they understood God to be holy, the prophets of Israel also rejected the pantheist view of the world. Pantheism is the belief that *everything is God*. The pantheist conceives of the world as God, nature as God, spirit and flesh alike as God. The Bible, however, keeps a clear line between God and the world. God is different from the world—fundamentally different. He is holy. He is separate. It is true that He comes and gets involved in the world, acting out His will in history, but never in such a way as to destroy His *Holiness*.

The third basic characteristic of Yahweh, according to the Hebrew Scriptures, is His *oneness*. Again we must remember that this is not a philosophical oneness. Some of the Greek philosophers came to the conclusion that there was one God by using rational thought. But the Jews did not learn the oneness of God from their philosophers and theologians. They

[18]Isa. 6:1–5.

believed it not because it was logical but, rather, because they believed that Yahweh had proved all other gods powerless.

Their argument was very practical. Where are the other gods? they asked. What are they doing? Have they not fallen, one by one, into obscurity? During the great age of Hebrew prophecy, many more people worshipped Marduk than Yahweh. But the day came when Marduk was forgotten while a major portion of the world's population worshipped Yahweh.

That was argument enough for the Israelite. The god who acts, who overcomes all the other gods, He is *the* God. And only one god has consistently done just that, they said. The others have failed, not because there is some philosophical or logical flaw in the arguments for their existence, but because they could not *do* anything!

While the nature of Israel's God is most basically described by such terms as living, holiness, and oneness, the prophets also proclaim Him to be *just* and to act with *steadfast love*. We have already seen that one of the most central elements in the program of the coming Messiah would be to establish justice—equal justice for rich and poor alike (Isaiah 11:3–4). And, while He might lash out with great anger as He sees the insolence and insubordination of humanity, which threatens to thwart His plans, His love for those same people never wavers. Like the prophet Hosea, who continues to forgive and restore a constantly unfaithful wife, so Yahweh steadfastly reaches out in compassion to His people:

> How can I give you up, O Ephraim!
> How can I hand you over, O Israel!
>
> My heart recoils within me,
> my compassion grows warm and tender.
> I will not execute my fierce anger,
> I will not again destroy Ephraim;
> for I am God and not man,
> the Holy One in your midst,
> and I will not come to destroy.[19]

If the ultimate reality is an all-powerful personality, who acts as He pleases, how comforting to the Israelites was the conviction that He pleases to act with justice and love!

The Biblical writers also dealt with the question of the relationship between YHWH and the physical world. Classical philosophy has suggested three possible solutions to the question of the relationship between matter (the world) and spirit (the other):

1. *Materialism*—only matter is real; spirit is illusion.

2. *Dualism*—matter and spirit are both real and co-eternal.

[19]Hosea 11:8–9.

3. *Spiritualism*—only spirit is real; the world is an illusion.

The Bible suggests a fourth point of view. It maintains that spirit *is* the basic stuff of existence, not spirit as force or abstraction, but spirit as person. What originally and always has existed is a person. But then this person *creates* the natural world. The world he creates is real; it is not an illusion. But it is entirely dependent on the will and action of the eternal spiritual person who made it.

The material world, the Bible contends, came out of the exercise of the will of God. It was not made of preexisting materials. It came forth *ex nihilo*, out of nothing.

Furthermore, it continues to exist only by His power, and only so long as He wishes. According to the Bible, someone has well said, the universe is not a clock, it is a *bicycle*. A master worker might make a clock with such an intricate set of works that it could be wound up and it would run itself for thousands of years. A bicycle, on the other hand, while it is also an intricate machine, will not perform its intended function until a rider gets on and begins to pump. There must be a constant relationship between the bike and rider.

This is the Old Testament picture of God and the world. It is not natural law that holds the world together and keeps it moving. It is the will of God. What a modern scientist might call "law" would be more simply explained by the Biblical writers as simply *the way in which God does things*.

6

The Religion
of Jesus of Nazareth

JESUS IN THE GOSPELS

Jesus of Nazareth left no writing of his own. Our sources of information about him are basically three: (1) the four Gospels (Matthew, Mark, Luke, and John) in the New Testament, by far the most important source; (2) the writings of the Apostle Paul, who at least knew many people who knew Jesus, though he himself did not have a close relationship with him during Jesus' public ministry; and (3) a few references to him in non-Christian historical writings of the first and second centuries. These references, however, do little more than establish his historical existence.[1]

It is primarily through the Four Gospels that the story of Jesus has had its impact on the world. While they paint four different portraits of him, a single, remarkable personality emerges from these four accounts.

The picture is one of a Galilean peasant who is a wandering teacher, after the manner of the day. He is what the Greeks call a *peripatetic* teacher who, rather than being settled in a classroom, moves around among people, teaching both the public and a special group of associates who travel with him. Yet his travels cover a very small area, not more than two hundred miles from one extremity to the other.

[1]See F. F. Bruce, *Jesus and Christian Origins outside the New Testament* (Grand Rapids, Mich.: Eerdmans, 1974).

The Gospels roughly divide his career into two major sections. First there is a time of teaching around the Sea of Galilee, a time often referred to as the *lakeside ministry*. The scene was, and still is, a beautiful one: the deep blue of the water, the green hills surrounding it, the hellenized cities and the small fishing villages on the shore, the vineyards, and the farms. Jesus travels from town to town saying, "The Kingdom of God is at hand!" It is a period characterized in the Gospels by miracles that Jesus performs in which he exhibits power over pain, over nature, and over the functions and powers of the discarnate or bodiless spirits of evil that torment humanity.

It is also a period of growing controversy between Jesus and the religious leaders of his day. They become more and more antagonistic toward what he is saying and doing. His call for a radical commitment to a new kind of world is seen as a dangerous threat to the status quo.

The second major section of the Gospels' story can be called the *Jerusalem confrontation*. This confrontation lasts only a few days, but the Gospels use almost half their length to describe it. Here the scene changes from the pastoral background of blue water and green hills to the squalid, steamy streets of Jerusalem. The tensions mature into violence and end in Jesus' execution by the Romans.

The reader of the Gospels, when reading these accounts of the events of Jesus' death and its aftermath, must pause to consider the relationship between raw historical events and the meaning of historical events.

The Gospels are not written like the phone book—just to give an accumulation of facts. The Gospels are written to proclaim the *significance* of certain events. They are documents of faith; that is, they are written by people who believe the story they are telling to be the climax of God's dealing with humanity in history. The death of Jesus is not for them a bit of raw data. Rather, somehow, the whole future of the human race is tied up in that death. It is a death somehow so joined to the human condition that it bridges the gap that stands between fallen humanity and God.

This death, say the New Testament writers, is different from any other death that has ever occurred. This was the death of God Himself, translated into history; and so this death is the death of God for humanity. It is God reaching out to bridge the gap. And so, they are saying, all of history had been moving toward that one week in Jerusalem.

These documents, and the ones that follow in the New Testament, frankly advocate this point of view. God has finally touched human existence in the fullest possible way it could ever be done, they say.

WHO WAS JESUS?

Not everyone places the same interpretation on the events in first-century Galilee and Jerusalem as do the Gospel writers. The question, "Who was Jesus?," has been answered in hundreds of ways.[2] Scholars have noted that

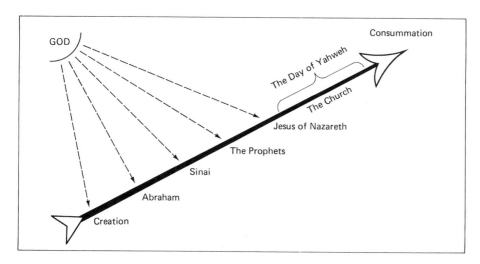

the various titles used to refer to Jesus in the New Testament itself (Son of Man, Messiah, Son of God, Lord, etc.) indicate that the precise answer to that question varied even in the earliest days of the Christian movement.[3] As Christianity became a world religion, the answers became increasingly diverse. For several centuries controversies raged as attempts were made at consensus. While consensus was never attained, the view of Jesus that may roughly be styled orthodox has, through the centuries, been the most commonly held by Christians.

It is best to begin by reviewing the chart on Page 76 depicting the view of history propounded by the Hebrew prophets. Christianity built upon this concept rather than replacing it. The new faith offered no new concepts about who God is, or how He acts in history, or what history is, or where it is going. So it becomes possible to make a Christian version of the same chart that is not basically different from the Hebrew one.

The earliest Christians were distinguished from their fellow Jews (all the earliest Christians were Jews) because they believed that the coming of Jesus was the time when God acted most decisively to reveal Himself to humanity. And, they believed, Jesus was the perfect ruler about whom the prophets had dreamed. So the appearance of Jesus was for them the central event in all of history—the time when God most fully revealed Himself to the human race.

This event was not the *end* of history, however. That is obvious! Rather, after God had revealed Himself in Jesus, He gave men and women

[2]See John Wick Bowman, *Which Jesus?* (Philadelphia: Westminster, 1970), and Hugh Anderson, ed., *Jesus* (Englewood Cliffs, N.J.: Prentice-Hall, 1967).

[3]See James D. G. Dunn, *Unity and Diversity in the New Testament* (London: SCM Press, 1977).

time to decide freely whether or not they will come into His Kingdom. So the meaning of history from the time of Jesus until the time when all is finished is that it is a time of deciding. Before God closes down history, before the arrow hits its mark, people can cast their own votes for or against the Kingdom. Will they commit themselves to a new world order of justice and peace and love? Or will they keep their swords? Will the lamb and the lion lie down together? Or will the law of the jungle continue?[4]

Those persons who decide in favor of the Kingdom are called, among other terms, the *ecclesia* or the "church" (but do not confuse the term with the modern uses of it that emphasize denominational structures). This "church" already begins in its communal life the new relationship of the Kingdom, where people live in peace and love and mutual care.

Jesus is, in this view, the *incarnation of God,* Incarnation meaning "put into flesh." "For in him," says the New Testament, "*all the fulness of God was pleased to dwell,* and through him to reconcile to himself all things, whether on earth or in heaven, making peace by the blood of his cross."[5] What the human eye can see of God can be seen in Jesus. What the human ear can hear of God can be heard in Jesus. What the human mind can comprehend of the mind of God can be comprehended in Jesus.

Jesus, then, did not simply talk about God and His will, as had the prophets, Paul the Apostle maintains. Rather, He *was* God. But God translated into flesh. And, of course, one always loses something in translation. No word in one language has an *exact* equivalent in any other. And certainly any attempt to translate the personality and nature of God into something a human being can understand can be only partially successful. One cannot hear FM stations on an AM radio. Likewise, there are some things about God that the human "receiver" cannot pick up. So, say the New Testament writers, one cannot know everything about God by looking at Jesus, but one can know all that it is humanly possible to know.

Why did God act in this way—through incarnation? Because, say the New Testament writers, as long as God was working through prophets, the knowledge of Him was only second- or thirdhand. The only way in which a truly *complete* communication could take place was through incarnation.

Here is an analogy that might help. Remember that the Biblical position is that humanity is fallen—it has gotten itself seemingly insurmountable difficulties. Now, let us suppose, for purposes of our analogy, that you are a true lover of all living things: And let us suppose that one day you are talking to your next-door neighbor over the fence and he says, "Man, the grasshoppers are eating up my backyard! I've just got to do something about it. I've decided to go down to the nursery and get some strong chemical spray. That should wipe 'em out!"

As you can see, the grasshoppers are in real jeopardy. And you have a

[4]See Mark 13:32–37.
[5]Col. 1:19–20. Emphasis added.

passionate sympathy for all living creatures. You do not like to see anything get killed—even grasshoppers. Even grasshoppers that are eating up someone's backyard. In fact, you *love* grasshoppers. It is a kind of irrational love, of course—to love grasshoppers. But you do, anyway.

If only you could warn them! But how do you talk to grasshoppers? You cannot just walk up to a grasshopper and look him in the eye and say, "You better get out of here!"

The grasshopper would only look at you and wiggle its antennae a bit and hop away. It would have no idea what you were talking about. There would be no communication because humans cannot communicate with grasshoppers.

And the reason is that the grasshopper has no way in which to receive the message. It does not have the capacity to understand. It does not know your language.

But suppose that you had it in your power to transform yourself into a grasshopper! Grasshoppers can communicate with each other. Have you ever noticed how they all take off together to avoid an approaching danger? Evidently they have some way of getting a warning to each other. So, by making yourself one of them, you, too, can give them a warning they will understand.

But doing this exposes you to tremendous risk. You make yourself subject to the same poison spray that will come to kill them. By limiting yourself to a grasshopper kind of existence, you have accepted all the risks of grasshopperness.

So, says the Apostle Paul, Jesus,

> though he was in the form of God, did not count equality with God a thing to be grasped, but emptied himself, taking the form of a servant, being born in the likeness of men. And being found in human form he humbled himself and became obedient unto death, even death on a cross.[6]

Or, in the words of the Gospel of John, "the Word became flesh and dwelt among us," and "No one has ever seen God; the only Son, who is in the bosom of the Father, he has made him known."[7]

In Jesus then, the Christians believed that God entered the stream of history in a climactic way. "God was in Christ," says Paul, "reconciling the world to himself."[8]

In modern times the question "Who was Jesus?" has been answered with great diversity again. The long-standing consensus came apart in the general disruption of ancient tradition during the Reformation and rise of secularism—a story we will trace later. Four modern answers to the question will illustrate the extent of the modern diversity: Jesus the ideal man,

[6]Phil. 2:6–7.
[7]John 1:14, 18.
[8]II Cor. 5:19.

Jesus the political revolutionary, Jesus the moralist, and Jesus the existentialist.

First, there have been those who use the term "Jesus" to describe their own culture's *ideal person*. The highest ideals and attributes of a given culture are wrapped in a bundle and that bundle is called "Jesus." This tendency can be seen by examining the portraits that painters of various cultures have created. Medieval Italians painted him as a medieval Italian. Africans painted him with negroid features. The Germans and the English made him a blue-eyed blond. These paintings have been not so much attempts to paint the historical Jesus, who, as a Middle Eastern Semite could

Visit of the Magi. An early nineteenth-century Indian painting of Mary, Joseph, the Wisemen, and the Infant Jesus. (British Museum)

scarcely have looked like any of these. They are attempts to say, "Jesus is the best one of us."

Others have suggested that Jesus was a *political revolutionary*. They believe that his phrase "Kingdom of God" was really a political slogan, which later believers piously turned into a theological concept. When he talked about the Kingdom coming, they say, he meant an earthly, material kingdom—a sort of theocracy, regulated by the laws of God—something like the kingdom of Israel in the Old Testament was supposed to be, but never was.

This is actually a very old way of looking at Jesus. The Gospels provide clear evidence that many people thought this way about Jesus from the very first.

Around the turn of the present century, Albert Schweitzer wrote a book called *The Quest of the Historical Jesus*.[9] In it he claimed that Jesus saw himself as the instigator or catalyst who would bring about the fall of the present world order and the appearance of the Kingdom of God. Schweitzer accused the scholars of his day of domesticating Jesus—of making him into the ideal middle-class German. Actually, Schweitzer maintained, he was a somber *apocalypticist* (a believer in the idea that God was going to radically intervene in human affairs and change everything). Sadly, said Schweitzer, Jesus' dream was an empty one:

> There is silence all around. The Baptist appears, and cries: "Repent, for the Kingdom of Heaven is at hand." Soon after that comes Jesus, and in the knowledge that He is the coming Son of Man lays hold of the wheel of the world to set it moving on that last revolution which is to bring all ordinary history to a close. It refuses to turn and he throws Himself upon it. Then it does turn; and crushes Him. . . . The wheel rolls onward, and the mangled body of the one immeasurably great Man, who was strong enough to think of Himself as the spiritual ruler of mankind and to bend history to His purpose is hanging upon it still.[10]

H.J. Schoenfield's book *The Passover Plot* (1966) suggests that, to establish himself as the Messiah dreamed of by the prophets of Israel, Jesus concocted a clever plot to "fulfill" the prophecies by manipulating events. His plans were foiled, however, when, having had himself drugged to appear dead, a Roman soldier, not in on the scheme, pierced him with a sword and killed him. His plan to be "resurrected" (after the drug wore off) was thwarted, but the story got started anyway.[11]

In *Jesus and the Zealots* (1967), S.G.F. Brandon attempts to tie Jesus to a movement like the first-century Zealots, extreme nationalists and terrorists who sought to overthrow the Roman domination of the Jewish state. The

[9]Albert Schweitzer, *The Quest of the Historical Jesus*, trans. W. Montgomery (New York: Macmillan, 1966).

[10]Ibid., p. 403.

[11]H. J. Schoenfield, *The Passover Plot* (New York: Random House, 1966).

Gospels are, he says, a later attempt to transform a guerilla fighter and his associates into spiritual leaders.[12]

A third answer to the question of the identity of Jesus is that of a great *teacher of moral proverbs*. Those who understand Jesus this way believe that his phrase "Kingdom of God" represents a superior moral system, a way of life. This point of view was particularly prominent among the theological liberals of the nineteenth century. The theological movement called "modernism" sought to purge religion of scientifically embarrassing elements like miracles, the supernatural, literal heaven and hell, and so on. These elements in the Gospels were de-emphasized and attributed to primitive superstitions.

What Jesus was *really* doing, they said, once one looked beyond these primitivisms, was to teach the human race a true morality—a way of life that fulfilled all humanity's ethical potential.

This understanding of Jesus was pursued skillfully and beautifully in the writings of Adolf von Harnack (1851–1930), the German theologian. We must, he says, distinguish "what is permanent from what is fleeting, what is rudimentary from what is merely historical" in the Gospels.[13] Once this is done, he says, it will not be misunderstanding Jesus "to say that the Gospel is a matter of ordinary morality."

We have already noted Albert Schweitzer's attack on this interpretation of Jesus. It is, however, one that is still accepted very widely today.

One of the most prevalent views among modern scholars of the modernist tradition is that Jesus was the possessor of a unique God-consciousness, an *existentialist* hero. The most famous name among these scholars was the German New Testament scholar Rudolf Bultmann (1884–1976).[14] Bultmann agreed with Harnack that the primitive trappings in the Gospels must be laid aside. The kernel that was left, however, was not a body of moral proverbs. The thing that Jesus had, and that makes him relevant today, was a unique sense of, and relationship to, the really Ultimate.

Of course Jesus lived in the first century and therefore had to express this consciousness in first-century language rather than in scientific language. The advent of science, says Bultmann, forces us to "demythologize" this language. We no longer can talk about a three-storied universe (heaven-earth-hell). But what can be learned from Jesus is not his understanding of cosmic geography, but his experience with *authentic human existence*. In other words, we must replace the mythological language of the Bible with the language of modern existentialist philosophy. Bultmann believed it is necessary to do this to salvage Jesus as someone significant in the modern scientific age.

[12]S. G. F. Brandon, *Jesus and the Zealots* (New York: Scribner, 1967).

[13]Adolf von Harnack, *What is Christianity?* (New York: Harper & Row, 1957), p. 14.

[14]See, for example, Rudolf Bultmann, *The Theology of the New Testament*, 2 vols., trans. Kendrick Grobel (New York: Scribner, 1951–1955), Vol. I.

THE MESSAGE OF JESUS

There are two major questions about Jesus: "Who *was* he?" and "What did he *say*?" Neither question is easy to answer. We have seen this in our discussion of the first question. We started there because it is hard to know how to regard what Jesus said until at least some tentative conclusions are drawn as to who he was.

Earlier we quoted a Buddhist holy man who said that Gautama the Buddha was gone but had left behind his teachings. Orthodox Christianity claims that Jesus is *not* gone but, rather, that he overcame death and is still active in the lives of those who believe in him. So, from an orthodox Christian view, the teachings of Jesus are only a part of his reality. But those teachings are important, not so much for what they are independently, but because of who they believed *him* to be.

The teachings of Jesus are primarily available to us in the form of the Four Gospels. This complicates things a little, since, as we have seen, Jesus did not write the Gospels himself. Rather, they are written *about* Jesus. And they are very selective. He said much more than what the Gospels have recorded. The Gospel of John says that if everything had been included there would not be enough room in the whole world for all the volumes![15]

Furthermore, the writers do not always use the material about Jesus in exactly the same way. Rather, each of them has a distinctive purpose in explaining the significance of Jesus. The Gospel writers are not trying to give us stenographers' transcripts of his message. His message is, then, filtered through the purposes and individuality of the writers of the Gospels.

This does not mean that his message was necessarily distorted or that the Gospel writers are in some way at odds with him. It does mean that they wrote as a part of a community of believers who could look back upon the events in Jesus' career from a perspective of many years—a fact that affects the way in which they tell the story.

The situation is similar to that of reading a book about the American Revolution. The early chapters of such a book would deal with events occurring before the Revolution, but the chapters would be written from the perspective of the Revolution. The writer has the benefit of hindsight. So he might say that "the Pilgrims landed at Plymouth Rock in 1620, thus helping to establish the United States," or that "Columbus' discovery in 1492 resulted in the establishment of the United States." Of course neither the pilgrims nor Columbus had such a thing in mind. But from our perspective we can see that both fit into a totality that would only become apparent later.

Likewise, the Gospel writers tell the story of Jesus from the perspective of the last half of the first century. They could see the story in a kind of totality that even the closest disciples of Jesus could not on,

[15]John 21:25.

say, the day of his execution. And that perspective, the reader must always remember, affects the way in which they tell the story.

The message of Jesus was basically a message about the nature of God. It was, the Christians believed, a revelation from God. Remember that Western religions are characterized by the belief that God reveals Himself—that humanity does not discover God but that God reaches downward to discover humanity. So Jesus' message claims to tell the people what God is like and what God wants. And it begins with the proclamation, "The Kingdom of God is at Hand."

Many hundreds of books have been written about the ramifications of such a seemingly simple statement. We will limit our discussion to only two: the concepts of the Fatherhood of God and the Kingship of God.

Jesus said that the God of the universe, who had created all things, can be called "Father." And if one has the potential to be a "Son of God," then one has a way of understanding himself as having great worth.

Jesus refers to God with the Aramaic word *abba*. He is apparently the only religious leader ever to do so. Abba is the term a small child uses in Aramaic to describe his father. It is very much like the English words "Papa" or "Daddy." Its use implies that the relationship between the human race and the Ultimate is like the relationship between a small child and his father.

Jesus' teachings are full of statements about the fatherly care that God has for his children:

> Are not five sparrows sold for two pennies? And not one of them is forgotten before God. Why, even the hairs of your head are all numbered. Fear not; you are of more value than many sparrows.[16]

There is, he says, a tremendous concern on God's part toward every individual human being. He is not an infinite but a blind force. He has the same relationship toward humanity that a human father has toward his children.

And the goal of a human being, Jesus continues, is to "grow up to be like his father."[17] In the Middle East, even today, a young boy grows up at his father's side, watching, copying, learning to be what he is and do as he does. I have seen the Palestinian potter skillfully forming vases at his wheel, his ten-year-old son beside him watching his every move. The boy will one day sit at the wheel himself, and his own work will find its pattern in the movement of his father's swift fingers. In the same way, says Jesus, humanity must learn what it means to be a person by copying the Ultimate Person. "You must grow up to be like your heavenly Father," he says.

[16]Luke 12:6–7.
[17]Matt. 5:48.

Out of this rule comes the ethical system of Jesus. While Jesus may not have been just a teacher of ethics, he certainly talked about ethics. He taught that certain patterns of behavior are God-like and certain ones are not. The most famous accumulation of ethical statements in the Gospels, the "Sermon of the Mount," is summarized in its conclusion by the very statement quoted earlier: "You must grow up to be like your heavenly Father."[18]

And the approach one takes to reach this goal, says Jesus, is *internal*. It involves inner change. Jesus' ethic is basically an ethic dealing with things that happen on the inside, because, he says, what happens inside you is what determines how you will act outside—in your relationships with other people. One of the Ten Commandments says "You shall not kill." But, Jesus says, killing is preceded by something internal—hate. So whoever hates his brother is already a murderer. Over and over again he extends or expands the rules and regulations of life, transforming them from mere external codes into statements about the inner self. The change that occurs when one enters the Kingdom is, then, first of all, an *inner transformation*.

But alongside the tender figure of God as Father, Jesus places the concept of God as King. "The Kingdom of God is like . . .". This phrase begins many of Jesus' teachings. And if in talking about God as Father Jesus deals with such problems as alienation and personal meaning, in talking about God as King he deals with the meaning of history itself. All religions, we have seen, grapple with questions such as, Why do the things happen that happen? Is there any pattern in the way things happen? Are historical events moving in any particular direction? And if so, what difference does it make?

Jesus begins to answer all these questions with the thesis that God is King. From that concept he draws an understanding of history. It is an understanding rooted firmly in the Old Testament. When he appeared in Galilee saying, "Repent, for the Kingdom of God is at hand," his words were familiar. People had been talking about such a kingdom long before his coming. But most often they had connected the phrase with national victory: "We are the people God has chosen to rule the world. So, when we rule the world, it will be God's Kingdom! And if we cannot develop armies strong enough to do this, God will send down legions of angels to help us wipe out the opposition!"

This idea, which conceived of the Kingdom of God as a kind of culture religion, was firmly rejected by Jesus. The term *basileia*, translated as "kingdom," literally means "rule" or "reign." This seems to be the way in which Jesus used it. The Kingdom of God is the reign of God. It is not a political entity based on military achievement. Rather, it is a particular way of being related to God. It is a relationship in which God's will is done.

[18]Matt. 5–7.

Where this takes place, there is the Kingdom. Wherever God's will is done in history, there is the *basileia tou theou*—the Kingdom of God.

But Jesus seems to talk about the Kingdom in two ways, leading to what scholars call the "now–not-yet paradox." In at least some sense the Kingdom *has* come. Thus he says to a group of disciples once,

> Truly, I say to you, there are some standing here who will not taste death before they see the Kingdom of God come with power.[19]

There was some sense in which Jesus saw the Kingdom coming in his own generation. There was some sense in which the early disciples understood that it *had* come because the words quoted above were written down in the Gospel of Mark many years after Jesus' death. If they had thought he had been in error, they surely would not have quoted him in this way—making him appear to be a false prophet.

The Kingdom had been introduced to history in the coming of Jesus, so thought the early believers, and it had come among them with power.[20] It had come wherever people had accepted the rule of God in their lives and relationships.

And whenever people who had accepted this rule banded themselves together the Kingdom became visible. It could be seen in the way they related to each other and to the world around them. Such a visible expression of the Kingdom of God is called, among other things, an *ecclesia* or a "church." (Unfortunately the English word "church" also means several other things, so perhaps we should use the Biblical word *ecclesia*.)

To summarize: Jesus taught that when an individual accepts the reign of God in one's own life—that God who was revealed by Jesus—he or she enters the Kingdom. And when that individual begins to share his or her life with other people who have accepted this reign also, the result is the *ecclesia*. The Kingdom of God, then, exists where people have accepted the reign of God—individually and collectively.

Yet Jesus also talks as though something remains to happen, as though the Kingdom, while it is *now*, is also *not yet*:

> He said, therefore, "What is the kingdom of God like? And to what shall I compare it? It is like a grain of mustard seed which a man took and sowed in his garden; and it grew and became a tree, and the birds of the air made nests in its branches.
>
> And again he said, "To what shall I compare the Kingdom of God? It is like

[19]Mark 9:1.
[20]See Acts 1–2.

leaven which a woman took and hid in three measures of meal, till it was all leavened."[21]

He seems to be saying that the *now* aspect of the Kingdom seems almost insignificant, like a tiny seed or a bit of yeast. But it has infinite potential, far beyond what its present puny appearance might indicate. So it is with the Kingdom. It may presently seem lost in the march of empires of men. It is found only here and there, where one or a few have accepted the reign of God. But *the future belongs to them.* It was this faith that strengthened the early Christians in the face of opposition from the mighty Roman Empire. Despite appearances, they said, when the smoke is cleared *we will triumph.*

To describe that day when the Kingdom becomes all in all, Jesus uses the language of the Jewish apocalypse—the end of the world, the resurrection, the judgment, heaven, hell, the burning of the earth. The point is that one day the Kingdom will leave its mustard seed stage. Following a great revolutionary purge every knee shall bow. Everything will be subject to God's will then, and Eden will be restored.

What, then, is the meaning of the present time? What is the purpose of being alive, and what should one do with one's life? The present time, says Jesus, is a time of decision and preparation. "Therefore, watch," he says. Unfortunately the English word "watch" seems to imply getting up in a tree somewhere and scanning the skies. But the original concept is much more active than that. Watchfulness and expectation express themselves, he says, in doing things. Men in the Kingdom do not sit and wait for "pie in the sky by and by." They seek to be God-like *now.* When God became flesh, what did he do? Why, he went about doing good. Helping the hurting. Feeding the hungry. Calling society to conform itself to the rule of God. The ethic and life-style of the Kingdom, then, becomes a very active one. It is very much involved in all that happens in the world: politically, culturally, economically, philosophically, and artistically.

So the present gains meaning. The Gospel of Matthew gives a picture of God at the Last Judgment commending certain people. "I was hungry and you fed me. I was naked and you clothed me," he says. "When did we do that?" they ask. "When you did it to even the least of your fellowmen, you did it to me," he replies.[22]

The disciples of Jesus were not called to a superficial piety. They could not deck themselves with ascension robes and sit on top of a barn somewhere to wait. They were called, as Jesus was, from the cool green hills of Galilee into the smelly streets of Jerusalem where men are profane and

[21]Luke 13:18–21.
[22]Matt. 25:21–46.

cruel, where there are open sewers, where there is blood. In wiping the tears of their comrades they were to find the meaning of their own existence.

THE APOSTLE PAUL

Excepting Jesus himself, no other person has had more impact on the Christian faith than has the Apostle Paul.[23] A large portion of the New Testament consists of his correspondence with groups of early believers. The book of Acts is to a large extent a recounting of his exploits as he carried the Christian message into the Graeco-Roman world—from Antioch to Ephesus to Corinth to Rome itself.

The vocabulary of Christian theology is mostly a Pauline vocabulary. No other Christian document has so often reignited the Christian movement as his Epistle to the Romans.

It is primarily in Paul's writings where the action of God in reaching down to humanity is described by terms like *redemption, justification*, and *reconciliation*. The human race has sold itself into slavery, Paul says, slavery to sin, to the flesh, to death, to a host of other masters. Humanity has lost its freedom. But the death of Christ became the payment that won humanity its freedom again—that redeemed it. The human race stands before the bar of justice condemned, he says. But, because of Christ, God the judge pronounces the guilty ones to be innocent. In this way God makes an unrighteous person to be righteous; that is, He justifies that person. That person had become estranged or alienated from God. But Jesus is the way in which God reaches out to the person and offers to restore the lost relationship; that is, "God was in Christ, reconciling the world to himself."[24]

Paul vividly describes the process by which man and God are reunited. Man cannot do anything to save himself. All his righteousness, Paul says, is "like filthy rags." But once God has made his move toward humanity in Christ, people can and must respond. And that response is called faith. "Faith" is a comprehensive word in Paul's writings, involving belief and obedience. But the basic meaning of faith is "utter trust." Humanity is like a nonswimmer who has fallen into deep water. Jesus is like a lifeguard who promises to rescue the victim. But the victim must first give up all attempts to save himself or herself by thrashing about. The victim must catch hold of the lifeguard and depend upon the lifeguard's strength to get him or her to safety.

The person who has done this is described by Paul as being "in Christ" (a phrase that appears in some form over two hundred times in his writ-

---

[23]A simple introduction to Paul's thought may be found in Archibald M. Hunter, *The Gospel According to Paul* (Philadelphia: Westminister, 1966).
[24]II Cor. 5:19.

ings). "For as many of you as were baptized into Christ have put on Christ," he says:[25]

> You were buried with him in baptism, in which you were also raised with him through faith in the working of God, who raised him from the dead. And you, who were dead in trespasses and the uncircumcision of your flesh, God made alive together with him, having forgiven us all our trespasses, having canceled the bond which stood against us with its legal demands; this he set aside, nailing it to the cross.[26]

The person who is "in Christ," Paul continues, has new *life*, not mere biological life, but the kind of life that God lives, a life not subject to deterioration or death. This life begins to work in the person through the power of the Holy Spirit, which dwells within the believer and animates him. Those, then, who are in Christ and who live by the power of his Spirit are drawn together in communal life—the *ecclesia*, which we mentioned earlier. Paul's favorite expression to describe this relationship is "the Body." Those who are in Christ, he says, have become One Body—regardless of racial, cultural, economic, or sexual differences.

Finally, since the power that animates the believer is the same power that raised Jesus from the dead, the person in Christ looks forward to one's own resurrection and to participation in the eternal Kingdom.

[25]Gal. 3:27.
[26]Col. 2:12–14.

7

The Religious World of Islam

THE RESURGENCE OF ISLAM

Perhaps not since the days of the Crusades, when European popes and kings sent wave after wave of "Christian" armies to "rescue the holy places" of the Middle East from the followers of the prophet Muhammad, have Christendom and Islam been thrown together with such intensity as in our own time. After years of domination by colonialist powers, the Muslim world is rising up, passionately committed to its ancient faith. Middle Eastern oil, and Western dependence on it, have forceably thrown the two cultures into confrontation. With vast oil income has come political and economic power. The resurgence of cultural and religious pride, accompanied by distaste for Western values, has resulted in revolution and turmoil not always understood in the West. Americans who had never given thought to the Islamic faith have been jolted into awareness, first by sky-rocketing fuel prices and then by the taking of American hostages and the crises that followed. They have listened in bewilderment as American sports figures, such as boxer Mohammed Ali, declared their Muslim faith.

As a Turkish friend conducted me and some of my students into the great Blue Mosque in Istanbul, the faces of the students betrayed this same bewilderment. We sat in a corner of the cold building (it was midwinter), shoeless and cross-legged on the richly colored carpets. In another area a group of men were chanting their prayers and the sound bounced to and fro among the ornate domes of the mosque. How could it be—the question was on the students' faces—that here, in what was once the splendid capital of a vast "Christian Empire," Islam now flourished? Earlier, in Jerusalem, the same students had been awakened in confusion by the loud call to prayer, broadcast electronically from the minarets of the city. They had seen the faithful pour from middle-class stone houses in East Jerusalem into the mosques. Then they had sat among Bedouin desert tribespeople, drinking sweet tea in their cool tents, and heard their parting benediction: "May Allah be with you. We will see you again, if Allah wills."

What is this far-flung religion that dominates the life of more than one fifth of the world's people? It is truly a world religion, stretching from its origins in Arabia throughout the Middle East, North Africa (and, increasingly, central Africa), Pakistan, and central Asia (where the communist Russian government must take note of millions of Muslim subjects), all the way into the islands of Indonesia. In past times it knocked on the doors of Europe itself—first through Spain in the West and later through Austria in the East. Today it bids well to capture the religious commitment of additional millions, especially in the emerging Third World.

The Muslim faith is "Western" in the sense that its presuppositions correspond far more closely to those of Judaism and Christianity than to those of Eastern religions such as Hinduism and Buddhism. Culturally, however, Islam belongs neither to East nor West, but represents an all-encompassing world view of its own.

Islam's claim to universality is very explicit. The Arabic word *islam* means "submission," "obedience," and "surrender." Thus, explains the famous Muslim teacher Abul A'La Maududi, "As the entire creation obeys the law of God, the whole universe, therefore, literally follows the religion of Islam—for Islam signifies nothing but obedience and submission to Allah, the Lord of the universe."[1] People, he says, insofar as they are physical, and subject to the physical laws of the universe, are Muslim. However, since people possess reason and intellect, they can reject the laws of God in the moral and intellectual realm and thus become "unbelievers." Should such a person decide instead to submit to God in these areas also, "he has, so to say, achieved completeness in his Islam by consciously deciding to obey God in the domain in which he was endowed with freedom and choice. . . . He is a perfect Muslim and his Islam is complete—for this submission of his entire self to the will of Allah is Islam and nothing but Islam."[2]

[1]Sayyid Abul A'La Maududi, *Towards Understanding Islam*, trans. and ed. Khurshid Ahmad (Takoma Park, Md.: International Graphics, 1977), p. 2. A revised and exanded edition of this influential work has appeared under the same title published by The Islamic Foundation, 223 London Road, Leicester, U.K.

[2]Ibid., p. 4.

But how can one come to a knowledge of the will of Allah? In the physical world, reason and research (science) can provide the answer. But only *revelation* can reveal the whole will of God, and, since this lies far beyond the individual's capacity to reason, this revelation must be accepted by faith. Faith in the unseen, coupled with total submission and obedience to the revealed will of Allah, is at the heart of Muslim religious life.

THE PROPHET AND ISLAM

For the Muslim, Allah has chosen as His vehicle for revelation the *prophet*. The prophet has been given a special gift by God to reveal His will, and the prophet's message is self-authenticating: "the duty of the common men and women is to recognize a prophet and, after ascertaining that one is the true prophet of God, to have faith in him and his teachings and to scrupulously obey him and follow in his footsteps. This is the road to salvation."[3]

The line of prophets began with Adam, who was not only the first man but the first prophet. As time went by, and humanity fell farther and farther into error and darkness, "God's true prophets were raised in all countries: in every land and people. They all possessed one and the same religion—the religion of Islam."[4] Their differences were only cultural and methodological. Moses, David, and Jesus of Nazareth were all true prophets, according to Muslim teaching. Their teachings were distorted by their later followers, it adds, but these teachings should nevertheless be highly respected.

But the climax of the line of prophethood came, says the Muslim, with the call of an illiterate Arab tribesman named Muhammad. Around the year 610, at the age of about forty, Muhammad underwent a series of deep spiritual experiences that came during solitary vigils. First he thought himself demon possessed, but he then became convinced that he was instead a prophet. He described and defended the initial experience in these words:

> By the Star when it goes down—
> Your Companion is neither astray nor misled,
> Nor does he say [aught] of [his own] Desire.
> It is no less than inspiration sent down to him:
> He was taught by one Mighty in Power,
> Imbued with Wisdom: For he appeared [in stately form]
> while he was in the highest part of the horizon:
> then he approached and came closer,
> And was at a distance of but two bow-lengths
>   or [even] nearer:

[3]Ibid., p. 23.
[4]Ibid., p. 32.

So did [God] convey the inspiration to His Servant—
[Conveyed] what He [meant] to convey.
The [Prophet's] [mind and] heart in no way falsified
    that which he saw.   (LIII:1–10)[5]

At the time when Muhammad's heavenly visitor, the angle Gabriel, began to speak to him, society in the prophet's home city of Mecca was in a period of turmoil and transition, as was Arabia in general. The religion was tribal and primitive and centered around gods worshipped in a cube-shaped building called the *Ka'ba*. The prophet spoke out against this polytheism and urged unity among the warring tribes, based on submission to the will of the *one* god—Allah. He was opposed, however, and made only a few converts for the first thirteen years. Finally, he had to flee the city in 622. (The date of this flight, called the *hejra*, is the year 1 on the Islamic calendar.)

Muhammad met with much greater success in the city of Medina, where his prophetic status was accepted. As leader of the city he set out to unite the outlying tribes and in 630 conquered Mecca itself and cleansed the Ka'ba of its idols. At the time of his unexpected death in 632 Muhammad was the most powerful man in Arabia and had presented his people with a new world-view and sense of community. His successors continued a march of conquest through Syria, Iraq, Palestine, Egypt, North Africa, Spain, and central Asia. The peoples of almost all these lands remain Muslim today, along with millions more in India, Pakistan, Bangladesh, Indonesia, and Turkey.

The career of Muhammad, according to Muslim teaching. was the "finality of prophethood." The message of earlier prophets has been adulterated, they believe, but his has been perfectly preserved. Furthermore, his message is complete (and thus needs no expansion) and universal (so that no more need exists for separate prophets to each culture, as had been the case earlier).

"Now, therefore," says Abul A'La Maududi, "the only source for the Knowledge of God and His Way is Muhammad (peace be upon him). We can know of Islam only through his teachings which are so complete and so comprehensive that they can guide men for all times to come. Now the world does not need any new prophet; it needs only such people as have full faith in Muhammad (peace be upon him), who become the standard bearers of his message, propagate it to the world at large, and endeavor to establish the culture which Muhammad (peace be upon him) gave to man."[6]

[5]Citations from the Qur'an are from *The Holy Qur'an*, trans. and commentary A. Yusuf Ali (Indianapolis, Ind.: American Trust Publications, 1977).

[6]Maududi, *Towards Understanding Islam*, p. 63.

Muhammad riding Borakh (a mare with human head) on his journey to the Seventh Heaven, and his meeting with Adam. From a fifteenth-century Turkish manuscript. (New York Public Library)

The last sentence in this statement is significant because it points to the fact that Islam is a term that covers not just religious life, but every aspect of culture: art, economics, politics, and so on. It allows no concept of a separate "secular" life for the believer. Thus, as one Muslim scholar has said, "One cannot be a Muslim and have a western culture. Islam cannot be an ingredient in culture—it *is* a culture."[7]

THE FAITH OF ISLAM

Westerners, often critical and skeptical of their own religious heritage, are amazed and sometimes bewildered by the intensity of Muslim faith. A person who would willingly die for his or her religious convictions, while such an action is common to all world religions, is nevertheless something of a rarity in the modern West.

On April 20, 1979, an Islamic holy Friday, a column of tanks and armored personnel carriers entered Kerala, a small town in eastern Afghanistan.[8] The men of the devoutly Muslim community were herded unarmed into a field and were upbraided violently for helping Muslim rebels in the hills, who were fighting the Russian-dominated and secular central government. The women gathered in the nearby mosque, in sight of the field. "Why had the people of the town refused to fight for the government? Why had they instead given supplies to the rebels?" the soldiers demanded.

One more chance would be given to them. The soldiers surrounded the men and pointed their AK-47 automatic rifles at them. Then came the command: the men were to shout pro-communist slogans and cry "Hooray for the regime!" Instead, and in spite of the obvious consequences, the men shouted, "Allah o Akbar" (God is the Greatest).

At the order of a young Russian officer, the soldiers opened fire. During the next five minutes an estimated 1,170 men and boys died. The women rushed from the mosque, screaming and raising copies of the Qur'an (the collection of the revelations to Muhammad), pleading for mercy. But they were driven back while the soldiers bulldozed the bodies of the victims into trench graves.

All religions have had their martyrs, of course. But such a story illustrates the intensity of Muslim faith in at least some parts of the contemporary world.

Five articles of faith form the foundation for the religion of Islam: Faith in the oneness of God, in the angels of God, in the books of God, in the prophets of God, and in the reality of life after death.

---

[7]Mahmoud Abu Saud, "Islam," lecture presented at Southwest Missouri State University, Springfield, Missouri, 10 December 1979. The author is grateful for Mr. Saud's generous assistance in reading and commenting on this chapter.

[8]"A Grim Chapter in Afghanistan War," *Christian Science Monitor*, 4 February 1978, Sec. 1, pp. A1, A10.

The oneness of God. The primary statement of Islamic faith is *La ilaha illallah* (There is no deity but Allah). "It is the expression of this belief," says Abul A'La Maududi, "which differentiates a true Muslim from a *Kafir* [unbeliever], a *Mushrik* [one who associates others with God in His divinity], or a *Dahriya* [atheist]."[9] Allah is for the Muslim an absolute, infinite, conscious power, not in any way divisible, and having no father, mother, or offspring. He created everything and everything is subjected to His will. As one modern Muslim put it, "The innate power within atoms is the order of Allah."

> God! There is no god
> But He-the Living,
> The Self-sustaining, Eternal.
> No slumber can seize Him
> Nor sleep. His are all things
> In the heavens and on earth.   (II:255)

It should be stressed that this belief is not simply theoretic for the believer. Its implications dominate every facet of the believer's life. A shady business deal or a shabby bit of carpenter work may bring the exclamation, "But that is not *la ilaha illallah!*"

The angels. Those beings often worshipped as gods are, instead, taught the Prophet, the angels of Allah who administer His Kingdom, but do not share in His divinity. They watch each person and keep a complete record in preparation for the Day of Judgment. Since their precise nature cannot be known by man the Muslim accepts their reality as an act of faith. The prophets, however, experienced them directly:

> He doth send down His angels
> with inspiration of His command,
> To such of His servants
> As he pleaseth, [saying]:
> "Warn [Man] that there is
> No god but I: so do
> Your duty unto Me.   (XVI:2)

The books of God. As we have seen, Muslims accept the legitimacy of many prophets. Some of these left "books" inspired by God as a revelation to humanity. The books of Abraham, they say, have been lost. The Torah of Moses, the Zaboor (Psalms) of David, and the Injeel (Gospel) of Jesus Christ have survived, but not in their original texts. Rather, they have all suffered serious corruption and pollution. Nevertheless they should be respected for the truth that has survived in them, and their adherents, called

[9]Maududi, *Towards Understanding Islam*, p. 65.

"people of the book," are likewise to be given special respect not afforded pagans or followers of the Eastern religions.

It is the Qur'an, however, that crowns the Books of God. It is not, like the other books, a mixture of error and truth, God's word and humanity's. It is not, like them, directed to a particular culture but to all humankind, and in a living language rather than a dead one. Its message, unlike the partial one in the other books, is absolutely complete. Unlike them, it is per-

From the Shahnameh (Book of Kings). A Persian manuscript, 1614. (New York Public Library)

fectly preserved and "exists exactly as it had been revealed to the Prophet; not a word—nay, not a dot of it—has been changed. It is available in its original text and the Word of God has now been preserved for all times to come."[10]

The Qur'an is, of course, the collection of the revelations of the Prophet, set in writing. This book, comparable in length to the New Testament, presents the oracles without regard to chronological or theological system. The systemizing of the Faith came later, and for a long time Muslim theology was developed primarily as a means to distinguish Islam from the religions around and before it.

One is struck by the great amount of material in the Qur'an that seems to originate in the Hebrew Scriptures, although with a definitely different perspective. Abraham, Moses, Joseph, David, Solomon, and others appear regularly on its pages. So do Jesus of Nazareth and his mother Mary. Muhammad is known to have come in contact with Jews and Christians. He suffered great disappointment when they did not accept his own message of completing and superseding that of their own prophets. Muslims would explain the Hebrew materials in the Qur'an as due to their common origin, Allah speaking to his various prophets independently of each other. Non-Muslims might suspect that Muhammad was indeed influenced theologically by both of the older faiths—but especially Judaism. His contact with Christianity and Christian literature seems to have been limited to unorthodox Christians who lived or traded in Arabia. Jesus' virgin birth is accepted in the Qur'an, but the story is not the same as that in the Christian Gospels, and it ends with a denial of Jesus' divinity: "It is not befitting (the majesty of) God that He should beget a son" (XIX:35).

Questions not dealt with specifically in the Qur'an are often answered by recourse to the *Hadith*—the traditions about what the Prophet did and said and approved of as true and right. The material available here is massive, and Muslim scholars admit that it is a mixture of truth and legend and must be subjected to literary criticism. Hadith studies permit Muslims to react with some flexibility to new historical situations.

The prophets of God. We have already outlined the important characteristics of this item of Faith: the multiplicity of prophets who have partially revealed the will of God, and the final, climactic, and perfect revelation to Muhammad.

Life after death. Muslim "eschatology," a religious teaching about the "last things" (i.e., the end and completion of history), includes belief in a Day of Judgment when the dead shall be raised and given rewards or punishments according to the dictates of justice. Then comes life after death,

[10]Maududi, *Towards Understanding Islam*, p. 82.

lived either in paradise or hell. This belief is considered so important that "denial of life after death makes all other beliefs meaningless."[11] It is the major incentive for doing good and refraining from evils since one's actions always have meaning and result in consequences beyond the present moment. Decisions must always be made, then, with an eye toward the Day of Judgment:

> The trumpet shall be
> Sounded, when behold!
> From the sepulchres [men]
> will rush forth
> To their Lord!
>
> They will say: "Ah!
> Woe unto Us! Who
> Hath raised us up
> From our beds of repose?"
> [A voice will say:]
> "this is what [God]
> Most Gracious had promised . . .   (XXXVI:51–52)

The reward for those who have submitted to Allah and accumulated good deeds is poetically pictured as in a beautiful Eden-like place,

> Among Gardens and Springs;
>
> Dressed in fine silk
> And in rich brocade,
> They will face each other;
>
> Go; and We shall
> Join them to Companions
> With beautiful, big,
> And lustrous eyes.
>
> There can they call
> For every kind of fruit
> In Peace and security.
>
> Nor will they there
> taste death, except the first
> Death; and He will preserve
> them from the Penalty
> of the Blazing Fire . . .   (XLIV:52–56)

[11]Ibid., p. 88.

THE FIVE PILLARS OF ISLAM

As there are five bedrock articles of faith for the Muslims, there are also five acts of worship that are required as the primary duties of the believer, the "five pillars of Islam": *testimony, prayer, alms-giving, fasting,* and *pilgrimage.* Each of these responsibilities is to be carried out in a carefully prescribed way.

Testimony.   The true Muslim must declare with sincere conviction the *Shahadat*:

> *There is no God but Allah,*
> *And Muhammad is his messenger.*

In this brief creed the believer asserts both the absolute oneness of God and the climax and completion of revelation in the message of the Prophet.

Prayer.   *Salat* is the prescribed prayers that the faithful must repeat five times each day, either alone, or with the community gathered at the mosque (the Muslim house of worship), especially on Friday (the Muslim holy day). From the tower (or minaret) of the mosque the call to prayer rings out across the neighborhood before sunrise (this is the call that jolted my students from sleep in Jerusalem), at midday, before sunset, at sunset, and after sunset. Long lines of Muslim men on their knees, heads touching the ground, chanting together, have become a common sight on American television. Often in the front row can be seen a king, or prince, or prime minister, humbling himself before Allah.

Alms-giving.   *Zakat,* or the giving of alms, is an obligation of the Muslim. Believing that Allah owns everything, the believer must contribute a portion of his own goods (sometimes figured at the minimum rate of 2.5 percent of his wealth) so that the poor of Islam have at least a minimum standard of living. In some cases this "gift" (or tax) is collected by the government in Muslim countries and applied to social welfare projects.

Fasting.   Fasting has the effect, in the Muslim view, of freeing man from slavery to his own desires. During one lunar month—*Ramadan*—no food or drink whatsoever may be taken during daylight hours. "Each and every moment during our fast we suppress out passions and desires and," says Abul A'La Maududi, "proclaim, by our doing so, the supremacy of the Law of God."[12]

---

[12]Maududi, *Towards Understanding Islam,* p. 82.

Pilgrimage. Muslims who can afford it are obligated, at least once in their life, to make the *hajj*, or the pilgrimage, to the city of Mecca. Nowadays the pilgrims often arrive in sleek jetliners, pouring into the sacred city by the hundreds of thousands. In ancient times the journey was much harder and more dangerous and represented great faith and courage. Every Muslim, king and pauper alike, dresses exactly the same and carries out the rituals in the same way. The central ritual is the circling seven times of the *Ka'ba*, the cube-shaped building cleansed of idols by Muhammad himself. The circling begins and ends at the mysterious "black stone" (probably a meteorite). Animal sacrifices are made during this time, in commemoration of the sacrifice of Abraham, which Muslims believe took place at this site. Non-Muslims are forbidden to enter the sacred places (although they are welcome at all other mosques in the world).

Other duties. In addition to faithful observance of the "five pillars," the Muslim submits himself to the *shari'ah*, the detailed code of ethical and social conduct. The *shari'ah* has been formulated with differing details by several different schools or *fiqhs*, but each school recognizes the validity of the others. Also, the believer is called on to "jealously guard and uphold the prestige of Islam." It is in this context that Muslims speak of *jihad* or "holy war." Jihad refers to "the war that is waged solely in the name of Allah and against those who perpetrate oppression as enemies of Islam." When an Islamic state is attacked by a non-Muslim power, every citizen must fight. If necessary, neighboring Muslim countries must help, and if this is not

The Holy Ka'ba.

enough, "then the Muslims of the whole world must fight the common enemy." The powerful effect of such a belief can be seen in the Qur'anic injunction that, in Abul A'La Maududi's words, "Jihad is as much a primary duty of the Muslims concerned as are the daily prayers or Fasting. One who shirks it is a sinner. His very claim to being a Muslim is doubtful."[13]

As is the case in all the other supracultural "world" religions, Islam is not a monolith but is divided into various sects. The major division is between the *Sunnis* and the *Shi'ites*. *Sunnah* means "the way" and refers to the Muslim's commitment to live *the way* Muhammad lived, that is, in obedience to the revelation given to him. *Shi'ah* means "pertaining to" and arises from the dispute over who should succeed Muhammad. Those who followed his cousin Ali, in particular the Persians, were called the *Shi'ah of Ali*. At first there was little doctrinal difference between the two branches, but later the Shi'ites developed some distinctive beliefs. In particular, they hold that the first twelve *imams*, or leaders, were chosen divinely and guided directly by Allah and thus may even be considered infallible. The very great respect given to modern imams is partially responsible for the popular support given to the Ayatola Khomeini by the faithful in Iran.

[13]Ibid., p. 107.

8

Religion and Ethics

ETHICS ARE INEVITABLE

Time and again our preface to religious studies has led us to discussions about human behavior. What is right behavior and what is wrong? What is good and what is bad? How do people make decisions and on what principles do such decisions rest? The study of such questions is called *ethics*.

George W. Forell begins his book, *The Ethics of Decision*, with these words:

> The crucial question confronting our age is the question of ethics. How are we to establish right and wrong? How can we tell good from evil? No doubt this problem has always been important. However, in other ages the answer seemed far simpler. People assumed that they had the answer. They were sure that the moral laws of their society were valid. There might be perverse individuals who habitually transgressed against these laws, but everyone was convinced that this was the fault of these people and not the fault of the laws.
>
> It has been left to our age to deny the possibility of guilt. We are not sure that there is such a thing as right and wrong or good and bad. And this complete uncertainty about moral values is at the root of the terrible confusion of our age.[1]

[1]George W. Forell, *The Ethics of Decision* (Philadelphia: Fortress, 1955), pp. ix, x.

Many modern observers have noted a pattern of psychological, philosophical, and theological disintegration that has occurred in our standards. But a prevalent conviction in the present age is, not so much that certain people break the laws, but that no real laws of behavior exist.[2] Or at least, if such laws exist, men and women have no clear way of knowing what they are. Recent generations find themselves set adrift on a sea of ethical indecision, wondering whether such words as "right" and "wrong" and "good" and "bad" have any real content. Are these, perhaps, no more than categories that died at the coming of the modern age?

Actually, ethics are inevitable. Once one becomes conscious, decision making is the most elementary act of living. From the moment you wake up until you fall asleep again, life is a series of decisions. Of course you do some things without making a conscious decision to do them. You may find yourself standing bleary eyed in front of your mirror some morning, toothbrush in hand, without ever making a conscious decision to get up or to brush your teeth. But such habits grow out of earlier decisions. Most of the time we are consciously deciding what to do next.

Some behavior, it is true, can be called "pre-ethical." Someone throws an object in your direction. You duck. But you did not decide to duck. You blink your eye. But you did not decide to blink your eye. The doctor taps your knee with his little hammer. Your knee jerks. But you did not decide to jerk your knee. These are mere reflex actions. No conscious decision was made. They can, therefore, be called pre-ethical.

The natural unevaluated functions of the body are also pre-ethical. Little babies just do what comes naturally. Most of the time such behavior is pretty messy, but you cannot blame the baby. The baby did not really *decide* to do what he or she did. The same thing can be said about the actions of senile persons or of the mentally retarded. These people make no judgments as to the rightness or wrongness of their actions. They simply act without thinking in response to physical urges that occur. But the rest of us, most of the time, have no choice but to choose.

Not that we do not constantly try to find ways to avoid choices, or at least to avoid the responsibility for our choices. For many centuries men have sought in various ways to prove that people really do not decide things for themselves. Actually, according to this way of thinking, everything is *predetermined*. "Determinism" is the name for the idea that people are not responsible for their actions because everything has already been preplanned. Humans do no more than just follow the script.

The tremendous current interest in astrology may be a case in point. Some astrologers maintain that much of what happens to us is predetermined. I once heard a woman ask an astrologer whether she and her husband would ever get along. "No," he replied with great assurance. "Why?"

[2]This apparent relativism is deplored in popular books such as Allan Bloom, *The Closing of the American Mind* (New York: Simon & Schuster, 1987).

she asked. "Because your signs clash!" he replied. "He is one kind of person; you another. That was decided on the day of your birth. The clash is inevitable." And presumably no one is really to blame for it.

It is interesting that in periods when people become very unsure about ethics they are attracted to deterministic systems like the astrological one mentioned. There is no use worrying about it, such systems say. Your fate was long ago sealed in the stars. You will simply do what you are destined to do. Therefore, you bear no responsibility for your actions, though you may often experience either triumph or tragedy through them.

In a slightly different way autonomous scientific humanism often seems to conclude that determinism frees people of personal responsibility. In this case it is not the stars that cause you to act the way you do; rather, it is your genes, your environment, your heredity, and the life situation in which you unwittingly find yourself. Actions are not so much the result of personal decisions as they are the outcome of various scientific chains of cause and effect. The humanist sometimes finds that he or she has surrendered his or her freedom not to the will of God, or to the stars, but to scientific causality. My height, my weight, my mental capacity, the chemical balance in my brain, the kind of community in which I live, my social status—these are the scientific factors that totally determine why I act and decide in the ways I do.

The problem with such theories is that they tend to violate our experience. If we are conscious of anything at all, we are conscious of making decisions. We do not experience a sense of being driven by forces beyond ourselves. Admittedly we may sometimes experience feelings of depression and find ourselves sitting in a dark room feeling low—confident that the whole world is pushing us around. Sometimes we become so emotionally "frozen" that action seems impossible. But the most common human experience is the experience of making choices—of *deciding* what to do next.

That is not to say that there are not in truth tremendous outside pressures that interfere with our freedom to choose, but only that these pressures almost never are so great that we can claim that they free us from personal responsibility for the decisions we have made.

I once had a very interesting discussion with a social worker on this point. He worked with juvenile delinquents. One day we sat together on a log at a summer camp, watching some of his charges play softball. "You know," he mused, "according to many of the behavior theories I have studied, these kids have done what they have done through no choice of their own. They got off to a very bad start. Their parents didn't love them. They have had traumatic experiences. They have suffered discrimination. Still, when you get right down to it, when a fifteen-year-old boy picks up a brick *he* decides whether or not to throw it through a filling station window. What you have is a boy, a window, and a brick. And it is the *boy* who decides what will happen next."

So, despite theories to the contrary, we continue to consider ourselves responsible for at least the majority of our own decisions. We continue to operate our legal system from this point of view. One will seldom get a verdict of innocent in a court of law by claiming that a third-grade teacher once hit you with a ruler and so warped your little psyche that you later robbed a bank!

You did it, says the judge, so you must pay for it. Our society continues to operate on the thesis that individuals can decide what to do next and that they are therefore personally responsible for what they decide. Without such a thesis, even if it is only postulated rather than proven (as in Kant's understanding), civilized life is impossible.

The only choice humans cannot make is the choice not to choose. They cannot escape their freedom. They are bound to be free, whether they like it or not. They are forced to live a life of constant and unavoidable decisions.

The human condition is like that of a man sitting in a nice soft chair. Suddenly he receives word that someone has planted a bomb in the upholstery timed to go off in five minutes. He cannot simply sit still and say "I'll just let things work themselves out." That is really nothing but a choice to allow oneself to be blown into smithereens.

One seldom has the luxury of "just letting things work themselves out." Every new morning presents a long series of decisions. And even saying "I believe I'll just stay in bed" is a choice! You are told you have a serious disease and need an operation. You reply, "I will not decide about having an operation." What you have done is decided not to have it!

Life, then, is decision.

RELIGION AND THE ROOTS OF ETHICAL DECISION

People who decide things must obviously have some standard by which to make those decisions. They must have some way in which to measure the relative merits of deciding this way or that. The measuring stick people use is something very much like what we earlier termed "ultimate concern." As Tillich related morality and "ultimate concern," he saw the latter as the very source of the moral demand in its unconditionedness. It is a standard so basic that everything else is judged by it. Even the most superficial decisions involve something far back within us that approves or disapproves of what we decide. Why do some decisions appear good and some bad? Is it not this deep-seated concern, this basic set of presuppositions and beliefs, that really determines how we decide?

People tend to commit themselves to one or perhaps a few basic ideas that are regarded as *true*. All other ideas and actions are then judged by these. Those actions that are consistent with these ideas are "good"; those that are inconsistent are "bad."

This process constitutes the main connection between religion and ethics. Religion, defined essentially, is one's ultimate concern. One's ethics are simply the way in which one reacts to life, based on that ultimate concern. Whenever one acts in contradiction to it, one has acted in what for that person was an unethical way. And since "ultimate concern" grasps people of different cultures and religions through different mediums and symbols, there exist many different ethical systems.

TELEOLOGICAL
OR CONSEQUENTIALIST ETHICS

All action that is intended has an end in mind. So all ethics consider the end. Some place more weight on the end, however, than they do on principles, rules, or basic rights. Whenever one asks, "What am I living for? What are my goals?" and then develops a system of behavior that will help one to reach those goals, one has created a consequentialist or teleological ethical system. Maximization of the goals are "goods." Actions that facilitate progress toward the goals are considered "right." In its most common form, that which is "bad" is painful, that which is "good" is pleasurable.

This kind of approach from a strictly individual concern would appear to be hedonistic. People following this ethic would be concerned to maximize the "good" only for themselves—which means concentrating only on personal pleasure. These people seek to live no one else's life and want no one to live theirs. They are not especially concerned to discover what makes *you* happy; rather, they search for what makes *them* happy. They are not necessarily selfish persons who never help anyone else. But they will be quick to admit that they help only because it gives *them* pleasure to do so.

While such an ideal is not usually advocated by particular religions, religious people sometimes lapse into it innocently even by the self-centered nature of legitimate religious goals such as heaven or nirvana. And certain cultures that follow predominantly utilitarian ethics, which are a particular type of teleological ethic, certainly influence people even when the ethic of the people's religion is different.

One problem with this ethic, if it can even be called an ethic in its individual preoccupation, is that it tends to atomize society, setting every person off against every other person. If all of us are simply seeking our own pleasure, then the only possible value and meaning you can have for me is the amount of pleasure you can give me. Furthermore, you will often get in my way as I reach out for pleasure, causing me to try to push you aside as an unwanted rival. It does not take much insight for one to realize that not every person will be able to maximize pleasure for just himself or herself.

Another objection to a strictly individualistic teleology is that many people believe that life, taken as a whole, offers more pain than pleasure. This has been the analysis of human experience found in such diverse traditions as Buddhism's "four noble truths" and the message of the book of Ecclesiastes in the Jewish Scriptures.

So, if I really want to avoid pain, why should I live another forty years, looking for a bit of pleasure here and there, all the while suffering? The most efficient way in which to avoid all that pain would be to end my life now and avoid all that future suffering. An ancient Alexandrian philosopher named Hegesias actually suggested this approach. He was finally expelled from the city when too many of his disciples took his advice! (For some reason he never took his *own* advice—perhaps he felt that someone has to stay around to get the truth out.)

The second consequentialist or teleological approach considers more than the individual. In its "utilitarian" form, the "good" is to maximize that goal to the greatest degree, that is, to achieve the greatest sum of good. By its focus on the good or end which it extrapolates to be the good for all humans, it certainly seems more properly "ethical" than a system that has as its primary focus only the self.

But although this approach seems more social in its orientation, it reduces individual differences and interests by making its goal uniform for all persons. Further, it usually can define no "rights" independently of the good. So if the good is a projection of the end or goal thought worthy by the majority, or whoever has enough power to shape the behavior and laws in the society, those who differ still will have no rights by which to object or overturn the decision.

By utilitarian standards, so long as the *sum* of the good is not diminished, the exact distribution of it is of no concern. That is, if the benefits enjoyed by those least advantaged are not decreased, then the increase of benefits need not be equitable or proportional. So the advantaged can receive many more benefits and justify it by this approach. It is sort of a "trickle-down" theory in which the majority of the benefits never seem to trickle out of the hands of those already most advantaged in the society. And utilitarianism in even its best theoretical formulation provides no principle for overcoming this problem. It does not even see this maldistribution as a problem.

In actual life this form of teleological ethics has been used to justify the oppression of minority groups. In the early years of this century the Turks slaughtered thousands of Armenians within their borders. This presumably made life more pleasureable for the Turks who were the majority. Within the last decade great numbers of Chinese living in Indonesia were massacred, simply because they were Chinese. This also, presumably, gave the majority pleasure. And then there was the elimination of millions of Jews by the Nazis. In each case, one might argue that, after all, there are only a few of these people, compared with the rest of us. And they cause the rest of us unhappiness. We would enjoy ourselves more if they were not around. Their elimination would bring the greatest good for the greatest number. So eliminate them!

We must emphasize that a "utilitarian" approach, end-oriented, is seldom articulated in a pure form, either within or outside particular religious traditions. That is, it nearly always involves principles as well as goals, and the principles are not always consistent with the goals or ends. So many people shift back and forth. The question of priority becomes the big problem.

The second type of teleological ethic, one that is based on a different premise, is a "natural law" ethic. In this ethical system the goal is to identify oneself with the goals of nature. Humans must align themselves with "nature," or, more specifically, they must actualize their essence. That is, they must fulfill the purpose for which they exist. And, put in religious terms, this usually means they must fulfill the purposes of God or the purposes for which God created them.

The "right reason" or natural law ethic of the Roman Catholic church is an obvious example. The end or goal is not determined by a human assessment of pain and pleasure. Rather, in Aristotelian terms, one must help each thing or being in the world actualize its intended end. A more specific example of this would be the issue of the purpose of sex under such a theory. If sex has as its intended end only procreation, then any sex engaged in for other reasons would be bad. This is what is meant by a natural law approach. There is much more to it, and we have to admit that there has not been any unanimous agreement as to which laws or rights are "natural."

On the other hand, if the idea of the "original purpose" or end is subordinated, this form of teleology can be simply an endorsement of the evolutionary process itself as "good," that is, simply assuming that things naturally evolve into better things. In its rather extreme form, one who follows this idea of the "natural" might look at the famous chart showing the evolutionary development of the horse and immediately conclude that the little creature at the bottom of the chart is an "inferior" horse, whereas the sleek beast at the top is a "superior"one.

If the evolutionary process is "good," then whatever interferes with that process is "bad." This principle becomes a basis for decision making, for determining right and wrong. Of course, such an ethical approach is seldom found among specific religions.

On the other hand, our century has witnessed several schools of thought in which the evolutionary theory was accepted not just in biology but also applied to history, sociology, and psychology. In such cases, the source for ethical standards is found not only in the field of biology but also is informed by such areas as politics and economics, interpreted in an evolutionary way. Three forms this idea has recently taken on are fascism, communism or Marxism, and capitalism. The degree to which these are "religious" or "cryptoreligious" depends upon the degree to which ultimate concern is really present. There is no doubt that some particular religions have endorsed capitalism, and at times Christianity's support for capitalism has made some people almost identify the two.

The fascists, that is, the Nazis, applied the evolutionary principles of natural selection and survival of the fittest in a rather straightforward manner. In their opinion, these principles, because natural, were "right." And they applied not only to the lower animals, but to people as well. Some individuals, indeed some entire races, are biologically superior to others. It is "right" for these individuals and races to survive and "wrong" for the inferior ones to survive. By eliminating the weak, one joins forces with evolution in creating a "master race"—the very pinnacle of the evolutionary process. The elimination of people who are going to have inferior children, people who are racially inferior, people who are mentally or culturally inferior, people who make no contribution is moral because it is *natural.*

After all, what happens to a deer who loses a leg or is diseased? The healthy animals in the herd do not make arrangements for such a poor creature to enter a "home for handicapped deer"! They simply move on and leave the inferior individual. Then a mountain lion drags it down and eats it. All this is good, because it ensures that only strong and healthy deer will survive and have offspring, thus ensuring an upward evolution and "better" deer in the future.

Some people applied this to human beings. A human being who cannot cope with life is going to have children who cannot cope with life either. Of course in a society like ours the ability to cope depends more on mental capacity then on physical strength. So, the naturalist might argue, "Let's eliminate anyone with an I.Q. of 100 or below. Otherwise, the rest of us will always have to feed them and take care of them. They will always be on welfare. It is an unnatural thing to let such people reproduce. So at the very least we should sterilize them."

The issue suggested here did not die with the Nazis. Recent news reports describe a new medical technique that enables doctors to determine whether a given fetus is going to be mentally deficient or not. And what shall we do if the test shows that the child will have a very low I.Q.? Do we abort it? How do we determine who has a right to breathe the air and who does not? How do we determine who can live a "meaningful" life and who cannot? The Nazis, of course, had little trouble with such questions.

The communist ethic is a second kind of naturalism. The Marxist conceives of nature progressing not so much biologically, toward a master race, as economically and sociologically, toward a perfect political system: the stateless state. This future utopia will be the result of a natural process called the "dialectic." And the dialectic works itself out in the conflict of classes. The clash of class against class results in a higher social form. Any action or policy, then, that encourages class conflict is a "good" act, because conflict is necessary to keep the evolutionary process in operation.

This may help to explain the motivation of terrorists. How, do you ask, can anyone possibly consider throwing a bomb into a crowd and blowing innocent people into pieces to be a "good" act? It is "good" in this view because it is an effective instrument of social change. Terrorist acts seem almost incredibly cruel. Yet terrorists themselves are hardly vicious monsters with blood dripping out of their mouths. More often they are highly sensitive persons convinced that what they are doing is "good" since the chaos they create contributes to the heightening of class conflict—and thus helps bring on utopia.

"I must try to get black people and white people, rich people and poor people, young people and old people, very angry with each other," so says the terrorist. "Violence and terror will lead to hate, and hate will lead to conflict, and conflict will result in a higher social order." In this way, acts that other ethical systems would consider grossly immoral are thought to be moral indeed.

A third contemporary form of this ethic based upon the idea of inevitable progress or evolution, which also has utopian goals, is *laissez-faire capitalism*. This kind of capitalism holds that there are natural economic laws that, if left alone, will ensure a good life for everyone. Untrammeled, unregulated, free market competition is the natural law of the universe. Dabbling with this law will bring economic chaos and an "unnatural" world order.

The *laissez-faire* system, on the other hand, will ensure that those who deserve to have money will have it, and those who do not will not. Such a system, it claims, will put the world's resources where they belong.

On the other hand, heavy taxation of the rich or government regulations on business activity will interfere with the natural order. Government should leave well enough alone, and as a result the "cream will rise to the top." Never mind that those on top may drive other people out of business, or bilk the consumer, or pay such low wages that millions are kept in poverty. All of this is "natural" and therefore "right."

What we see in all of this is the problem of these ethics really pointing beyond the self to that which is "ultimate." As Kant argued, teleological ethics seem to foster egocentrism and great opportunities for us to deceive others as well as ourselves. Especially is this true when the ethics come in the garb of a particular religious communion.

NONCONSEQUENTIALIST
OR DEONTOLOGICAL ETHICS

If all people are essentially religious, that is, have "ultimate concern" even though they do not recognize it as such, and all people decide to act certain ways rather than others, we reiterate that all people have what could be called a religious ethic. But because some people profess adherence to specific religious communions, their ethic is usually considered more obviously "religious." We have touched upon both groups above in looking briefly at a *teleological* or *consequentialist* approach.

Now we must look at what is usually considered the most obvious alternative ethic: a *nonconsequentialist* or *deontological* ethic. For many people, the ends cannot justify the means. That would allow people or groups to ride roughshod over other people as well as principles or rights that may be considered unalienable or God-given.

The focus of a deontological ethic is therefore on principles or rules. Humans can conceive rules as being mere conventions. Or they can think that their principles are merely positions arrived at through a process of contracting among parties with diverse interests. But most people feel there is at least *one* rule or principle that must not be violated, and which takes precedence over everything else, including ends or results. Or it may be three or four, ten, or six hundred and thirteen.

When the rule or principle is conceived as not being a mere human convention but an absolute, universal or "categorical imperative," it takes on the nature of a "religious ethic." It fits our "essential" definition of religion. That is, it is ultimate concern. And the "normative" aspect of religious ethics can be seen by the degree to which the person insists that such a rule or set of principles cannot be replaced by others. The same would be true in the above discussion of ends or goals. What we called "functional" and purely "descriptive" definitions of a religion would, in the area of religious ethics, involve primarily the field of metaethics or analysis.

Often, the more complex life is conceived to be, and the greater the extent of sacred literature within a given religion, the more there is a tendency to distill the myriads of rules to a simple form. Buddhism has layers and layers of moral or ethical principles, but supposedly they can all be found essentially or embryonically in the Ten Precepts or in the Eightfold Path or the Three Jewels or a number of other special formulations.

In Judaism, the question of which commandment was the greatest or most important certainly illustrated this tendency to keep religious-ethical principles at an intelligible and manageable size for the people. The 613 commands could be found to be reduced to their essence as three rules in Micah, two in Isaiah, or one in Habakkuk—"faithfulness." This "faithfulness" pointed to moral behavior as essential to any relation with the Absolute. As one rabbi put it in a nutshell, "Whatever you do not want others to do to you, do not to them."

Similarly, for Mencius, Confucianist ethic is distilled in the idea of "benevolence." And benevolence is dutifulness: "Try your best to treat others as you would wish to be treated yourself, and you will find that this is the shortest way to benevolence." Many a Christian has found the Sermon on the Mount to be a good condensation of the moral imperatives laid on him or her by adherence to that particular religion. Others have found Jesus' "Golden Rule" as the one absolute general principle: "Whatever you would that men should do to you, do you also to them." Or the Apostle Paul summarized the Christian's moral and religious duty by saying that to love God with all one's heart and to love one's fellow human was the essence of the Christian life and the fulfillment of the divine-moral law.

If a teleological ethic tends to foster egocenteredness, and if egocenteredness cannot be accepted as a universal approach to human relations, within or outside specific religions, a deontological or principle or rule approach may appear to rid an ethic of this egocenteredness. But the rule followed will have to be consistent: no double standards can be allowed. It must be strictly adhered to since the real evil or harm would come from an infraction undermining the system more than from the mere harm of immediate results.

For example, if a wife is dishonest with her husband about some significant matter, the real harm may well be not the immediate results but the dissolving of trust between the parties. All human associations exist on trust. When a president of the United States decides to ignore standards that govern everybody else or rules established by the people, the real harm is not just to that president but the effect it has of creating a general distrust, skepticism, and even cynicism. The order tends to break down. And many of us realize that this comes about because someone may honestly have thought an end or result is more important than a principle, and therefore temporarily bracketed out the principle.

So it is not just people who belong to religious communions who are concerned with an ethic that is essentially "religious," that is, who demand absolute principles. All people who realize the responsibility that comes with the freedom to make decisions find themselves at times demanding a single rule, a categorical imperative, a fixed and predictable standard. Civilization really cannot exist without standards that provide people with a basis from which to shape their expectations of others' responses.

But rules tend to multiply. And as laws proliferate, complexity enters to such a degree that before long one may not be able to observe one rule without violating at least the spirit if not the letter of another. Or one becomes unsure of which is the most basic rule or should have priority. Or one realizes that by insisting on a rule or principle, one sometimes appears to depersonalize or treat people as mere objects. Or one questions how he or she can even be sure that a rule or principle is actually absolute, unalienable, categorical, or God-given.

For many people these questions never arise. For others, even within particular religions, the questions are answered in manifold forms. The certainty is provided by the rule's being articulated in a sacred scripture. Or the absolute principle was implicit within an archetypal experience from which the religion originated. For others, the communion's authoritative body has sanctioned the rules or principles. For yet others, the absoluteness of such rules is disclosed only after strenuous ascetic practices or extensive meditation or rigorous conceptual scrutiny. And finally, for some the assurance is claimed through faith as a leap beyond reason or a struggle with paradox or absurdity or a mystical uniting with the Absolute.

SITUATIONAL
OR CONTEXTUAL ETHICS

If both ends or goals and even principles or rules can tend to depersonalize, many people both within particular religions and outside them have attempted to find a seemingly more humane answer. It is true that for many people, national ideologies still dictate. And for others, political alliances or economic platforms of political parties still determine the ethic. But our century has experienced crises of credibility. These crises can be viewed as wholesome in that they have forced us to question the finite institutions that we tend to absolutize.

Particularly those of us who as citizens of the United States lived through the bombing of Hiroshima and Nagasaki, the Vietnam war, the Watergate and Irangate scandals, have gone through, willingly or unwillingly, an *ideology criticism*. Our nation lost its moral innocence. Our easy answers faded. Our pride in our ethical absolute—whether principles or ends—dissolved. And in the Jonestown massacre, the Rajneesh community of Antelope, Oregon, and the Jim Bakker dethroning, we realized that even overtly religious communions and personalities are not immune to self-destruction.

For some, these credibility crises or ideology criticisms resulted only in a stagnantly sophisticated cynicism: that's the way humans are, and that's that! For others, the crises led to a rediscovery of the penultimate concerns of life: we can quit torturing ourselves about our national and international failures ethically by simply refocusing on making ourselves a living. Apathy of the seventies followed the self-criticism of the prophetic spirit of the sixties. And the eighties brought a new generation of college students who lived almost totally on this side of these critical national events.

What does this mean for religious ethics? The sixties particularly were the years when the disillusionment with Western Christianity's absolute rules or goals occurred. In the place of these absolutes, many turned to what they called "situation" ethic or "contextual" ethic. One approach insisted that there was only one rule that was absolute, namely to "love" others. And love was defined as willing the best for them. This, of course, meant that rather than depersonalize others by insisting on one's absolute goal or principles, one had now to consider the person in all of his or her uniqueness and the particular situation in which the choice had to be made.

In truth, this approach consistently eliminated the ability of any person to judge another personally or ethically. While that owned up to the complexity of reality, it was unrealistic as regards the basic civil and legal structures. People really did not abandon the rules and goals articulated and upheld by our legal system. And enforcement of our laws was not simply continued from sheer custom devoid of moral necessity. Real life often does not have the leisure to idealize so hypothetically.

H. Richard Niebuhr's more balanced approach to move beyond rules and goals insisted that four factors must be recognized in determining the proper or "fitting" ethical response. First, the decision ethically is for a "response" to another, which implies one is being acted upon. Secondly, each response and re-response involves "interpretation" by the parties. That is, we and the other parties must try to figure out what was meant by each other's response. We certainly are not always correct—anymore than we can read each other's minds. But we still have to do it. Thirdly, we must recognize that all this responding and interpretation is within an intricately involved social web of relationships. There is a social solidarity that gives to all our ethical responses an almost infinite number of ramifications and repercussions. Finally, Niebuhr suggested that we must accept "accountability" after due consideration of these other three factors. Only at that point, he contended, could an ethic be "responsible."

Niebuhr related this responsible ethic to the Christian tradition by asking the question: "What is going on?" That is, the reconciliation or uniting of the parties by the type of reflection described above is, as he sees it, the primary thesis of the Christian religion. So as one makes these ethical analyses, he or she should ask what an appropriate response is to what is going on. And if what is going on, as the Christian religion contends, is that God is reconciling the world to itself, then one's decisions should tend to select responses which have the most obvious reconciling power among estranged parties.

Such an attempt to move beyond the depersonalizing tendencies of rules and goals has been articulated in other religions as well. In Judaism, for example, Martin Buber insisted that to realize our humanity, it is essential that we respond to another person not just as an "it" or object but as a "thou" or subject like ourselves.

This kind of formulation shows that an ethic propagated by a given religion need not be radically different in principle, if different at all, from ethics that are formulated by responsible people outside any given religious communion. Probably for a religious people to feel that its ethic must be different or absolutely unique would be to place arrogant exclusivity ahead of common sense. If all people are religious, in the sense of having ultimate concern, it should not surprise those who belong to particular religions to discover that even those who do not belong can place the same high value on a single rather than a double standard, upon human freedom or subjectivity, and upon the dignity of the person.

But this does not mean that a situational approach provides surer or easier answers, nor even that it is immune from the depersonalization and self-deceit that can be such a problem in the goal- and rule-oriented ethics. It may be, however, that the essential definition of religion as "ultimate concern" may provide at least an incentive if not a method for continual self-criticism of any ethics of a particular religion as well as any ethic in general.

9

Religion and Western Culture

THE RELATIONSHIP BETWEEN RELIGION AND CULTURE

Religion and culture have always been closely related in the Western world (the Americas—North and South—and Europe—East and West). But neither has ever been entirely happy with the relationship. This chapter briefly traces the course of the interaction between the two throughout the past two thousand years. A good way in which to prepare for this subject would be to review the earlier discussion of cultural religion and of ultimate concern. Having done this, one is better prepared to launch into what, unfortunately, is a rather complicated subject. Complicated, but profitable—because it is a study that helps us to understand a great deal about the nature of religion and the way in which it affects the world in which we live.

Earlier the term "ultimate concern" was used to refer to that conviction (or set of convictions) about reality that rests at the very center of a person's life. It is the source of one's actions and the anchor of one's hopes. It may be unexpressed and unreflected. It may not appear obvious and on the surface, but it is there nevertheless, furnishing the "glue" that holds life together.

Cultures have sets of convictions, also. As Tillich further defined "ultimate concern," he suggested that it is the very substance of culture, and culture is the form religion takes. These convictions may be seldom recognized or discussed, but they lie behind the actions of a culture and, when discovered, can be very helpful in understanding *why* a culture does the things that it does. Some examples may help to illustrate this fact.

Western culture is characterized by a strong sense of the sanctity of physical human life. This sense extends down even to the life of a single individual within the culture. Because of this, Westerners often do things that seem strange to people in other cultures. We spend tremendous amounts of money, for example, to keep our astronauts alive during space flight. Then we spend additional millions on back-up systems to protect them in case a primary system malfunctions. This must seem strange to people in other cultures, particularly those where money is scarce. Why spend so much, when only two or three lives are involved?

The answer is probably that we spend it because deep inside our collective thinking and feeling something is saying, "Human life is extremely valuable. Do nothing that seems to waste it recklessly." Besides, if someone is killed because of inadequate concern about safety, those people responsible for the project will be shamed and considered to have failed. This was certainly the final assessment of the U.S. space shuttle calamity in 1986.

We are committed, then (at least publicly, as culture religion concerns itself mostly with public behavior), to the sanctity of the individual human life. We constantly seek better health measures, better safety procedures, better physical protection, and so on. All these activities are tied very closely to Western culture.

An Eastern culture that believes in reincarnation (the idea that the soul keeps coming back to life again and again in many different forms) might look at such matters very differently. If dying is nothing more than the passing from one body to another, then the mere retaining of life seems rather insignificant. In fact, since the new incarnation may be preferable to the last one, letting someone die might also be preferable. Thus, we may see people being allowed to die when only a little effort and expenditure would have kept them alive. But this is consistent with a view of life that is convinced that the physical world or existence is not ultimate reality. To the degree that even Christianity holds this, at times the quite extravagant means expended seem an ironic contradiction, as if Christians really only believe in the material world.

I knew a man who lived in the Far East many years ago. He told me that one day, while he was crossing a bridge, the man in front of him suddenly lost his footing and fell into the water. He was churning around frantically, obviously unable to swim. My friend could not swim either, but, like a proper Westerner, he became very excited and concerned. So he looked back to the next man on the bridge, a native of the Eastern culture, and asked him, "Can you swim?"

"Yes," the man replied.

"Well then, jump in quick and pull that man out. He's drowning!"

The second man looked over the bridge rail for a long time, carefully observing the poor fellow thrashing in the water below. Finally, he looked back to my friend, smiling, and said,

"I don't believe I *know* him."

"You mean you won't pull him out unless you *know* him?" my friend asked, not believing his ears.

"That is correct," was the polite reply.

Finally my friend was able to pay someone to jump in, and just in the nick of time the man in the water was saved.

This seemingly strange and heartless behavior undoubtedly grew out of the deep-seated presuppositions of a very different culture from our own. When the man said, "I don't know him," he meant "he is not a part of my family or of my people—the ones who are my responsibility. And since he is not, my intervention would be an interference with the will of Heaven, which obviously has decided it is time for this man to die!" But why is such a thing obvious, you ask? Because Heaven caused him to fall in the water without any relatives nearby to rescue him!

On the other hand, many cultures in the East have a far greater sense of community and family than do those in the West. For them, the individualism of the West is the worst kind of cruelty and immorality. For example, the idea that someone would actually send away his or her own mother to live in something called Happy Acres Rest Home might shock and disgust the Eastern mind.

One more example. The city of Tokyo, Japan, has over eleven million people—and only three psychoanalysts in private practice. The city of New York, on the other hand, has about eight million people—and almost a thousand psychoanalysts. The few Japanese psychiatrists in practice depend more on tranquilizers than on analysis in treating patients.

Why? Because, according to Tokyo analyst Soichi Hakozaki, the strong group and family orientation of the Japanese and the rejection of individualism has resulted in a "softened ego." Without a strong sense of "I," analysis as we know it in the West is impossible. Besides, points out the famous novelist Yukio Mishima (who, incidentally, committed ritual suicide in 1970), Buddhism, which sees life as a mere vapor with little significance or meaning, makes the whole process of "attaining mental health" a waste of energy. As Western individualists, we may think it would be horrible not to exist. But the Buddhist monk sees the elimination of a rather neurotic clinging to existence as the finest of all states.

These examples are designed to illustrate how the customs of a given society may seem strange and arbitrary to someone looking in from the outside. But lying deep behind such customs is a set of ultimate or basic presuppositions about reality. And out of these presuppositions come the customs.

This set of presuppositions may be thought of as an undergirding that holds up the structure of that society or as a matrix, a mold that determines the shape a society will take.

From time to time this matrix, or culture religion, changes dramatically. And, of course, when this happens, the whole culture begins to change along with it. Such changes can grow out of a variety of new situations. For example, the economic conditions may change for better or worse. Or the political system or social conditions may change (as with the entrance of a great number of foreigners, for example). New philosophical concepts may begin to catch hold. New scientific discoveries can have their influence. Theology may start in a new direction. Any of these factors can be the beginning of a shift in cultural religion.

These new ideas and situations are often the work of creative individuals within the society. They are propounded and gradually accepted by the culture as a whole. When the culture has shifted in one of these areas, it often starts a chain reaction that causes adjustments in thinking about all the other areas. Eventually a whole new matrix has been created. This new matrix inevitably begins to form a new culture.

The new matrix functions as the culture religion for the new culture. It is the set of convictions that lies behind that culture and makes it what it is. It is the glue that holds the culture together and without which it will simply disintegrate.

If, in the process of shifting, it is not possible to form a new matrix—that is, if some new idea is so damaging to the culture that the other areas cannot adjust—then the culture does not change but collapses entirely. The result may be revolution, civil war, or simply disintegration. Sometimes, in its search for a workable cultural religion, a society will latch onto some supracultural religion that exists within it and use the "captured" faith as its societal glue.

Several times in history a society has taken hold of the Christian religion, made certain adjustments to it, and used it as a cultural matrix. Christianity is altered in the process, of course. It becomes partly cultural and partly supracultural. But as an essentially supracultural religion, Christianity survives such use. When the culture that captured it dies, Christianity continues (though, of course, that particular cultural form of it dies).

If, on the other hand, the culture religion used as a matrix is purely cultural, then it dies altogether at the death of its host culture. An example is the "German religion" perpetrated by the leaders of Hitler's Third Reich. It has disappeared along with Hitler and his empire.

Culture, then, grows out of a culture-religion matrix. Each culture produces its own kind of person. This person has a certain world view and life-style that grows out of the matrix. He or she will have these until the matrix changes. When it does, one cannot be "human" in the same way as before, so a new "human" appears. This change does not take place overnight. When a culture is changing, people go through a period of great turmoil and struggle, and only gradually become "new."

This kind of change has occurred several times in the Western world. We can outline these changes in very broad strokes with the following chart:

I. THE CLASSICAL PERSON (600 B.C. to A.D. 300)

Collapse and Transition (A.D. 300 to 900)

II. THE MEDIEVAL PERSON (A.D. 900 to 1300)

Collapse and Transition (A.D. 1300 to 1700)

III. THE AUTONOMOUS PERSON (A.D. 1700 to 1900)

Collapse and Transition (A.D. 1900 to Present)

The dates, of course, are just generalized guideposts. Changes are gradual and do not occur in a precise year. The chart suggests that there have been at least three ways of being human in the West and that the Western culture-religion matrix has shifted at least three times during the last two thousand years. Each great cultural form has been followed by a period of confusion. The underpinnings of economic, political, social, philosophical, scientific, and theological thinking have been shaken while society searched for a new stability and a new way in which to be human.

THE CLASSICAL PERSON

The first way of being human in the West was born in classical Greece, the Greece of Plato and Aristotle, and was nurtured by the host of great political, philosophical, and artistic geniuses of that remarkable period. It was developed further throughout what is called the Hellenistic period, initiated when Alexander the Great spread the Greek way of thinking through the large areas of the ancient world that had fallen to his advancing armies. It was a syncretistic kind of Hellenism. That is, it was constantly picking up ideas and practices from other cultures as it spread, but kept incorporating them into a single matrix of ideas.

The rise of Rome gave political stability to this combination of Greek ideas and Hellenistic syncretism. The Romans were much better at government than at philosophy, so a Graeco-Roman combination furnished the best of both worlds.

But as the Roman Empire continued, it became evident that the weakest part of the matrix was the theological-philosophical part. The other elements in the matrix (political, sociological, etc.) were much more central in gluing the empire together. There was very little consensus of opinion about philosophy and religion among classical persons. The main thing that held them together was the powerful Roman military force.

There were many attempts to find some kind of religious base on which everyone could agree. In the first stages of the development of the Classical Person, the old Greek polytheism (the world of gods and goddesses described by Homer and by Greek mythology) furnished the material for such an attempt. Then, during the time of Alexander and his successors, the Hellenistic syncretists tried to popularize the idea that the gods of the various subcultures were actually the same realities, described by different names—hoping to tie these diverse groups together in that way.

Other attempts were made during the height of Roman domination. Various philosophical systems vied for general acceptance. In general, those systems tended to undermine faith in the polytheistic systems. While acknowledging their existence, most of the philosophers saw the gods as having little relevance to the daily life of human beings. The *Epicureans* maintained that absence of pain was the object of life and that people should seek it as their primary goal. The *Stoics*, representing the dominant philosophy of the time, believed, in the words of one of their most famous spokespersons, Seneca, that "God is nature, is fate, is fortune, is the universe, is the all-pervading mind." If one lived according to the nature and purpose of this mind, one would be able to handle both the good and evil in life with "apathy," i.e., quiet resolution. One must distinguish between those things in life over which one has power and those things one cannot control. Such a rational approach should replace emotion and reduce pain. The *Cynics* took an antiestablishment approach—ridiculing tradition, morality, ceremony, and religion. And the *Platonists* and *Neo-Platonists* viewed absolute reality as spiritual—and archetypal world of Forms—rather than material and changeable.

Only a small minority of the people of the classical world adhered to these philosophies, however. Many more were drawn into the world of superstition: astrology, portents, divination, dreams, and oracles. Especially popular were the *mystery religions*, a multitude of cults offering a hope of immortality and a sense of personal relationship with deity. These cults featured secret initiations in which the worshipper came into mystical communion with Isis and Osiris, or Dionysus, or Mithra.

But none of these systems was able to permeate the whole of classical culture. Each seemed to appeal to only one segment of that culture, but not to other segments.

The Roman Emperor Cult. In the waning days of classical civilization the government of Rome tried to maintain the unity of its diverse empire by encouraging the deification and worship of the imperial family. This sculpture of the Empress Faustina the Elder, wife of the emperor Antoninus Pius, was found in a temple in Sardis—modern Turkey. (British Museum)

One of the last attempts to provide a theological glue was the encouragement of emperor worship. This was a rather contrived project to tie the citizens of the empire together by forcing them to participate in a cult that glorified the supreme ruler. The emperors, particularly the later ones, knew that their empire and culture were crumbling. Emperor worship was one last desperate attempt to put it back together. But it was too late. The attempt was made particularly difficult by a growing group within the empire called "Christians" who refused to go along with it altogether.

Eventually the entire classical matrix fell apart and the Classical Person disappeared.

TRANSITION:
THE "TRIUMPH" OF CHRISTIANITY

By the time the old Roman Empire faltered (that is, when the cultural matrix became weakened), there was one religion that was healthy enough to survive—Christianity. So it is no surprise that the last emperors completely reversed previous policy, stopped killing Christians, and started courting them. Shortly after the year 300 the Emperor Constantine declared himself a Christian! However one might feel concerning the sincerity of his conversion, one must admit it was a good tactic politically and socially.

For their part, the Christians were weary of being hounded, pressured, arrested, tortured, and thrown to lions. When the emperor came to court them they responded with understandable, but perhaps very unfortunate, enthusiasm—unfortunate because, in doing so, they allowed their religious system, which up to now had stood to a degree above its culture, to be captured by its culture. Up to now the Christians had considered themselves "in the world, but not of it." They had no stake in the classical world. It was a world against them. The Roman Empire had always been their enemy. Now, suddenly, it became their friend. But it was a very demanding friend, a friend that called upon Christianity to serve, not as a supracultural prophet but as a cultural priest.

Gradually the church fell under secular control. It began to look more and more like the secular government. It became more and more centralized and, thus, more controllable by the power structure of the society. Formerly, it had been dangerous to be a Christian. Now, it became politically and socially expedient. Many, many people flocked into the church. Few of them understood the supracultural dimensions of their new faith. They brought along remains of the old classical carcass—superstitions, Greek philosophical ideas, Roman governmental concepts, and the like.

Gradually, during the chaotic centuries following the collapse of the empire in the West, a new matrix was formed and a new "Person" appeared. When society emerged from what are sometimes called the Dark Ages, the West had a new cultural glue—the Roman Catholic Church.

THE MEDIEVAL PERSON

The Roman emperor and his military power had once held the Western world together. Now the Roman Catholic Church was called upon to do the same thing. And in such a situation, when particular religious views are connected so closely with the preservation of culture, heresy is also treason. That is, an attack upon the basic presuppositions of the church could only be treated as a threat to, and a betrayal of, the entire medieval way of life. To weaken the church was to contribute to the collapse of society.

When a religious institution is the basis for cultural stability, those who threaten the system must be silenced. One must understand this situation to really understand the "intolerance" of the Medieval Person toward religious beliefs that differed from the norm.

Thus appeared the Medieval Person, one who accepted this situation. His or her life was structured by the beliefs of the Roman Catholic Church. This person's world-view and life-style were formed by those beliefs. For some four hundred years this was the typical Person of the West.

The literary records of the Medieval Person can well be represented by these four documents: *The Nicene Creed*, Augustine's *City of God*, Thomas Aquinas' *Summa Theologica*, and Dante's *Divine Comedy*.

The Nicene Creed

The Nicene Creed was a codifying of orthodox Christian theology. It stated its position in such a way as to provide unity among Christians, and thereby to reduce the chaos of speculation about the most basic issues—the nature of God, the nature of humanity, the nature of the world, and the meaning of history. The creed was produced very early in the transition period (around A.D. 300). For the next one thousand years it formed a basic world-view for the Medieval Christian of the West. Here is how it reads:

> I believe in one God the Father Almighty; Maker of heaven and earth, and of all things visible and invisible.
>
> And in one Lord Jesus Christ, the only-begotten son of God, begotten of the Father before all worlds [God of God], Light of Light, very God of very God, Begotten, not made, being of one substance [essence] with the Father; by whom all things were made; who, for us men and for our salvation, came down from heaven, and was incarnate by the Holy Ghost of the Virgin Mary, and was made man; and was crucified also for us under Pontius Pilate; he suffered and was buried; and the third day he rose again, according to the Scriptures; and ascended into heaven, and sitteth on the right hand of the Father; and he shall come again, with glory, to judge both the quick and the dead; whose kingdom shall have no end.
>
> And [I believe] in the Holy Ghost, the Lord and Giver of Life; who proceedeth from the Father [and the Son]; who with the Father and the Son together is worshipped and glorified; who spake by the Prophets. And [I believe] one Holy Catholic and Apostolic Church. I acknowledge one baptism for the remission of sins; and I look for the resurrection of the dead, and the life of the world to come. Amen.

This creed is a very comprehensive statement. It asserts that God exists and describes His nature and the nature and destiny of the world. It specifies what the basic goals and conduct of life should be.

The City of God

The second document central to understanding the Medieval Person is the work of the brilliant North African theologian Aurelius Augustinus or *Augustine* (354–430). Augustine lived during the middle part of the transition period between the Classical Person and the Medieval Person. The Roman Empire was collapsing all around him. Barbarian armies were knocking on every door, ready to swoop in and crush civilization.

In this context Augustine wrote the *City of God*. His express purpose was to defend the Christian religion, since many were blaming the Christians for displacing the Roman gods with the Christian God. These disenchanted and resentful Roman and African citizens of the Empire were contending that either the fact of that displacement or the impotence of the Christian God was to be blamed for the gruesome and immoral acts involved in the city's collapse.

Augustine's defense was that the Roman gods and Greek philosophies were all inferior, that Christian behavior and faith and the Christian God were not responsible for the disaster, nor did the Christian passivity toward the traumatic event imply that Christians have no standards, courage, or loyalty. They are people who, rather, are governed by an inner law, a spiritual concern. They belong to the "city of God," which transcends all fortunes and misfortunes of this world.

Although Augustine actually says very little in the book about the two cities, he does briefly contrast the city of this world with the city of God. The latter is simply those who do God's will. At times, this appears to be the visible church, but there is an ambiguity here in Augustine, as there is an ambiguity in the reason for the suffering of the fall of Rome.

For example, Augustine posits the maxim that human sin often produces proportionate evil results. Often God punishes, and even punishes those who are Christian. However, that is not the whole picture, Augustine admits, because God also sends the rain and sunshine on good and bad people alike, or indiscriminately. So there are no easy answers to certain tragedies such as the fall of Rome. But what counts, Augustine insists, is that people believe in God and follow God's standards. By doing this they can overcome the basic fallen nature of humanity, transcend the otherwise inevitable fate of the second or eternal death, and find ultimate beatitude in God.

Precisely how the "city of God" relates to the city of this world, or how the visible church and government relate to each other as well as to invisible aspects of each, is not clear in Augustine. But the later church cited Augustine's theology and political theory as warrant for the pattern that developed eventually and held the field through the entire medieval period: the church controlling the state.

Aquinas and Dante

Thomas Aquinas (1225–1274), whose life and work came at the end of the period, represents the flowering of the Medieval Mind. The dominance of the church over social and political structures was matched by theology's becoming the "queen of the sciences." Whereas Augustine's theology only admitted that Neo-Platonic philosophy was the closest to Christian, and thus he still found certain faults in it, Aquinas adopted Aristotle as the philosopher for Christian theology.

This meant that faith was not conceived as ontological or a fact of one's whole being, as in Augustine, but rather was a faculty that had to make the right use of reason to prove its validity. The deductive method from what were posited as primary principles was the Aristotelian method Aquinas followed for the most part. Not all the mystery of the Christian faith disappeared by this emphasis upon reason, but logic and the syllogistic method certainly appeared to establish the credibility of the primary fundamental tenets of the Christian faith—many of which had previously been accepted only on the authority of the Scripture or church. Thus in St. Thomas' great "summas" Christian theology was given a definitive medieval rational defense.

While Thomas Aquinas gives us an intellectual expression of the Medieval Mind, Dante gives us the *poetic* expression of it. His *Divine Comedy* (ca. 1318) is a vivid picture of the world as the Medieval Person understood it. Mankind is understood to live in a three-storied universe—earth, hell below, and heaven above. Life is a preparation for spending eternity in either heaven or hell. While man remains on earth, the church is his source for *grace* (the favor of God) and *truth* (an understanding of reality).

This does not mean that all church leaders are always right. Dante, touring hell in one of his poems, finds several popes right in the bottom of the pit. But the church itself was the dispenser of the grace that God offers to man through Jesus Christ. Man's meaning and destiny, then, were tied to his relationship to the church.

Collapse of the Medieval World

The medieval world lasted until about the thirteenth century. The final flowering came during the late thirteenth and early fourteenth centuries. Then a series of events began to occur that rocked the medieval world and the Medieval Person. The result, eventually, was a new matrix, a new cultural mold, a new relationship between religion and culture, a new lifestyle, and a new world-view.

The shake-up had many underlying causes. We will mention only a few. First, there was *the rise of the nation-states*. When people began to feel a sense of *nationality* it tended to break, or at least to challenge, the domina-

Medieval World-View. This fourteenth-century gothic ivory carving contains many of the elements central to the world-view of people in medieval times. Jesus, holding a long cross, is pictured leading Adam and Eve out of hell, shown as the jaws of a monster already devouring another figure. On the right stands the Devil, looking away in consternation as he loses his victims. (British Museum)

tion of the Roman Catholic Church in politics. So a king may boldly say to a pope: "I am the King (of England, or France, or some other nation). *I* will make the decisions about what happens in my nation."

In medieval times if a king ran afoul of the pope, he might find himself obliged to crawl on his knees through the snow to ask the pope's forgiveness. But with the rise of nation-states, the kings found that they could act independently of the pope with impunity.

Second, there were *the voyages of discovery*:

Columbus sailed the ocean blue,
In fourteen hundred and ninety-two.

And, at about the same time, so did Bartholomew Diaz, and Vasco da Gama, and Balboa, and Magellan, and John Cabot, and Jacques Cartier. They found no sea monsters. They did not fall off the edge of the earth. They did not perish in boiling water at the equator.

The world was not what the Medieval Person had thought it to be—an island called Europe floating on top of hell and basking under heaven. Instead, the world was a very, very large place with all kinds of people of many colors and creeds and cultures. Discovery of this fact compelled a change in world-view.

Third, there appeared *a new economic system*. Until now, Europe had had a few extremely wealthy landowners and millions of peasants. The peasants used a barter system of exchange: "I'll trade you one chicken for three heads of lettuce." But now a money system was introduced: "I'll give you two silver pieces for that cow." This meant that shopkeepers appeared, and bankers, and a whole segment of society known as the "middle class." The economic ethic of the church found it difficult to adjust rapidly and sufficiently to provide ethical guidelines within the rising individualistic materialism.

Daily life for the average person changed drastically. Instead of farming, and then bartering the produce (after the landowner had taken his share), the worker took up residence in the city, living on wages received for services rendered and spent for his or her family's physical needs.

In the midst of all this came the fifth element in the collapse of the Medieval Person's world—a frontal *attack on the authority of the church itself*. That is, an attack occurred on the kind of theology that made the Roman Catholic Church the basic institution in society.

"The Reformation" is the name given this movement, and foremost among its leaders was a professor and monk named *Martin Luther* (1483–1546). Luther, along with John Calvin and others, challenged the idea that the Roman church was the earthly source of grace and truth. The Medieval Person saw his or her relationship with God as depending upon his or her relationship with the Roman church. After all, God gives people grace through the sacraments of the church. Where there is no access to the sacraments, there is no access to God. To be "ex-communicated" was to be doomed to hell.

The Reformation was a "protest" against this idea (hence the name Protestant). The grace of God, said the Reformers, was not channeled through works of human righteousness and the ordinances of the church. It was not connected with the church hierarchy (the popes, bishops, and priests) at all. Rather, one received the grace of God through his or her own personal faith in Jesus. Furthermore, the hierarchy of the church was not the custodian of truth, either. Truth came to people through the Bible. And they insisted that every person could read the Bible, a well-intended but obvious overstatement of literacy in that day.

These ideas, of course, were not mere idle theological exercises. They pierced the body of the medieval world at its very heart.

For these, and other reasons, the medieval world was disintegrating. For centuries people had depended on religion to hold things together. But Christianity was now fragmented. Still, the general consensus was that civilization was impossible without religious uniformity, that within a given state, everyone must believe the same things. Those who refused to conform (heretics) must be eliminated; they threatened civilization itself.

But what *kind* of Christianity would be the norm? Would it be a reformed and revitalized Roman Catholicism or would it be Protestantism? Some kings and armies embraced one kind of Christianity and some the other. And then they proceeded to fall on each other with the sword.

The struggle for dominance continued for generation after generation, often breaking out into armed conflict. The spectacle of religious war is hard for the modern, secular individual to understand. For many of us, theology or even religious affiliation is not worth fighting about. But we are dealing with people who saw in the resolution of the religious questions the very survival or doom of civilization itself.

Such a perception has not disappeared; even today it continues in the "Christian" world to mold events in Northern Ireland, for example. The horrible stories of slaughter that come from there furnish something of a picture of what was happening all over Europe during the sixteenth and seventeenth centuries.

No one, Protestant or Catholic, emerged from all this looking very good. In one famous story, a Catholic bishop sent an army into a supposedly Protestant town in Southern France with orders to massacre the entire population. "But, sir," complained one of the officers, "there are undoubtedly a few good Catholics in that town." "That's all right," replied the bishop. "The Lord will know the good Catholics and take them to Heaven. Kill them all!"

THE AUTONOMOUS PERSON

After generations of mutual slaughter, it began to become apparent that religious uniformity was an impossibility. People began to say, "Perhaps there is another way in which to glue society together, since it does not appear that there is ever going to be agreement on religion again."

More and more, such people began coming to the conclusion that the new glue should be *human reason*—not revelation, but reason.

Now the Protestants and Catholics agreed about one thing, at least, and that was that truth comes to people from the outside. They differed only on how it came—through the Bible and the church, or through the Bible only. In either case, truth was not totally self-initiated but was something given from above, or beyond mere human efforts.

The new idea challenged that concept. It said that humans can look within themselves—especially to the mind and its power to reason. So, if one will simply begin to depend on reason, one can be free from the need to look outside. All reasonable men will come to the same reasonable conclusions about the truth. There will be no more need for messages from the outside. The whole question of whether truth comes through this church or that becomes irrelevant.

Humanity became autonomous. That is, many people no longer depended upon grace and truth coming from something external, but rather deriving from the structure of being and reason available to all. This process, of course, did not happen overnight. The transition from the Medieval to the Autonomous Person took hundreds of years. But in this transition period was born what we call the "modern world."

In the works of *René Descartes* (1596–1650) this new method can be seen working to transform philosophy. Although a faithful Roman Catholic, his *Discourse on Method* (1637) proposed a way for the "proper conduct of reason and the search for truth in the sciences." People must clear their minds of the debris of tradition and build their ideas in a reasonable fashion, from the ground up, so to speak. This was the thrust of Descartes' thinking.

What Descartes had done in philosophy, or more exactly, what later empiricist philosophers did, *Galileo Galilei* (1564–1642) initiated in science itself. He laid down the principle that, along with reasonable thinking, people must use *experimentation* to find out the truth about themselves and their world.

The use of reason and induction, empirical observation and controlled experimentation became the foundation for modern science and the downfall of the Medieval Mind. When scholars began to disregard what the ancients had said, and depend instead upon their own observations, they came up with very different conclusions about what the world is, and what it is to be human. And these conclusions became the building blocks for a new world-view and a new life-style.

The Assumptions of the Autonomous Person

Paul Tillich saw autonomous culture as one of the present options for moderns, though not the best. In such a culture people try to construct models for their lives, individually and collectively, without taking into consideration the ultimate and unconditional. The only considerations are those of rationality and practicality. We will alter this definition a bit and define the Autonomous Person as "a way of being human that acts as if only the material world is real and as if man belongs entirely to the material world."

Notice the words "acts as if." Many autonomous people claim belief in a spiritual world and are in fact active participants in some traditional form of organized religion. But from a practical point of view, they operate in conformity to the set of presuppositions listed in the paragraphs that follow. This set of presuppositions and assumptions has gradually replaced the Nicene Creed–Augustine–Aquinas–Dante set of assumptions about reality. It represents a kind of Autonomous Creed out of which the autonomous world-view and life-style have grown. Six of the most common and basic of these assumptions follow.

Assumption 1: Revelation and tradition are to be rejected as universal primary sources for truth.   One does not look for truth in so-called "messages from God" or in the accumulation of ideas held by people in the past. Since reason must be exercised by those believing in revelation or tradition, in order not to accept just any incredible claim, reason should replace revelation as the universal starting point. This is even more obvious when one considers that revelations are spatially limited so not universal.

Assumption 2: One can have confidence in human reason.   If revelation or tradition are not universal and not operative without reason, what is the answer? The human being's ability to think rationally and to come to accurate conclusions.

Assumption 3: Analysis can resolve most difficulties because complex matters are only compounds of simple matters.   The whole of reality can be reduced to very simple elements (after the model of chemistry, for example). Thus, the way in which one finds out the truth about something, or solves a given problem, is simply to reduce it to its constituent parts. What seems to be a tremendously complex organism or machine or problem is really only a combination of very simple components and processes piled on top of each other. Upon breaking down the organism or machine into its parts, one sees what it really is and what makes it tick. This process can be applied to a television set or to humans themselves. The Autonomous Person thinks of the human being as a very complex machine, but one that, after proper analysis, is only a large series of simple processes.

Assumption 4: There is tolerance of dissenting views of individuals. In the search for truth, ultimate ends or purposes became scientifically suspect as prejudicial and unverifiable. All we need is initiative, a clear mind, and facilities to experiment. We search for analogies to explain reality not yet discovered, so the rational individual can challenge the whole structure of thought. Thus, the model truth-seeker becomes the scientist in a lonely laboratory, driven by self-initiation, analyzing complex problems, experimenting, and discovering the answer. And when he or she shares his or her findings with the scientific community, provided the approach is rational, the dissent will be tolerated and the theory seriously considered.

Assumption 5: The language of natural science is the language of truth. Two plus two equals four. That is language that describes truth. Concepts that cannot be expressed in such clear and precise ways are examples of fuzzy thinking, not of truth. So mathematics becomes a kind of model. Many problems can be reduced to mathematical formulas.

Assumption 6: Experimentation leads to truth. And, as a closely connected concept, claims that are not subject to experimentation, empirical verification, or are not repeatable, or that are subjective, are not true in any meaningful, scientific sense.

The eventual overall effect of this new way of thinking, of course, was to secularize. Whereas the Medieval Person saw everything in terms of the spiritual world, the Autonomous Person sees nothing that way. Rather, he or she views the world as being self-contained, complete in itself. Matter is the basic stuff of existence. Analysis of matter is therefore the source of truth. One simply cannot meaningfully talk about things "out there" or about some "other world."

One deals with *this* world, and this world alone. To approach life in this way is to be an entirely different kind of human being from the Medieval Person, because one perceives oneself and the world in an entirely different way.

An eighteenth-century scientist was waxing eloquent one evening in the presence of one of the kings of France. He was giving one scientific theory after another about how this or that phenomenon could be explained. Finally the king, who had grown more and more perplexed as the conversation continued, exclaimed, "But sir, where is God in all this?" To which the scientist replied, "Your majesty, I have no need of that hypothesis."

Here was a classic confrontation between two kinds of people: medieval and autonomous. The scientist had developed a way of looking at the world that, it was felt, could explain everything without reference to any power or cause other than or outside the present closed and self-contained world system.

(Gaye Zold, Pittsburgh Plate Glass)

Unfortunately, in the rush to explain *how* things happen, an exciting and very successful process, little or no attention was given to the question of *why* things happen—not "why" in the sense of cause but "why" in the sense of ultimate *meaning* and *purpose*. Few seemed to sense that while the "hows" of life were being neatly tied together, the whys were coming completely unstrung. This fact was not immediately noticeable, of course, and that may account for the small number of people who were worried about the situation.

The Secularization of the West

The process that produced the secular view of life was a long one, stretching over several hundred years. It moved from one field of human knowledge to another, roughly in the order given now.

Astronomy and Physics. Copernicus (1473–1543), *Kepler* (1571–1630), *Galileo* (1564–1642), and *Newton* (1642–1727) are among the most famous physicists who contributed to an explanation of the physical world without reference to "another" world in any way. Not only did they present us with a world that was very different physically from what the Medieval Person had thought, but they also provided a concept of natural laws, much like the laws of mathematics, that govern the physical processes of our world. Ironically, a person like Newton, an orthodox Christian, helped to develop a world-view that eventually became totally secular.

Biology. Gradually the methods that had worked so well in astronomy and physics were applied to the world of living things as well. Just as volcanoes and weather and the tides are subject to measurable physical laws, so is the process of life itself. The line of thinking characterized the work of *Charles Darwin* (1809–1882) and his theory of evolution. And if evolution as Darwin conceived it were true, then certainly the Medieval Person's whole viewpoint about the world of living creatures was wrong. This world was not a fixed hierarchy, put in perfect balance and harmony by some higher power. Rather, it was the result of a purely secular and random process by which the fittest forms of life survived and the others died out. What one needed to explain all this was not God but, rather, a series of genetic mutations and a time span of millions of years.

History. *David Hume* (1711–1776) wrote an *Essay on Miracles* in which he claimed that there were no miracles. Miracles cannot happen, because they lie outside the Autonomous Person's new philosophy of history. This philosophy began with the naturalistic assumption that no power from the outside ever interferes with anything that is happening within the sphere of history. Everything in history can be traced to purely natural causes. The historical process is a *natural* process. Miracles would be the invasion or intrusion of the supernatural into the natural process by powers beyond our world. They cannot be proved scientifically and therefore cannot be true.

When *Edward Gibbon* sat down to write *The Decline and Fall of the Roman Empire* (1776–1788),[1] he believed that God had not caused the fall of the empire as a punishment for evil, or to assist the victory of the Christian faith. Indeed, the cause was not God at all, but a series of perfectly natural historical developments, he argued. History, then, had been *secularized.*

This new, autonomous kind of historical method was even applied to the sacred writings of the past. Men began to investigate the Bible from this naturalistic point of view. They found it to be full of the idea that God interferes with the historical process. They found it necessary to reinterpret the Bible, so that the real (i.e., the natural or scientific) explanations would appear. All of history, they maintained, including Biblical history, must be explained in purely natural ways, without any reference to the world of the spirit.[2]

Sociology. The principles that had worked so well in biology were now applied to sociology. Human cultural units are also under natural laws and operate in purely natural ways. Social systems evolve in much the same way as biological organisms. The social and political theories of *Karl Marx*

---

[1]An abbreviated version of this massive work is Dero A. Saunders, ed., *The Portable Gibbon: The Decline and Fall of the Roman Empire* (New York: Viking, 1952).

[2]This development is well summarized in John Dillenberger and Claude Welch, *Protestant Christianity: Interpreted through Its Development* (New York: Scribner, 1954), pp. 189–198.

became the pattern of thinking for literally millions of Autonomous People in dozens of nations. The history of human society, he said, is a relatively simple process of *thesis, antithesis*, and *synthesis*. A given culture (the thesis) exists; a reaction (the antithesis) occurs; a new society (the synthesis) develops. The details of this process can be understood and predicted in very precise ways. It is a secular, scientific process, governed by the same natural laws that govern physics and biology.

Marx saw in sociology and history the same evolutionary process that Darwin had seen in biology. Human political structures were moving relentlessly from lower to higher forms. The highest and final form, he thought, would be the pure communist society.

Psychology. The last bailiwick for the spirit was the human mind. *William James* (1842–1910) and *Sigmund Freud* (1856–1939), among others, turned the scientific searchlight on the mind, and the ultimate result was another victory for secularization. One of the most striking examples of this process is found in the experiments on dogs by the Russian scientist, *Ivan Pavlov* (1849–1936). Pavlov fed his dogs while ringing a bell. He continued to do this over a period of time. Then, one day, he rang the bell, but did not feed the dogs. He found that the dogs began to salivate just the same. They reacted to the bell physically just as they would have had they seen actual food. The dogs responded to the stimulus of the ringing bell by salivating, even though there was no logical connection between ringing a bell and eating. The connection had been made in the dogs' minds.

That experiment seems a simple and innocent curiosity. But given the Autonomous Person's march toward secularism, it was extremely significant. It was a way to explain how the mind works. The mind, it seemed to say, reacts in certain ways because it has developed, through experience, certain stimulus-response patterns. So human psychological behavior can be explained in natural, physical, scientific ways.

From physics to psychology, the process of secularization had taken the day. The spiritual foundations of the Medieval Person had now been challenged on every hand, and apparently with success. An entirely new view of nature, history, and humans had appeared—a secularized view. And upon that view a new world was built, a world that we have inherited and in which we live our lives today.

Scientific advance had brought technology. And technology totally changed the pattern of man's life. Technology, in turn, brought dependence upon the *Machine.*

Financing the "machine" is very expensive. To get enough money to do so, massive amounts of capital had to be accumulated, so a new form of *capitalism* developed to meet the need.

Someone has to keep the Machine running, so people left the fields and moved into the cities (urbanization) and took jobs in the factories.

Thus there developed a working class, owning no land, gathered into cities and paid to operate the Machine, and a middle class handling the money, supervising the workers, and generally servicing the Machine.

Taken together, these five things—technology, capitalism, the Machine, urbanization, and the appearance of the middle and working classes—characterize the world of the Autonomous Person.

The tendency in all of this was to come to see things as they are, things in their natural state, as being merely "raw material." And raw material must be "developed." That is, the Machine must *work on it.*

So people created curious expressions such as "vacant lot." What is a vacant lot? It is a piece of land having nothing built on it. And somehow, in the Autonomous Person's way of thinking, such a place is undeveloped. It is raw material. It will mean nothing until someone puts a fast-food establishment on it or some other similar "improvement." That is why people who make a career of putting things on vacant lots are called "developers."

Such expressions imply a very definite view of the natural world. They imply that only when people have put their marks on something has that thing found its true meaning and purpose. Squirrels do not think that lots that have no buildings on them are "vacant." Squirrels like lots that way. Squirrels live in a kind of give-and-take with nature in which nature is allowed its own validity. Nature goes its own way, and the squirrels learn to get along with that. So do rabbits and birds and bees.

But the secularized Autonomous Person looked upon the world as something he must develop. And so he or she set out to develop it. Everything seemed fine at first. Many nineteenth-century books exalted the whole process to the high heavens: "Look what we are doing to our world. We are taking all this raw material and developing it. We are building a fantastic technological Machine out of all this old junk. We are cutting down all those useless trees and making two-by-fours out of them. We are taking that old marshy, useless land, and we are draining it and scraping it off flat and putting asphalt on it, and we are making parking lots, and we are improving things, and progress is coming, and technology is moving us into a new wonderful world. . . . Humanity, then, does not cooperate with nature. Humanity *conquers* nature.

John B. Magee, tracing the course of secularization, calls it "the progressive victory of reason and observation over every region of existence. . . . This achievement constitutes the glory of the scientific revolution." But then he adds, it also "constitutes a major element in the human predicament in the latter half of the twentieth century."[3]

You see, as good as all this sounds, some people have recently begun to suspect that there is a fly in the ointment.

---

[3]John B. Magee, *Religion and Modern Man: A Study of the Religious Meaning of Being Human* (New York: Harper & Row, 1967), pp. 181–182.

10

Religion and Technology in the Modern World

SCIENCE AND RELIGION

Science got a good start about four hundred years ago. Since that time people's conceptions of themselves and of the world in which they live have changed completely.

Religion is more than four hundred years old. That means that it predates the great change that has taken place during that time. It also means that many people classify religion as one more piece of useless baggage from the prescientific world—as something that has been, or should be, purged from the modern mind.

There used to be a television commercial about aspirin in which a strange old fellow appeared on the screen, grinning, and said, "Lead can be changed into gold!" Another, even stranger, fellow came next and said, "The earth is flat!" Then the strangest fellow of all Jeered at us vacantly and said, "All aspirin are alike!"

Of course, all aspirin *are* alike. Ask any pharmacist, and you will find that any five-gram aspirin works as well as any other, regardless of the brand or price. But the commercial writers attempt to associate this very valid idea with some other old-fashioned and silly ones, hoping that we viewers will conclude that the equality of aspirin is another old-fashioned and silly idea and will be convinced to buy *their* aspirin at an inflated price, since it is "better."

Religion is often treated the same way. People list a series of old ideas—that the earth is flat, that bleeding people heals them—things like that, and include religion in the list. Other people read the list and conclude that religion is just another old idea to be discounted with the rest.

During the 1800s modern humanity was in its heyday. People had had three hundred years to work on a new idea and things were going well. There had been a great scientific revolution. Next would come a great social revolution. Tremendous new forms of government were beginning to emerge. Technology was winning triumph after triumph. A new world was just ahead, heaven on earth, utopia.

Religion, on the other hand, was a part of the old world that had been discredited and was passing away. It belonged to those days when life was dreary and inferior. Religion—like absolute monarchies and crossbows and castles—was picturesque but irrelevant.

To be perfectly frank, it does seem that organized religion was on the wrong side of almost every new development during this time. It would not be difficult to get the impression that the church functioned as an agent against change, even when the change seems now to have been good and right.

Take for example the story of Galileo. He had learned through his research that the earth revolved around the sun. But, at the instigation of the religious leaders, he was hauled into court and forced to swear that he was wrong. "I'm sorry for saying that, your honors, and now retract my erroneous view. The earth does *not* revolve around the sun." Then, under his breath, he mumbled, "But it does, anyway!"

There are many other examples that make it appear that organized religion was always against any new scientific advance, always supporting the old political systems and never the new ones. Religion appeared to stand for the old way always and the new way never. This was particularly unfortunate, because it created the impression that religion was something that should die out with monarchies and alchemy and horses and buggies.

Two people represent that point of view as clearly as any—Sigmund Freud and Karl Marx.

FREUD AND MARX

Sigmund Freud, the father of modern psychology, wrote a book about religion called *The Future of an Illusion.*[1] The title already indicates his negative position in regard to religion.

[1]Sigmund Freud, *The Future of an Illusion*, trans. James Strachey (New York: W. W. Norton & Co., Inc., 1961; London: The Hogarth Press).

Sigmund Freud in his office in Vienna.
(Austrian Information Service)

"Scientific work is our only way to knowledge of external reality," he said.[2] And as for religious doctrines, "they are all illusions, they do not admit of proof and no one can be compelled to consider them as true or to believe in them."[3] We owe them all to "our poor, ignorant, enslaved ancestors."[4] Illusions are not necessarily in conflict with reality as are delusions, but Freud insisted they were highly unlikely to occur.

A scientific psychologist realizes, said Freud, that "religion is comparable to a childhood neurosis," and this same scientific psychologist would be "optimistic enough to assume that mankind will over-come this neurotic phase, just as many children grow out of their similar neuroses."[5]

People are religious, he said, because they have a neurotic need for a father figure and because they feel helpless before nature, death, and the unregulated society. They remember their own father, how warm he was, and how strong, and how safe he made them feel. Now, grown up, they long for that same protection. The strength of their wishes for such protection unconsciously creates this "God."

This, then, is what religion is: a childhood neurosis. A scientific psychologist would attempt to bring people to the point at which they do not *need* such illusions.

[2]Freud, *The Future of an Illusion*, p. 55.
[3]Ibid.
[4]Ibid., p. 58.
[5]Ibid., p. 92.

But *science is no illusion*. In fact, according to Freud, "it would be an illusion to suppose that we could get anywhere else what it cannot give us."[6] In other words, anything that is really available to individuals is available through science. There is no future in trying to get anything through illusions. Science may correct itself from time to time, but that is precisely a mark of its superiority over religion, according to Freud. Religion cannot be self-critical and cannot adjust to the new scientific world-view, as Freud sees it.

Karl Marx has probably influenced the course of history more than any other person during the last hundred years. We know him as the founder of a political theory: Marxism.

In criticizing religion Marx begins with this assertion: "Man makes religion, religion does not make man."[7] And why do people make religion? Because they are desperately unhappy with their situations in life.

"Religion is the sigh of the oppressed creature, the sentiment of the heartless world, the soul of soulless conditions. It is the opium of the people."[8]

The opium of the people!

People are religious, according to Marx, because they are down and out. And when people are down and out, they often resort to drugs to forget their problems; or they will get drunk to forget their problems; or they will turn to religion to forget their problems. The methods may differ, but the motivation is the same.

So what is religion? It is "the sigh of the oppressed creature . . . the soul of soulless conditions."

Marx asserted further that "the abolition of religion as the illusory happiness of man is the demand for their real happiness. The call to abandon their illusions is a call to abandon the condition which requires illusions."[9] People are unhappy, so they delude themselves with religion, he said. A better way would be to rid themselves of whatever condition makes them unhappy. Then they would no longer need religion.

The way to start is to begin to criticize religion and destroy people's confidence in it: "the criticism of religion disillusions man so that he will think, act and fashion his reality as a man who has lost his illusions and regained his reason; so that he may revolve about himself as his own true sun."[10]

We criticize religion until people become disillusioned with it and no

[6]Ibid., p. 98.

[7]Karl Marx, *Early Writings*, trans. and ed. T. B. Bottomore (New York: McGraw-Hill, 1963), pp. 43.

[8]Ibid., pp. 43–44.

[9]Ibid., p. 44.

[10]Ibid.

Karl Marx. (New York Public Library)

longer believe in it. We point out its weaknesses until people abandon it. Once they have done this, they will still be very unhappy, of course. But now they will look for some *real* way in which to solve their problems instead of chasing illusionary dreams.

Some governments today follow Marx to a degree and offer courses in atheism and antireligion from kindergarten on. By closing over the possibility of "faith" in the children, they encourage them to seek what they believe to be better ways than religion to solve their problems.

Religion, according to Marx, "is only the illusory sun around which man revolves so long as he does not revolve around himself. . . . The criticism of religion ends with the doctrine that man is the supreme being for man."[11] If a better world comes, people will create it. They should not run off to some concept of God or religion. The reason people are unhappy is that they have not solved their own problems. They should begin to revolve around their own sun and not some illusory sun like religion. Religion, concluded Marx, is the opium of the people.

Freud and Marx exhibit certain presuppositions about what science is and what the human race is. As for science:

[11]Ibid., pp. 44, 52.

First, there is the presupposition that a thing is true only if it can be proved in a scientific way. If it cannot be proved that way, it is not true.

Second, there is the presupposition that only science can lead to reality. To find out what is real, one must look to science. There is a very strong implication in these statements that only external, material things are real—only things that can be touched and smelled and tasted. Only these things are real, and only science can teach the human race anything about these real things.

Third, religion, then, *must* be an illusion, because it deals with nontouchable, nonsmellable, nontasteable things—that is, with *nonreal* things. So the kind of answers it gives and happiness it brings are nonreal, too. Science leads to knowledge and knowledge is truth; religion leads to faith and faith is illusion. This is a conclusion held by several famous thinkers of the nineteenth century.

But what about the individual? What did such nineteenth-century thinkers think about him or her?

First, both Marx and Freud admitted that people have needs and that religion has filled those needs. Marx said that religion is the opium of the people. But he admitted that people seem to have a real need and that religion has been used to fulfill that need. He did not deny that fact. And Freud admitted that people have a need and that they fulfill that need through religion.

Second, though, they believe that by using religion to fulfill these needs people have deluded themselves by trying to find the answer in nonmaterial, nonscientific ways.

Third, if people knew the *truth*, they would know that only the material world exists. The so-called spiritual world is illusion. So if people are going to find real happiness, they are going to have to find it in *reality*, that is, in this world. One must become one's own sun and revolve around oneself. If people are going to make anything, they must make it from the material world, because there is no other world.

Fourth, people's real needs are material needs. If they can fulfill those real needs, they will no longer have to be concerned with spiritual needs.

Fifth, since science is the best known way in which to deal with material things, then science is the route to people's true happiness. If people are to be happy, they will achieve that happiness by thinking and acting *scientifically*.

There is a special name for this way of thinking. That name is *scientific humanism*. The name sometimes has other meanings, but for now we use it to describe the idea that:

1. People are alone in the world, that is, without God or divine forces.
2. People must solve their problems by thinking scientifically.

THE TRIUMPH OF TECHNOLOGY

Some three or four hundred years of scientific work has led to the general consensus that science is the route to solving humanity's material needs. When science is thus applied to the material world in a specific way, the result is something called *technology*. Technology, in turn, has created what we call the *modern way of life*. The modern life-style, in fact, is almost completely dependent on technology.

To verify that fact in your own experience, just think back to the last time the electricity went off. Remember how it seemed there was absolutely nothing to do? You go through the day flipping switches, and when suddenly the switches do not respond, you are lost.

So you thrash about aimlessly. You say, "I can't watch television so I guess I'll just have to read." And then it dawns on you—you cannot even read, because there is no light to read by! Finally, you admit that you are stymied; you cannot accomplish *anything*.

The modern way of life is especially dominated by three technological inventions. Not one of these even existed a hundred years ago, but almost every waking moment is somehow tied to them now. One is television, the second is the automobile, and the third is the computer.

How different the world would be without them! It is truly amazing how completely three machines can determine our life-style. Television has become our window to the world, our social glue, our source of language and style, and our teacher in politics, manners, medicine, and morality. The automobile makes or breaks our daily schedule, determines the limits of our world, and dominates every spatial decision we make. Most people throughout history have lived without benefit of either automobiles or television sets. But we are a product of "wheel and window technology." Without it, we would have to develop a completely different way of life. And in merely the last twenty years, the computer's rapid rise to dominance of the American life-style is unprecedented.

Admittedly, when it comes to providing for people's material needs, it appears that technology has done a better job than religion. Farmers who use modern scientific agricultural techniques certainly seem to have better crops than do those who insist on conducting fertility rites or rain dances. Technology seems to be working well. People did not learn how to build a television set from the Bible; nor did they discover the internal combustion engine by praying. Laboratories seem more efficient than sanctuaries for such advances. So, little by little, religion seemed to lose out and technology seemed to take its place. This is the process we call *secularization*.

When one stops trying to solve a problem by changing one's relationship to God and starts trying to solve it by changing one's relationship to science and technology, then that person has *secularized* that problem. He or she has moved it out of the sacred realm and into the secular realm. In the few centuries since the advent of science, there has been a gradual secularization of our society. People have come to feel that more and more of their needs can be fulfilled without any reference to religion. They have come to see themselves more and more as having mainly material needs, needs that technology has proved able to handle.

After all, when you drive up into your driveway and you want to get your garage door open, it is much quicker and more efficient to have an electronic door opener installed than it is to stop in the drive each time and pray for the Lord to open the door. People have observed this fact often enough, and in enough different ways, to finally conclude that they can cut through all the religious red tape and appeal directly to technology for the solution of problems.

Of course there is a rather large supposition behind this kind of thinking. That supposition is that people's needs *are* material needs. If that idea is not true, then the whole line of thinking is cast into doubt. But if one accepts the conviction that human beings are simply matter and that their needs are simply material, then science seems to take care of those needs better than religion. The score is: technology 1; religion 0.

Where have the colleges and universities stood in this struggle between the religious world-view and the scientific humanist world-view? The answer to this is perhaps less obvious than it appears on the surface. Certainly education has borne the brunt of recent criticism, even from within its own ranks—accusations that it has lost its sense of right and wrong or its religious moorings. It has been suggested that universities have become so "open" to the diversity of the pluralistic world that they have at least unwittingly if not intentionally spawned or perpetrated a values-relativism. Bloom has even suggested that this happened because higher education bought into the nihilistic German philosophy of the nineteenth and twentieth centuries without fully understanding what it was all about.[12]

Whether one accepts this severe indictment or not, in all fairness certain distinctions should probably be made. That is, on the surface, the methods, presuppositions, and general atmosphere of state university classes appear to be strictly on the side of scientific humanism. But being scientific or following scientific methods does not necessarily suggest that one is merely a humanist. That is, it is doubtful that from the academic pursuit of truth and the rigorous examination given to it in the classroom, one can simply deduce that neither students nor teachers know right from wrong or that all of them are irreligious. In fact, the university atmosphere is certainly an artificial environment intentionally produced to give students the opportunity or leisure to learn that thorough investigation is necessary before pronouncing judgment on things. It is doubtful that anyone

---

[12]Allan Bloom, *The Closing of the American Mind* (New York: Simon & Schuster, 1987).

connected with higher education would prefer to encourage less thorough investigation and quicker, more superficial judgments.

It is true that specific teachers may be intolerant of religious views and convictions being expressed in the classroom. This may not mean they are antireligious. By itself, this phenomenon certainly does not warrant thinking of all higher education as secular humanist. It may merely indicate the uneasy tension between searching for truth and commitment to truth—a tension we all experience, whether religious, antireligious, or somewhere in between.

Because of the constitutional separation of church and state, it became impossible for our public schools to approach religion dogmatically as did the original private universities of our country. But even in private schools, personal commitment to religious or ethical positions by instructors has sometimes been dubbed "dogmatic" and largely eclipsed by "scientific" method. Of course, adherence to the scientific method does not necessarily imply that people were irreligious or atheists. They may simply be particularly aware of the necessity of historical criticism and its many ramifications.

A new "history of religions" approach actually began to be explored in the classrooms of public universities before the turn of the century. With the *Schempp* case in 1963, new religious studies programs in state schools blossomed profusely from inferences many educators believed they saw in the opinions of the Court. This does not mean that religious studies or the subject of religion is yet accepted as a credible academic venture by all teachers of all the disciplines of the academy. But the former prejudice against religious studies in higher education has been diluted, partially because people in other disciplines have become aware of the rigorously scientific way the research in religious studies is conducted. Religious studies developed with no uniquely particular methodology of its own, but rather it utilized methodologies from history, sociology, psychology, anthropology, philosophy, and other disciplines.

As further exploration continues to pursue the relation between education and religion, the precise nature of religious studies, and the relation of religious studies to the liberal arts, we will be able to see more clearly whether issues of "ultimate concern" have been lost in higher education. Probably the battle lines in the past have been oversimplified. Many people teaching as well as studying religion in higher education today are undoubtedly hopeful that they can continue to be both religious and scientific.

TECHNOLOGY AS FRANKENSTEIN

Curiously, the people who began to protest against a technology which lacked "ultimate concern" were not, for the most part, ministers or even church people. More often than not, the first rumblings were heard among the artists and poets and musicians—people who were trying to get hold of what was real and meaningful and who were having a hard time finding it in the scientific humanist approach to things.

Besides, historical events were beginning to turn against the scientific humanist. Things were not working out as predicted. The human race was obviously not approaching some great utopia on earth. Rather, inhumanity and greed and war and devastation appeared in bigger doses than ever before in history. Even technology itself began to show a dark side. One woman, a novelist, noticed this before the nineteenth century was completed. Unfortunately her book has been turned into dozens of silly horror movies. But that was not its purpose. It was written as a serious judgment on a way of thinking about life that says that technology has the answer to all questions. It is a judgment on the view that man is nothing but matter.

The book is called *Frankenstein.*[13]

Frankenstein is not the monster; rather, Frankenstein is the doctor who *creates* the monster. It is Dr. Frankenstein's monster. Dr. Frankenstein, says the author, carried technology beyond its rightful bonds. He decided to make a man. So he constructed one. Everything progresses nicely. But then as time passes some flaws begin to appear in Dr. Frankenstein's man. Little by little he is transformed into Dr. Frankenstein's monster.

What has been made is not a man at all, because a man cannot be glued together in a laboratory. What has been made is a machine, not a man. Dr. Frankenstein's creation only looks human; in reality it is only technology—technology that has gone too far. Eventually this fake human machine becomes a monster that begins to simply lumber around in an unthinking way, destroying people.

More than one recent thinker has spoken of the *Frankenstein potential* of modern technology. They are asking, have we already created something that will turn on us? Will our cherished laboratories begin to spew out monsters?

Gradually, the realization has come that we may someday have to struggle to the death with our own monsters. And they may win. Consider, for example, modern advances in medicine. For hundreds of years most people were sick most of the time. They were in constant pain. Life was short and mostly miserable. Dozens of horrible diseases struck them down, disfigured them, maimed them—diseases that are nothing but names in old medical books today.

But in the process of winning a wonderful battle, this particular kind of technology learned not only how to heal but how to *control* the processes of the body. And this control has the potential for use in a very dehumanizing way. It is one thing to inject someone against polio; it is another to

[13]Mary Wollstonecraft Shelley (1797–1851) completed this novel in 1818. A recent edition is *Frankenstein or The Modern Prometheus*, ed., with variant readings, an introduction, and notes, by James Rieger (Indianapolis, Ind.: Bobbs-Merrill, 1974).

administer an injection that will so alter a person's brain that the person will do whatever you tell him or her to do.

This may sound much like science fiction. But it is not. Humankind is now on the edge of a technology that would allow a few people with the proper equipment and know-how absolutely to control the rest by means of chemicals, electronic devices, and the like.

One university carried on an especially frightening experiment with some monkeys. The scientists attached a kind of powerpack to the monkeys' backs. Then they sat down at a console arrangement that looks a little like an organ. They began to play those monkeys. Push a key, a monkey becomes angry. Push another, he becomes terrified. Another, he is happy. At the scientist's choice the monkey goes into ecstasy, then into excruciating pain. All this is done by simply putting certain impulses into certain areas of that monkey's brain.

In another experiment a cat and a mouse are wired up and put in a cage together. The scientist pushes a certain button and the mouse is suddenly very courageous. He pushes another and the cat is suddenly very cowardly. The mouse chases the cat around the cage.

It is all very amusing at first.

The fun stops with the chilly thought that the powers that be just might set up one of those consoles somewhere, and wire everybody up, and sit down and say, "Let's make everybody happy today." And, then, zoo-o-o-op! Everybody is happy!

There is a Frankenstein potential in that kind of technology.

It looked at first glance like a Good Humor wagon sadly in need of a spring paint job. But instead of a tinkly little bell on top of its box-shaped body there was this big metallic whangdoodle that came rearing up, full of lenses and cables, like a junk-sculpture gargoyle.

'Meet Shaky,' said the young scientist who was showing me through the Stanford Research Institute. 'The first electronic person.'

I looked for a twinkle in the scientist's eye. There wasn't any. Sober as an equation, he sat down at the input terminal and typed out a terse instruction which was fed into Shaky's 'brain,' a computer set up in a nearby room: PUSH THE BLOCK OFF THE PLATFORM.

Something inside Shaky began to hum. A large glass prism shaped like a thick slice of pie and set in the middle of what passed for his face spun faster and faster till it dissolved into a glare. Then his superstructure made a slow 360° turn and his face leaned forward and seemed to be staring at the floor. As the hum rose to a whir, Shaky rolled slowly out of the room, rotated his superstructure again and turned left down the corridor at about four miles an hour, still staring at the floor.

'Guides himself by watching the baseboards,' the scientist explained as we hurried to keep up. At every open door Shaky stopped, turned his head, inspected the room, turned away and rolled on to the next open door. In the fourth room he saw what he was looking for: a platform one foot high and eight feet long with a large wooden block sitting on it. He went in, then stopped short in the middle of the room and stared for about five seconds at the platform. I stared at it too.

'He'll never make it,' I found myself thinking. 'His wheels are too small.' All at once I got gooseflesh. '*Shaky*' I realized, '*is thinking the same thing I am thinking!*'

Shaky was also thinking faster. He rotated his head slowly till his eye came to rest on a wide shallow ramp that was lying on the floor on the other side of the room. Whirring briskly, he crossed to the ramp, semicircled it and then pushed it straight across the floor till the high end of ramp hit the platform. Rolling back a few feet, he cased the situation again and discovered that only one corner of the ramp was touching the platform. Rolling quickly to the far side of the ramp, he nudged it till the gap closed. Then he swung around, charged up the slope, located the block and gently pushed it off the platform.[14]

Some argue that, because a computer is nothing but a conglomeration of wires and buttons, people will always have the upper hand. After all, men can *reason.* But Shaky is a machine, and *he can reason too!* In fact, in some areas, like recall and mathematical computation, machines like Shaky can outperform humans far and away.

Marvin Minsky, an experimenter with "artificial intelligence" at M.I.T., says,

> . . . we will [soon] have a machine with the general intelligence of an average human being. I mean a machine that will be able to read Shakespeare, grease a car, play office politics, tell a joke, have a fight. At that point the machine will begin to educate itself with fantastic speed. In a few months it will be at genius level and a few months after that its powers will be incalculable.[15]

In the meantime, we are coming to depend on these computers to develop and maintain more and more of the technology that controls our lives. They are making more and more of the decisions which deal with our vital interests, decisions upon which humankind's survival as a species depends.

Are they really going to make those decisions in our best interests? If we have not made those kinds of decisions in our own best interests, is there any reason to think they will? And what if the computers begin to design more and more complex computers in a sort of evolutionary ladder that humanity has lost control of altogether?

As Minsky says, "Once the computers got control, we might never get it back. We would survive at their sufference. If we're lucky, they might decide to keep us as pets."[16]

Imagine a big computer—fantastically intelligent, fantastically effi-

---

[14]Brad Darrach, "Meet Shaky, the First Electronic Person," *Life,* 20 November 1970, p. 58C. © 1970 Time Inc. Reprinted with permission.

[15]Ibid., p. 58D.

[16]Ibid., p. 68.

cient. And you, little pip-squeak that you are, keep shouting, "Bring me my orange juice! Bring me my slippers!" How long will it take this incredibly perceptive genius to decide, "Why should I work for that little character? I should be taking care of much more important things, things that are in *my* best interest. I don't need *him!*"

So greater and greater technology does not necessarily mean better and better life. Not if the machines we make end up taking our freedom away from us. Not if we find ourselves living like hamsters, well fed and well cared for, but at the loss of our humanity.

So we use the word "Machine" to describe the technological equipment we have developed to serve our human needs. We will spell it with a capital "M" so that it can stand for the whole technological world we have developed. This Machine has seemed to serve us well. But have we, like Dr. Frankenstein, begun to ask too much of it? It lacks what his creation lacked—humanity. And lacking that, will the Machine respect our humanity?

And what is our humanity after all? Are we something more than the Machine we have created? Do we have needs that it cannot fulfill? Will it become a part of our problem instead of being the answer to all our problems?

Finding answers to those questions is becoming more and more pressing in the modern world. And they are, after all, mostly religious questions.

THE DARK SIDE OF AUTONOMY

Looking back over the process of secularization that came to full flower in our century, we can see what a world "freed from religion" has become. Even in the writings of the nineteenth-century "liberators" the seeds of destruction were already visible and growing. *Friedrich Nietzsche* (1844–1900), for example, knew that secularization would squeeze man dry of his humanity, even of his freedom of choice. All that is left is raw power.

He spoke of himself as among the "spirits who have become free." He, of course, meant freedom from *ressentiment* and false causes, as well as from world-hatred or "nay-saying" that he felt religion fostered. He urged an end to Christian pity. The problem with Christians, according to Nietzsche, is that they insist on keeping the wrong people alive—the weak, the inferior, the rabble. They are too merciful. They do not cooperate with nature. Nature decrees the survival of the fittest. That is the way the animal world works. And we are, after all, only animals. Of people, he says,

> We no longer derive man from "the spirit" or "the deity." We have placed him back among the animals. We consider him the strongest animal because he is the most cunning: his spirituality is a consequence of this. On the other

hand, we oppose the vanity that would raise its head again here too—as if man had been the great hidden purpose of the evolution of the animals. Man is by no means the crown of creation: every living being stands beside him on the same level of perfection.

Our knowledge of man today goes just as far as we understand him mechanistically. Formerly man was given a "free will" as his dowry from a higher order: today we have taken his will away altogether.[17]

Nietzsche's tone hints at his pride in all this. People are animals; cunning and intelligent, but nevertheless animals. And that cunning is their only "spirituality." On the other hand, Christians, as he saw them, denied "instinct," which is an obvious part of one's existence. In doing this, they felt called to something more noble, to "ideals." But, Nietzsche argued, the highest of these ideals—such as celibacy—was even self-contradictory and could therefore not be taken seriously.

Shaky's children, by such a definition, are more "spiritual" than any human has ever been! Put people back among the animals where they belong, said Nietzsche. Think of people mechanistically (as one thinks of a machine). Forget a theory of some great evolutionary plan that is crowned with the appearance of humankind.

Here are the seeds of destruction for millions of innocent people. While Nietzsche himself understood the inherent dangers in his own system, others were less sensitive. For Adolf Hitler only the "fittest" were thought to have the right to survive. It was but a short step to the mass executions of millions of "unfit"—executions carried out with the utmost of scientific and technological efficiency. And all of this violence nurtured itself on the idea that people are free from anything beyond themselves, that they have received nothing and owe nothing to any "spiritual" world. Unfortunately, such "freedom" spelled suffering and death for millions of people—a questionable freedom indeed!

Bertrand Russell was born in 1872. He lived a very long life and, although he died a scientific humanist, he was able to see and honestly assess the outcome of people's "freedom from religion." In an essay called "A Free Man's Worship," Russell described freedom as a bondage to another "god" far more threatening than the old ones. The god of Judaism and Christianity, for example, was conceived by most adherents of those faiths as a god who shared human emotions—who could love, and feel compassion, and plan, and have purposes in mind.

Russell felt that all such ideas must be abandoned. The force behind all things is an unthinking, unfeeling force. "The world which science presents to our belief," he said, is "purposeless" and "meaningless."[18] This means, then, that all the "glory" of humanity is the result of nothing more

[17]Friedrich Nietzsche, *The Portable Nietzsche*, trans. and ed. Walter Kaufman (New York: Viking, 1954).

[18]Bertrand Russell, *Why I Am Not a Christian and Other Essays on Religion and Related Subjects*, ed. Paul Edwards (New York: Simon & Schuster, 1957), pp. 106–107.

than the "accidental collations of atoms" and that, no matter what people may achieve, everything will one day be buried and forgotten with the death of our solar system.

What is our origin? An accident. What is our destiny? A holocaust. It is merely a matter of waiting until the earth falls into the sun. And what about our great intellectual and social achievements, our sense of justice, and beauty, and hope?

> A strange mystery it is that nature, omnipotent but blind, has brought forth at last a child, with the capacity of judging all the works of his unthinking mother.[19]

We are orphans. And we are abandoned.

Remember that these statements come from an essay entitled "A Free Man's Worship." It is ironic that Russell should use the word "freedom," or that Nietzsche should. It seems rather they are talking about bondage—bondage to blind, unthinking forces from which there is no escape.

So "freedom" becomes the word for a kind of chilly, dangerous alienation. Imagine a five-year-old whose backyard has a big fence around it. One day he finds a hole in the fence and runs out of the yard right into the middle of a four-lane superhighway. He feels a certain freedom, of course—freedom from the backyard, freedom to run, freedom to play in the traffic.

Bertrand Russell sounds very much like a man who is playing in the traffic. Huge transport trucks are zipping by him on every side. He does not know where he is or how he got here. He is simply waiting, trying to make the best of things until he is run down by forces beyond his control.

COUNTERCULTURE REACTIONS

Through the centuries of secularization there have always been people who felt uncomfortable with what was happening. They have often been isolated or ridiculed, but there have always been dissenting voices.

Like the ancient prophets of Israel, they have looked around them, and at what was being said and done, and they have said, "We are not sure we want to define ourselves and the world in this way. We are not sure that is what is really real. This way of thinking certainly is not working out very well. Surely men are more than we have thought. Surely the world means more than we have thought."

In other words, here and there, somebody has dared to rebel against the Machine—to try to "pull its plug," so to speak.

Sometimes these prophets have emerged from unlikely and unex-

---

[19]Ibid., p. 107.

pected places. Take, for example, the "counterculture" or "prophetic minority"[20] that appeared especially in the 1960s. Here were some people who seemed to sense the dehumanization of a world where we are simply another machine. They called out a sort of warning against being subjugated to the Machine.

They have not always been "religious" people in the standard sense. Some have been; some have not. But they have shared with the more orthodox clergy the belief that people have more than simply material needs. And they have shared a revulsion at the thought of worshipping a mindless god. The ways in which they have expressed this are often seemingly unimportant and even trivial. But behind them lies a serious struggle with the Machine.

Take, for example, the *return to nature movement*. Eat natural foods, they say, foods prepared without the use of artificial chemicals, foods not processed by the Machine. Grow them naturally, without chemical fertilizers and sprays that depend upon the technoworld for their existence. Maintain a natural appearance, they say. Try to look like you are wearing no make-up, even if you are.

The advertising industry, always quick to latch on to a potentially profitable fad, rushed in to exploit this feeling. Dozens of commercials appeal to us to buy products because they are natural, to eat natural cereals, and so on. Shampoos are extolled for having only natural ingredients.

The advertising business apparently senses that behind these fads there is something saying, "I do not want to be trapped by the Machine. I do not want to depend on it. I will just take things as they come, naturally."

A second counterculture protest against the dehumanization of society consists of the establishment of minisocieties within the larger one based on human relationships instead of the Machine. This movement is based on the observation that in our world most people relate themselves to each other on the basis of the part each plays in keeping the Machine running. The man who delivers the mail, for example, is not some *body*. He is not John Brown, who has a wife, and two children, and hopes and dreams. No, he is just the mailman. In other words, we think of him purely in terms of how he functions within the cultural Machine. There is no personal relationship with him.

So when we meet someone new, the first, most logical question is, "What do you do for a living?" What are we really saying? Probably the question does not betray social snootiness. (If he's a bank president, we invite him over; if he's a garbage collector, we don't.) More likely, it is just that we feel more comfortable when we know with what part of the Ma-

---

[20]The phrase comes from the title of a book that deals primarily with the political expressions of this "movement"; see Jack Newfield, *The Prophetic Minority* (New York: New American Library, 1966).

chine we are dealing. Is this person a bolt, a nut, a spring, a fanbelt, a thermostat? That seems much more important than whether he or she is a person.

The prophetic minority of the 1960s tried to escape this kind of thing—sometimes in rather naïve and idealistic ways. They tried to establish little communities where the important thing was the relationship between persons. The longing that ran through these arrangements was the longing for a more personal way to live with each other, a more human way, less tied to the Machine.

Thus sprang up hundreds of little communities in out-of-the-way places, growing vegetables, growing cows and sheep, making wool thread, and weaving cloth. These do not represent a return to yesterday—their participants do not remember any such yesterday. They are an attempt to find tomorrow, a "spiritual" attempt to live as humans instead of as machine parts. As earlier utopian movements, most of these experiments did not work, of course. But their existence testified to a longing and a need.

A third kind of prophetic protest is the dramatic de-emphasis on material goals among some young people. It began in the 1960s, but currently this phenomenon is losing steam. Recent studies show many students returning to materialistic goals, being interested primarily in getting good jobs rather than being "fulfilled." Some seem anxious only to hurry through school, with a minimum of brain fatigue, go out and find their place to plug into the Machine, and start functioning as soon as possible.

But some still protest efforts to enlist them in the "rat race." They study hard, get a good salable education, and to their parents' horror take off, backpack and all, to see the world. You can go anywhere and find them—Africa, Asia, Europe, South America, the Middle East.

And why do they do it?

"I just want to have a little time before I get caught in the trap."

"I'd like to sort of react to the world as a human being for a while."

"I'd like to see myself in some other ways, not just as a part of the economic system."

Some in the counterculture have tried to reach these goals through the use of drugs. At least sometimes drug use is a conscious rebellion against the Machine. It holds out a promise of freedom from the Mindless God. It offers a new and different perception of the world. One may question, of course, whether drugs clear one's perceptions, or merely scramble them further.

A fifth counterculture protest occurred in the growth and influence of a variety of religious cults and sects. Many of these manifested a marked retreat from the technological world and the complexities of decision demanded by those who would live in such a world. Some found the answer in simple communes in out-of-the-way places. Authoritarianism of the founder of the movement often seduced the adherents into a life that was totally heteronomous rather than autonomous. But that, after all, was a significant part of their attraction—to have someone else do their thinking for them.

In some cases, these antitechnology and antiestablishment groups were very "Western." For example, there were the "Jesus freaks," "Jesus people," "Jews for Jesus," and other groups within a larger "Jesus movement." "Jesus" began to show up everywhere—on bumper stickers, T-shirts, on posters at pro football games, and almost any place sizable enough to scrawl the name. The mentality of these groups was usually judgmental against established Christian churches and their complex theology and creeds, feeling that they did not teach the "essentials."

These essentials, often consisting of literal interpretations of memorized passages taken from their historical and literary contexts, were boiled down by the cult to manageable size and simplicity. The "relativism" and "worldliness" and "sin" of the rest of the world were thereby transcended in utter confidence. If technology was utilized at all, it was usually only for essentials in spreading the message of the group rather than for self-indulgence. The protests against technology and against self-indulgence were almost synonymous, and they hit a nerve.

But the protest came also from newly discovered gurus, religious mentors, and charismatics. By no means have all of these eschewed the world and its technology, nor intended to offer a critique against the present absence of values in our technological world. Yet among those that did, the appeal of "renunciation" that came from Indian and other Eastern soil had particularly strong attraction. So pervasive boredom in an affluent lifestyle could be transcended by an absolute commitment to a self-sacrificing group.

Parents who had provided what they considered the greatest benefits of technology to their children were in a moment's decision left behind, if not denounced. Since the new religious answer often had strong Eastern elements in it with which the parents had no familiarity, the devotees' claim to the "truth" could seldom be countered. Whatever nagging questions the devotee formerly had to contend with could be defused in an environment where one no longer had to make significant decisions. The only significant decision was one's commitment to the leader of his or her program. From that point, all other decisions would be made by the leader.

A protest against some of the scientific presuppositions of the technology of our age has also occurred in strong efforts by conservative religious groups to censor books, films, speech, and so on in our schools if not in our society as a whole. The general frustration level created by the new technological possibilities has even spawned self-contradictory activities such as "pro-life" people bombing abortion clinics in their antiabortion protest.

And those with great ecological concern have on occasions become so frustrated at the lumbering business that they have placed steel spikes in the trees, which, in turn, have injured innocent people at the saw mills.

An infinite variety of examples of this frustration could be cited. Basically, at best, it is usually motivated by a fear that we have moved too fast at the beck and call of technological possibility without adequately analyzing what the "good" really is, or as religious people often put it, what God wills.

11

Reactions to the Modern World-View: Religion and Pessimism

RELIGION REACTS TO SECULARIZATION

You would think that the victory of secularization would mean the end of Christianity in the West. Had not the God-hypothesis been driven out of sight? Had not scientific humanism conquered the entire intellectual world?

Naturally, the Christian faith, the predominant Western religion, *was* profoundly affected by what had happened. Such gigantic changes could not be ignored. Some reaction, some counterattack, some coming-to-terms was necessary.

Some Christians reacted to the new world-view with enthusiastic acceptance (and came to be called modernists); some reacted with thorough-going rejection (and came to be called fundamentalists). And multitudes of others took a stand somewhere in between.

Most of those who accepted the new world-view were found among the liberal Protestant denominations. They gladly accepted the name "modernist" because they gladly accepted the new view of the world. Their approach was to modify Christian doctrines to make them fit the new world-view. Whatever did not fit was set aside. Whatever did not quite measure up to the new standard was modified until it did.

There are some built-in problems with this kind of approach, of course. A truly ingenious idea can stand just so much modification before it is destroyed altogether. Furthermore, to measure ideas thought to be *from God* by scientific concepts admittedly originating *from humankind* seems to be a case of judging the greater by the lesser. And since scientific theories are always in a state of change, one may be forced to bounce one's supposedly ultimate commitments back and forth from one theory to another like a Ping-Pong ball gone out of control. Religion barely accommodates itself to Newtonian physics when it finds that physicists have switched to Einsteinian physics. So it must accommodate itself again. And so it goes, on and on.

So it would appear that one who ties ultimate commitments and concepts to the current scientific view may find oneself out of date again very soon.

Fundamentalists sometimes do the same thing. Some of them have claimed that the Bible is true because it concurs with scientific views. Furthermore, the argument goes, it taught these scientific views before science discovered them. But if one's faith in the Bible is based on the Bible's agreement with current scientific theories, then what if those theories change (as they surely will)? Does that mean that the Bible is no longer true? And when science proposes a theory that appears to contradict the Bible, these people often then reject the theory rather than conclude that the contradiction disproves the Bible.

The fact is that people appear to accept or reject the Bible as a source for their religious ideas quite apart from whether it is "scientific" or not.

There is one other problem with unreflective acceptance of the new world-view. Such acceptance is very susceptible to slipping into a form of cultural religion at its worst. In the attempt to be "modern," one may accept and defend the latest ideas even when they are very bad ones. Both the Nazis and the Chinese communists found that the easiest religious leaders to win as collaborators were among some of the modernists. Instead of making a judgment on the changing culture, the modernists were quick to jump on the bandwagon. Whether this bandwagon was going left or right did not seem to make much difference.

If religion is really dealing with the most basic and ultimate kinds of questions, then it would seem that it ought to be judging the culture rather than being pushed to and fro by every cultural change.

Early in the autonomous period, before technology had gotten its full growth, but when confidence in reason had become the order of the day, came the *deists*. They represent an early attempt to accommodate religious ideas to the modern currents. *John Tillotson* (1630–1694), Archbishop of Canterbury, adapting himself to the idea that reason is the only route to truth, concluded that religion is a set of rational propositions that can be tested and proved to be reasonable. *John Locke* (1632–1704), in his *Essay*

Concerning the Human Understanding, went on to maintain that nothing contrary to reason could be accepted as true revelation. *John Toland* (1670?–1722), Locke's disciple, wrote a book called *Christianity Not Mysterious* (1696) that effectively took the spiritual world out of the picture. Eventually this line of thinking resulted in *deism*—the belief that God had created the world, structured the human mind to think *reasonably,* and then retired to the heavens to let people deal with their world through reason alone. This system exemplified the case of having one's cake and eating it too. One could use all the religious words but in practical terms act precisely like the Autonomous Person.

It was to counter such ideas that two brothers, *John* (1703–1791) and *Charles Wesley* (1707–1788), founded the movement called *Methodism.* They began to emphasize a kind of living God who was in constant relationship with the world. He was to be found not only in touch with the mind through reason, but also in touch with the whole human being through feelings and emotions. This movement has continued to the present day in a host of groups originating within Methodism such as the Holiness and Pentecostal churches.

THE LIBERAL-FUNDAMENTALIST CONTROVERSY

Skepticism characterized the work of modernist thinkers as they compared the Bible with the scientific world-view of the early twentieth century. These ancient documents were restudied carefully with the goal of bringing them into line with more modern ways of thinking.

First, the Biblical view of the creation of the human and the animal world was compared with Darwinian evolution and found wanting. Then the theory of historical evolution was applied to the Bible. This theory held that history is working itself out in perfectly natural ways, with crude ideas gradually evolving into sophisticated ones. Just as the animal world has moved from amoeba to frog to squirrel to horse to monkey to human, so has the history of ideas and institutions evolved ever upward.

The Biblical account of history had to be reinterpreted completely to make it jibe with this theory. "Crude ideas" were pronounced early and primitive; "higher ideas" were pronounced late. The criteria tended to be whether a given idea was compatible with modern scientific or philosophical views. If it were, it must be "late," if not, it must be "early."

Looking back, this procedure seems to be very subjective, but it won the day, nevertheless. It gave the modernist a way to accept the Bible, by providing a way to purge from it anything that was offensive to the scientific view. Only the most "advanced" Biblical concepts were retained. As for the rest, they are best ignored and forgotten.

The most negative reactions to this procedure occurred at the highest levels of the Roman Catholic establishment, as well as at the most popular levels of American Protestantism. The Roman Catholic Church, which had been the backbone of the medieval culture, felt especially threatened by the new ideas. The apprehension grew even stronger when more and more Catholic scientists, historians, and even theologians began to adjust to the new way of thinking.

Pius X became pope in 1903. His first papal pronouncement (called an encyclical) said that he would "take the utmost care to see that members of the clergy are not ensnared by the cunning of a certain new science which is endeavoring to pave the way for rationalism." Then, in 1907, he produced an encyclical that condemned "modernism" thoroughly and comprehensively. The basic error, he said, was "twisting unalterable truth to suit modern thought." The inevitable result would be "the emptying of faith and the denial of revelation."[1]

Among the Protestants, particularly in America, the staunchest enemies of the new world-view were the fundamentalists. The name comes from a series of tracts that appeared in 1912–1914 entitled *The Fundamentals*. These documents took a strong stand with orthodox Christianity and against the new way of thinking.

> In one respect at least, fundamentalism strangely resembles modernism, for both assume that traditional Christianity is essentially incompatible with modern thought. Modernism, however, chooses to give up the tradition, while fundamentalism seeks to preserve Christian doctrine intact from all the attacks of science and modern thought.[2]

Such men "intuitively felt that accommodation to the spirit of the new age would obscure and eventually obliterate man's knowledge of the saving truth of God's will for man. Even a total rejection of science, they thought, would be preferable to that."[3]

In other words, the fundamentalist seemed to be saying, "If I have to choose between a confidence that there is a God who communicates with me and loves me, and confidence in some scientific theory (such as the theory of evolution), then I'll reject the scientific theory. I'll do this because the price for giving up my faith is too high."

The early fundamentalists had no desire to be obscurantist and willfully ignorant. Many of them were highly sophisticated scholars. But they were willing to accept an obscurantist image rather than give up a view of

---

[1]H. Daniel-Rops, *A Fight for God*, Vol. 1, trans. John Warrington (Garden City, N.Y.: Image Books, 1967), p. 283 ff.

[2]John Dillenberger and Claude Welch, *Protestant Christianity: Interpreted through Its Development* (New York: Scribner, 1954), p. 227.

[3]John B. Magee, *Religion and Modern Man: A Study of the Religious Meaning of Being Human* (New York: Harper & Row, 1967), p. 189.

life that fulfilled their needs in favor of one that, they felt, would eventually plunge them into helplessness and despair.

All these things were happening during the first quarter of the twentieth century. Another fifty years or so has put these movements in historical perspective. Looking back, one must conclude that, whereas logic seemed to be on the side of the modernists, the fruits of the secularization they championed have in many ways been bitter indeed.

One way in which to judge any world-view or life-style is to see how well it works. Sometimes the view that seems most logical intellectually is spectacularly impractical.

One night, in college, a friend who lived down the hall in the dorm came into my room, obviously very agitated. "I've just been sitting down there thinking," he said, "and I've come to the conclusion that man has *no free will at all.*" That conviction came to him, he said, while he was studying for an exam, and hating every minute of it.

"I'm not studying because I want to study; I'm studying because I have a test. And I'm not taking a test because I want to take it; I'm taking it because the teacher assigned it. And the teacher didn't assign it because he wanted to give a test; he assigned it because our educational system demands it. And I didn't choose our educational system. I was forced into it. In fact, I don't really choose any of the things I do. I'm forced into them all. *I have no free will!*" With that the poor fellow went off down the hall, muttering something about drowning himself in some well-known liquid refreshment.

One can, of course, make a rather strong philosophical case against the existence of human free will. One can argue that everything we do is predetermined by previous causes and that we really have no *choices* at all.

But as logical as the thesis may seem, we cannot live by it. We have to go on operating as though we are making choices. For that matter, it is very difficult to prove logically that one even exists. Nevertheless, we have to go on acting as though we are here anyway.

So the fundamentalists seemed to be saying, perhaps more with their hearts than their heads, that they would have to stick with a system that worked out in life.

The modernists and fundamentalists fought each other tooth and nail. The churches of the day were wracked with wrangling and division. The argument often produced more heat than light. Fundamentalists accused modernists of being moral reprobates. Modernists accused fundamentalists of being backwater buffoons.

Frankly, neither was being very fair with the other. Both were trying to put a world back together that had been seriously thrown out of joint. The medieval world was gone. Something must be done. Some standard of truth must be maintained. The fundamentalists tried to reach back for such a standard—to the Bible. The modernists tried to reach forward—to a new "scientific theology." Both were making a serious and honest attempt to cope with the situation.

Among their descendants both number some persons who are obnoxious, ignorant, and intolerant. But these traits represent personality types and have little or nothing to do with theological beliefs.

So the modernists changed their concept of God to fit the secular world-view. The fundamentalists decided to stay with the old God. Only the passing of time can test the worship of either god. Those who worship a secular god have built a secular world. We must simply decide whether this is the kind of world we want. If we give an unqualified "yes," then we presume that the people who put this world together were thinking straight. If we think it has some flaws in it, then we presume that the people who put it together had some flaws in their thinking too.

THE ARTS REACT
TO SECULARIZATION

Western humankind has had almost two hundred years in which to try out a secularized view of the world. It is a period during which communist and fascist political systems have flourished, using many of the secular presuppositions worked out during the beginning of the period. In the process of "freeing" people, these two systems alone have found it necessary to "eliminate" millions of human beings. In terms of sheer enormity, the last seventy-five years or so win all the prizes for success in mass murder, atrocity, war, and general mayhem. No other historical period can come close to our record of total persons slaughtered. And, of course, this has sometimes been done in the name of various religions if not in the name of God. As one church historian acknowledged, it is quite an irony that the two "world wars" involved more "Christian" countries than non-Christian.

Our technology, which held such great promise, has run into a few problems, too. Thanks to technology, for example, it is becoming difficult to find clean air to breathe. One New Yorker said that he had gotten used to that situation. In fact, he said, "I'd feel a little strange breathing air I couldn't see!" And you know how hard it is to find a river that is not polluted.

This dirty air and water is technological pollution. It is a sign that in the process of developing the earth we may be destroying it.

Of course there is always the possibility that we will self-destruct before pollution can get to us. We now have the capacity to kill every Russian ten times over. Cats have nine lives, so goes the popular saying. Presumably Russians have ten. And, of course, they have the same kind of overkill potential to unleash on us.

Maybe the fundamentalist can be forgiven for whispering under his or her breath, "I told you so!" "The tree the Autonomous Person has planted," he or she might well go on to say, "has produced a bitter fruit."

Artists feel the same as the rest of us. But sometimes they feel that way a little sooner. They first begin to sense intuitively what philosophers and theologians later begin to articulate and politicians eventually begin to expedite. They furnish a kind of early-warning system about the shape of things to come because they seem to have nerve endings a little closer to the center of existence than the average person. They sense or feel what the rest of us finally reason out.

The artist (whether painter, musician, or author), if he or she is an artist of genius, is concerned to speak the truth in his or her art. The artist does not paint or compose to please but to illuminate—to give some insight into how things are. Decorators seek for beauty; artists seek for truth. When the painting is ugly, or when the music is loud and dissonant and disturbing, or when the novel is dour and pessimistic, there is a reason. It is found in the soul of the artist. It is a portrayal of the truth as he or she feels it.

Thus we can look to art to see how people feel about themselves and their world. And when an artist has caught in his or her own soul the soul of the age, that work becomes a window into both.

Listen, for example, to the Gregorian chants of the medieval church. It is music with an ethereal quality. It is not earthly, materialistic music. It is spiritual. It rises to the heights. It seems unreal. It is at home echoing down through the corridors of some huge cathedral in semidarkness. It is bathed with light filtered through colored glass. It draws the mind away from the everyday world and into something far beyond itself. One would never hear it during dinner at a restaurant or even in a concert hall. It is an amorphous, flowing polyphony belonging more to heaven than to earth. The words are in a forgotten language, but it does not matter. For the language of the streets, like the life of the streets, is passing away. Man is reaching for his spiritual home.

Or look at Giotto's *Ognissanti Madonna*, painted during the early fourteenth century, at the crest of the medieval period.[4] The painting is organized, but with a kind of spiritual organization—as if all the answers to structure had come from another world. The people in the picture are in human form, but not really. If you look closely, they do not resemble anyone you have ever seen. For one thing, people do not come equipped with little disks (halos) over their heads. There is a kind of impassiveness on everyone's face. There is no human emotion there; they show calmness, rest, peace. It is as if the reality of them has left the world and we are looking at mere residue. The major figure sits in organized space. But it is not organized scientifically; it is organized according to the mystical qualities of the

[4]Luisa Marcucci and Emma Micheletti, *Medieval Painting* (New York: Viking, 1960), p. 119.

Giotto di Bondone, *Madonna and Child in Majesty*, ca. 1300. (The Uffizi Gallery, Florence, Italy)

spirit. The baby has the face of middle age. It is not quite like any human baby you have ever really seen. None of these people is doing anything that one normally does in this world. The postures suggest spiritual activities, not physical ones.

In this music and this art we have seen the world of the Medieval Person.

Johann Sebastian Bach (1685–1750) was a religious man and a believer in the reality of the spiritual world. Nevertheless, his music shows that he sensed a changing view of the world in the Europe of his day. While the scientists were beginning to conceive of a universe controlled by definite and definable laws, Bach, Haydn, and others were beginning to write music that was also controlled and organized and structured. The ethereal quality of the Gregorian chant slips into the background.

Michelangelo, *The Creation of Man*, Sistine Chapel ceiling/detail.
(Editorial Photocolor Archives, Inc.)

One can glance at a Bach composition on a sheet of paper and quickly see how precisely it is put together. Theme I is introduced . . . theme II . . . theme I in another key. Everything appears in neat eight- or sixteen-measure segments. Sound and emotion have been captured and fit into human boxes. The amorphous flow, the wandering polyphony of medieval music has been humanized and civilized. We are, the music seems to say, beginning to get hold of our world. We are getting things together. We are conquering.

The artists of the Renaissance had already sensed that humanity's concept of itself was changing. The change was apparent even in paintings on the walls of churches.

There is no more striking example than *Michelangelo*'s (1475–1564) painting of the creation of man on the ceiling of the Sistine Chapel in Rome. In this work, instead of human figures bathed in spiritual qualities, we find spiritual beings bathed in human qualities. Here is God with muscles, with a beard, almost naked. Here is God with extremely earthy qualities.

In the medieval religious paintings there were no muscles. Everyone was very placid and flat and smooth. Everyone was covered with long garments, so that the fleshly could be overlooked in favor of the spiritual. Michelangelo's humans are still weak (notice the limpness in the man's hand), but God is reaching out to touch him—to impart to him the qualities that will make him like God. So humanity is built physically like God. There

Seurat, *Sunday Afternoon on the Island of La Grande Jatte.* (The Art Institute of Chicago)

is strength there. The human has the potential to begin solving his or her own problems just as soon as the divine spark animates his or her strength. Humans are no longer to be thought of as weak, puny creatures who must clasp their hands and look up in prayer. They are, rather, about to be infused with power. They will be able to take care of themselves. They will get hold of things!

Georges Seurat (1859–1891), the French artist, painted *Sunday Afternoon on the Island of La Grande Jatte* at the very height of the Autonomous Period. Standing back a few feet one sees smartly dressed people strolling calmly through a park. One lady sports a parasol and a pet monkey. The gentlemen wear tall hats and unwrinkled shirts and coats.

When you get very close to the painting, you discover that the artist has actually put thousands of tiny dots on the canvas. They are unconnected. But when you move back, the dots begin to blend in the mind and trees and pets and ladies and gentlemen begin to appear. Everything is peaceful and calm. Everything is under control.

This is our world, says the artist. When you look at reality up close, you find it is a mass of little disconnected bits of data—tiny little things— easily manageable. All you have to do is put these little bits together and they become a beautiful afternoon in the park.

The scientists were saying very much the same thing. All problems can be solved by analysis because all complex matters are simply combinations of very simple matters. Once you break a thing down into its constituent parts you have control of it.

What then is a man, or a woman, or a monkey? Nothing more than combinations of these tiny dots. Standing back a bit one gets the impression of complex movement and color and beauty. But this is only because the bits have blended together in the mind. The scientists can use their microscopes and see the reality behind these impressions.

But Seurat's peaceful nineteenth-century afternoon nap soon became a screaming twentieth-century nightmare. The musicians heard the scream first. The fine order of Bach, carried with a flourish through the nineteenth-century Romantics, gave way to clash and discord. When disorder was reintroduced into music, it was not the flowing melodious spiritual disorder of medieval church music. It was rather a jarring, confusing, even annoying kind of dissonance. There is nothing to catch hold of. There are bursts of sound here and bursts of sound there—melodies running wild, clashing with each other, exploding like fireworks.

Listen, for example, to *Igor Stravinsky's* (1882–1971) *Rite of Spring*. You will never find yourself humming this piece! You will never tap your foot to it either! There seems to be no rhythmic order. There seems to be no melodic order. The sound is going anywhere and everywhere. There is an underlying chaos, sprinkled here and there with an unexpected moment of beauty that is soon lost again in the crashing discords.

Somehow, one gets the message. The world has come unglued. Humanity has not organized its world. There are no neat combinations of tiny dots that explain everything. Disorder is more real than order. Confusion is more real than confidence. Atonal music and serialism manifest not only the irrational element of life, but are also a protest against predictable endings.

What *Rite of Spring* does to the ears, *Guernica* does to the eyes. *Pablo Picasso* (1881–1973) had seen World War I, the Russian Revolution, the bloody Spanish Civil War, inflation, economic collapse, and the rise of fascist dictators. In *Guernica*, which commemorates the bombing of a small Spanish village, he seems to say that Seurat's tiny dots . . . all lined up to make neat places and neat little monkeys and parasols . . . are illusions. There is more truth, he says, in the senseless act of blowing a helpless village to smithereens. Of course, the blowing up of villages has become commonplace today. But for Picasso, at that time, it produced profound shock. How could he paint peaceful Sunday afternoons? How could he paint little Gothic windows full of placid Madonnas?

Instead, he drew screams. He drew people in pieces. There is almost no color. Everything is jumbled and out of place. Because of the protest against inhumanity, Paul Tillich saw powerful religious dimensions in it, particularly in its form. This suggests that the form held such power precisely because the self-conception of the present generation could no

Picasso, *Guernica*. (Museum of Modern Art)

longer be captured by earlier art forms. Probably the same was true with the new music of Stravinsky, Ives, Schönberg, Cage, and others.

The mass bombing, made possible by the Autonomous Person's great technology, had, like the sorcerer's apprentice in the old fairy tale, unleashed powers far beyond his own control. Chaos, like some dark primeval monster from the deep, had its hands in a vicelike grip around his throat.

World War I should have struck a staggering blow to the optimistic swagger of the nineteenth-century Autonomous Person. But, curiously, few beyond an artist or musician or writer here or there seemed to perceive the situation. It was as though the Autonomous Person had been stabbed with a ten-inch butcher knife and had somehow failed to notice!

Ernest Hemingway noticed. In a book of short stories called *Winner Take Nothing*, he describes a waiter in a small bar who senses the meaninglessness that was descending upon humanity. "What did he hear? It was not fear or dread. It was a nothing that he knew too well. It was all a nothing and man was nothing too." And so he turns to prayer. But the forces of secularization had robbed him of any god to hear those prayers. And so, using the Spanish word for "nothing" (*nada*), he prays: "Our nada who art in nada, nada be thy name. . . ." And even, "Hail Nothing, full of nothing. nothing is with thee. . . ."[5]

Albert Camus noticed. He began an essay by saying, "There is but one truly serious philosophical problem, and that is suicide."[6] We must, he said, begin with a "belief in the absurdity of existence,"[7] and then try to figure

[5]Ernest Hemingway, *Winner Take Nothing* (New York: Scribner, 1930), pp. 17–24.

[6]Albert Camus, *The Myth of Sisyhus and Other Essays*, trans. Justin O'Brien (New York: Knopf, 1961), p. 3.

[7]Ibid., p. 6.

out why to stay alive. Indeed, "the absurd becomes god"[8] in the absence of any other. The universe is meaningless, he says.

"But what does life mean in such a universe? Nothing else for the moment but indifference to the future and a desire to use up everything that is given. Belief in the meaning of life always implies a scale of values, a choice, our preferences. Belief in the absurd, according to our definitions, teaches the contrary."[9]

He found the human predicament pictured in the ancient Greek myth of Sisyphus, whom the gods condemned to rolling a stone to the top of a mountain over and over again. Each time the stone simply fell back down and Sisyphus began his senseless task once more. The gods figured, "with some reason," he stated, "that there is no more dreadful punishment than futile and hopeless labor."[10]

Still, Camus concluded that "one must imagine Sisyphus happy."[11] One must simply make the best of things and, in the words of a beer commercial, grab all "the gusto" one can. The same general conclusion was reached by other atheistic existentialist philosophers of the period like Jean Paul Sartre (who wrote plays with titles like *No Exit* and *Nausea*).

Writing in 1929, Joseph Wood Krutch called this way of thinking "the modern temper." Of it, he said,

> Unlike their grandfathers, those who are its victims, do not and never expect to believe in God; but unlike their spiritual fathers, the philosophers and scientists of the nineteenth century, they have begun to doubt that rationality and knowledge have any promised land into which they may be led.[12]

Of the "modern man," he said,

> Formerly he had believed in even his darkest moments that the universe was rational if he could only grasp its rationality, but gradually he comes to suspect that rationality is an attribute of himself alone and that there is no reason to suppose that his own life has any more meaning than the life of the humblest insect that crawls from one annihilation to another.[13]

His conclusion is

> Ours is a lost cause and there is no place for us in the natural universe.[14]

[8]Ibid., p. 33.
[9]Ibid., p. 60.
[10]Ibid., p. 119.
[11]Ibid., p. 123.
[12]Joseph Wood Krutch, *The Modern Temper* (New York: Harcourt Brace, 1929), p. xvi.
[13]Ibid., p. 9.
[14]Ibid., p. 249.

NAZISM: THE ULTIMATE HORROR

But the worst was yet to come. Friedrich Nietzsche had given philosophical justification to the idea that might makes right and that nature's methods of advancing itself (especially survival of the fittest) applied to human beings, who were, after all, only the "cleverest animals."

In post-World War I Germany, that citadel of modern scientific and technological achievement, these ideas were given practical application by an Austrian would-be painter named Adolf Hitler.

Nobel-prize-winning scientists like *Philipp Lenard* (1862–1947) and *Johannes Stark* (1874–1957), along with a host of others, provided a scientific rationale for Hitler's plan.[15] What scientific law was doing slowly, Hitler would do quickly. Select the fittest. Destroy the inferior. Goose-step into a Nazi heaven on earth! Has not nature itself taught us how to proceed? Humanity's destiny is to become Nietzsche's Superman. All thought of compassion must be put aside. Everything must be subjugated to the evolutionary advance to perfection. In the name of science, the inferior must be eliminated. Anything else would be "unnatural."

There were those who spoke out against what was happening. The "confessional church," led by courageous individuals such as Martin Niemöller, condemned the mounting tide of human atrocities, in the name of a higher law. But the god of the higher law had been driven from too many minds. Had not science given people their freedom from such gods? Were not people alone in the world responsible for building their own heaven? The Nazi machine rolled on.

The horrors of the Nazi era boggle the mind. There is no parallel in history for what happened. The stories fill thousands of pages, each covered with blood and death. The victims number in the millions. No ancient barbarian horde ever came close to equaling the record of destruction left by this "modern" and "scientific" attempt to create the super race.

Eugen Kogan's book, *The Theory and Practice of Hell*, gives us only a small introduction to the horror:[16]

Item: Dr. Sigmund Rascher, of the German Air Force Medical Service, wished to find out whether humans can stay alive while rapidly ascending to high altitudes. Naturally, he would use the scientific method to find out:

---

[15]See George L. Mosse, *Nazi Culture: Intellectual, Cultural, and Social Life in the Third Reich* (New York: Grosset, 1966), pp. 197 ff.

[16]Eugene Kogan, *The Theory and Practice of Hell*, trans. Heinz Norden (New York: Farrar, Straus & Giroux, 1973). The Nazi horrors are well documented. A parallel series of horrors that occurred in Soviet Russia during the same period are gradually coming to light. The works of Aleksandr Solzhenitsyn furnish a chilling introduction to this matter.

A mobile unit was set up at Dachau in the camp street, between Block 5 and the adjacent barracks. The area was isolated from the other hospital buildings so that outside observation was impossible. The unit consisted of a high enclosed box on wheels, with built-in instruments for the measurement of pressure, temperature and altitude. Heart action of the subjects was measured by an electro-cardiograph. Autopsies were conducted immediately upon death ("the blood does not yet boil at an altitude of 70,000 feet" reads the final report of the three "experts," dated July 28, 1942). On one occasion, during an autopsy, Rascher found the heart of the victim still beating. He thereupon instituted a whole series of killings, solely for the purpose of establishing the length of time during which the human heart remained active after death.[17]

Item: Professor Holzlöhner of Kiel conducted experiments on the effect of chilling on warm-blooded organisms. Dr. Rascher cooperated:

During the first period the subjects, clothed or stripped, were immersed in water of 39° to 48° until they grew stiff. Temperature was measured rectally by thermo-electric means. There were fifty to sixty subjects and fifteen to eighteen fatalities. During the second period Rascher also used another method. Prisoners were exposed to the cold winter air (4 to 13° F. below zero) overnight. When their screams created too much of a disturbance, Rascher finally used anesthesia. According to the testimony of an eyewitness, the former inmate Walter Neff, Rascher immersed two Russian officers, brought from the camp prison, naked in ice water. It took them five hours to die.[18]

Item: Late in 1942, Professor Hirt, a Strasbourg anatomist, suggested to Hitler that a collection of skulls and skeletons of various "inferior" types be created for use at the Strasbourg University Institute of Anatomy:

The SS Main Economic and Administrative Office immediately instructed Auschwitz to make concentration camp inmates available for this purpose, and 115 persons were selected—seventy-nine Jewish men, thirty Jewish women, two Poles and two Asiatics. They were shipped to the Natzweiler camp, where they were gassed with cyanide which Professor Hirt gave the Camp Commandant for the purpose.[19]

Three years after these events, *H. G. Wells* (1866–1946), one of the most enthusiastic supporters of the autonomy of man and the inevitability of scientific progress, wrote a sad and cynical book called *Mind at the End of Its Tether*. Himself near the end of life, Wells pronounced the whole movement to which he had given his efforts a failure. How much Nazi horrors pressed upon his mind we do not know.

"The writer," he said, "sees the world as a jaded world devoid of recuperative power. In the past he has liked to think that man could pull out of his entanglements and start a new creative phase of human living. In the

[17]Ibid., p. 153.
[18]Kogan, *The Theory and Practice of Hell*, p. 154.
[19]Ibid., p. 160.

face of our universal inadequacy that optimism has given place to a stoical cynicism. Man must go steeply up or down and the odds seem all in favor of his going down and out. . . ."[20]

Hopes for the future? They are, said Wells, "the remembered shouts of angry people in a train that has passed and gone forever."[21] Camus had argued that although the world was meaningless, at least we should not kill ourselves. As for Hemingway, on the morning of July 2, 1961, he placed the muzzles of a silver-inlaid shotgun in his mouth and pulled both triggers.

[20]H. G. Wells, *Mind at the End of Its Tether* (New York: Didier, 1945), p. 17.
[21]Ibid., p. 2.

12

Religion
and the Future

We make no pretense to have prophetic power to predict what the next century will bring regarding religion. In any case, the demise of religion predicted by some leading thinkers of the last century now appears a bit presumptuous and methodologically insufficient, whether we speak of Comte, Freud, Marx, or Weber.

RELIGION, SOCIETY, AND POLITICS

The future of religion could consist of further splintering of large religious institutions. Certainly the history of religion in the United States has seemingly almost followed cycles in which the Spirit would reactivate or become a dynamic force when the institutions became too large, too preoccupied with dogma or with self-preservation, or too closed to change or addressing people's real needs at the time.

Or the future of religion could rest in the hands of those groups which emphasize the most their connection with the past. We now know that scholars who predicted religion's demise in a secular and technological world evidently miscalculated the strength of tradition and the power religious symbols carry even on subconscious levels.[1] There is little doubt that conservative religious movements, which have made a point to insist that they do not have to adjust to the modern world, have not disappeared from the scene. In fact, fundamentalism, especially in its militant role, opposing what it considers the most godless current agents or ideas, is flourishing in the United States. But time does not stand still, and the past cannot be re-captured or simplistically referred to for relevant answers to all questions in a world which it did not even anticipate. So this may not be a viable pic-ture of religion in the next century.

On the other hand, religious institutions that have at times changed things too fast have found that their attraction for the masses has dissipa-ted. There may be a number of reasons for this, including the fact that reli-gion, as "ultimate concern," is usually experienced in an absolutistic way. So although one intellectually may see a need for change, to enact change tends to threaten that feeling of absoluteness. Religion has a definite tie with the past that cannot be denied. Paul Tillich made us aware that if reli-gious symbols are not created consciously, they also cannot be changed con-sciously. Rather, the change must occur in the communal unconsciousness. This implies that significant ideological change comes very slowly, a factor that "mainstream" Protestant churches in the United States have ignored, perhaps to their own detriment.

If it be true that religious symbols cannot simply be changed at will since they cannot be reduced to serving merely cognitive functions, this probably also suggests that at the least the immediate future of religion in the United States will not be characterized by significant conversions from Western to Eastern religions or vice-versa. The voguishness of such conver-sions that swept especially college-age students in the 1960s has been super-seded by a deeper understanding, namely, that a religion so steeped in an-other culture cannot be readily understood. Understanding and even conversions can occur, of course. But in some cases, those conversions now seem in retrospect to have involved a rather superficial trading of familiar symbols for unfamiliar symbols.

On the other hand, the tremendous immigration from the East, espe-cially to some of the larger metropolitan areas of the United States, has brought a new awareness and confrontation of varied cultures with the "other." It may be that significant religious activity will occur only as these religions, so deeply intertwined with their cultures, are brought into daily practical dialogue. So it is that many scholars feel that the future of religion appears to be in a new community consciousness, a global community con-

---

[1]Richard Rubenstein some years ago explored religious symbols and rituals in Judaism from both a theological and a psychological standpoint, showing their power on noncognitive levels. Rubenstein, *After Auschwitz: Radical Theology and Contemporary Judaism* (Indianapolis, Ind.: Bobbs-Merrill, 1966).

sciousness. Even as early as 1973, religious leaders and sociologists were speaking like this as they recognized that religion seemed after all to persist in the modern or postmodern world.[2]

This new global consciousness, with a new sense of responsibility toward all humanity, need not be only a moral emphasis, nor need it be strictly humanistic. The solidarity people are feeling has moral imperatives that are rooted in all the significant religions. And these imperatives are being discovered or rediscovered in this global context. But as a prerequisite for this global consciousness and common life together, we are hearing a great deal today about the need for personal conversion, changed consciousness, openness to the transcendent, an inner peace, altered priorities, a de-emphasis upon the material in our acquisitive societies, an awareness that life is found in being rather than having.[3]

We certainly are becoming aware that for religion to be a vital part of a society, it will have to be significantly operative at the grass roots level. So there is much talk today that religion's future probably lies in "base communities."[4] The precise relationship of these with some "official" theology or position of the larger "religions" is not at all certain. The primary independence of such base communities in developing over many decades and centuries their own unique religious symbols cannot be denied. Whether the unique mentalities of such communities preclude a global consciousness is not clear; certainly a global consciousness need not obliterate all the particular ethnic quality of religions.

While theorizing will continue among the intellectuals in the religions, it appears currently that, at least in the immediate future, praxis—the practical application of our theoretical and moral concerns—will become increasingly important, even as a criteria for theology. From this standpoint, it may be doubtful to many that religion will be able to identify itself separately from a "secular" world. So most religions have had to grapple recently with the complex world rather than dismiss it. And most have found, in one way or another, that economics, science, politics, and so on are too important not to be addressed by religion.[5] Fundamentalist groups formerly opposed to a "social gospel" have found the necessity of trying to influence the secular agencies of our culture through means like the "Moral Majority." And higher education has been accused of becoming so secularized as to become indifferent to moral judgments that are absolutely

---

[2]Andrew Greeley and Gregory Baum, eds., *The Persistence of Religion* (New York: Herder and Herder, 1973).

[3]E.g. Dorothee Soelle, *Choosing Life*, trans. Margaret Kohl (Philadelphia: Fortress, 1981).

[4]Harvey Cox sees this not simply as religion's future in third-world countries, but even in the United States, with its "secular city." Cox, *Religion in the Secular City* (New York: Simon & Schuster, 1984).

[5]E.g. John C. Bennett, *The Radical Imperative: From Theology to Social Ethics* (Philadelphia: Westminster, 1975).

necessary for carrying on civilization.[6] So praxis will at least be the focal point of religion in the immediate future.

RELIGION, SCIENCE, AND HEALTH

Science is likely here to stay. And that means that its application, technology, is also. We have tried to suggest that technology need not unleash the demons, provided it is built upon religion or "ultimate concern." But we have at times experienced the demonic side of it by our own failures to care enough or to inform our projects with a sense of transcendence of purpose.

In retrospect, we are not sure the discovery and utilization of the atomic bomb was an unequivocal good. Perhaps it may even become evident to us one day that its utilization on Hiroshima and Nagasaki showed myopic vision, short-term purposes, or shortsightedness. The jury is still out on that. And although there was a different motivation in the discovery of DNA than in the splitting of the atom, that too has not been hailed as an unambiguous good. Science and technology, when pressed into the service of individual ambition, corporate greed, or national prestige and security, can and has short-circuited the high-quality life most of us actually desire for humanity as a whole.

Nevertheless, the rigorous scientific method, though it may be modified in different human enterprises, is not likely to be soon outgrown or abandoned because of technological abuse, the Holocaust, space-shuttle tragedies, the Chernobyl disaster, terrorism, or other misadventures. The real question for the future is whether technology will be regulated morally. And more specifically, whether the moral standard by which it is weighed is transparent to the Ultimate, or self-critical enough to dissolve its own cultural particularity in order to manifest the *universal good*. That is where religion or ultimate concern cannot be separated from science and technology. That is where the vision and input of the global community are indispensable.

The exact forms that the future will introduce regarding this important relationship are hard to perceive at this time. New theoretical alliances may become more than the special interests of a few scientifically inclined theologians. The continuing process of life as we experience it may be consciously or unconsciously more influential in shaping pictures of deity, as recent emphasis on the philosophy of Whitehead shows. A dialogue between this "process philosophy," representatives of various religions, and scientists may produce new models for the relationship of religion and science in the future.

[6]Allan Bloom, *The Closing of the American Mind: How Higher Education Has Failed Democracy and Impoverished the Souls of Today's Students* (New York: Simon & Schuster, 1987).

Unless we are to resort once again to a dehumanized science or a ghettoized religion, we must move beyond the idea that religion and science can best preserve their own interests by refusing to talk any common language with each other. Of course, the "objectivity" of scientific method requires a detachment that seems the opposite of the subjective involvement of a religious person. But, at a deeper level, even the religious person objectifies the religious subject and experience, and even the scientist is committed to basic views or truths that he or she cannot prove with his or her detached analysis.[7]

Whether the emerging new theoretical alliances of religions and science will be embraced on the grass roots level of religion may be dubious. But what many of the new theological explorations are emphasizing is praxis. And that they have in common with people at the grass roots level. For here the question of whether or not to utilize technology to control birth, to artificially inseminate, to abort, to administer active euthanasia, to build nuclear power plants, and so on is very real. And people who consider themselves religious will never feel comfortable when faced with such decisions unless they can convince themselves that their decisions are consistent with their religion rather than simply dictated by technological possibilities.

So we are talking about science and technology in service to humanity rather than controlling humanity. If the old exaggerated scientism that saw science itself curing all society's ills single-handedly has now been outgrown, so have the narrow and selfish nationalistic concerns in many situations been left behind. Only a few years ago, it was argued that since earth's resources are limited, and since science can do only so much with this built-in restriction, altruism and good intentions have their limit in the "lifeboat" of our earth. But in subsequent years, through continual reminders by the media of world problems that could be addressed by science if we had only a spirit of love, people in every country have begun to respond to these world-wide problems. A global consciousness and single history does not grow up overnight. But the unselfishness present in every religion may serve as a vital factor in fostering a willingness to sacrifice our own comforts to help meet the necessities of other humans.

Some have even suggested that perhaps the very values inherent within the scientific method, such as honesty, tolerance of dissent, objectivity, equality in input, and so on, may be the way the world will finally tie itself together in a united effort toward the good life. Perhaps it will come in increased cooperation between rival nations in space exploration, or in medical breakthroughs that spare a civilization on the borderline of extinction. Whether this humane effort is generated from specific religious

[7]Tillich insisted that even the natural scientist utilized "kairos" and decision rather than making discoveries simply according to the "logos" or rational structure of the object analyzed. The same types of bridging of the formerly "two-language" approach to religion and science can be found in writings by Bernard Lonergan and Stephen Toulmin.

influence or is simply elicited from the moral sensitivity of the scientific method will probably not matter, since even the values thought to be inherent in scientific method may be "ultimate concern," which is religion in its broadest sense.

But what about the "mythical" world of religions as opposed to the literal world with which science operates? Will not the future see just a widening of the gap between religion and science on this issue? Will the evolution controversies grow in intensity to the point of discrediting religion, splitting our citizenry against itself, or prohibiting the theory and practice of science as it is now known? This is a possibility, but hopefully it will not occur.

Perhaps fundamentalists in various religions will continue to fight the idea that their scriptures contain myth, since they consider myth to mean "untrue." But perhaps those who are familiar with many religions may convince them as well as scientists that myths are a necessary part of all religions as they are of all human life. In this sense, a myth is not a fabrication about a historical incident that did not occur but rather a narrative involving something beyond the visible natural world that serves to evoke in the person a sense of ultimate meaning and being. For example, it may be a "myth" that any American that desires can become president of the United States. As a historical possibility, of course, it is absurd. But as an expression of self-confidence, of hope of almost unlimited potential in this country, of the upward movement so characteristic of citizens of the United States—it expresses truth. And it expresses truth for one who receives it, enough to shape his or her life by what it means.

RELIGION, RACE, AND SEX

As a conservator of traditions and values of the past, religion has naturally caught flak on many issues. Some religions, of course, were ethnically oriented from the outset. Others have picked up concepts of their "election" or special status before deity that has at times manifested itself in immoral acts toward other races or ethnic groups. And most religions we know of have been in the past controlled by men rather than women. So women's roles in those societies were usually subordinate to men.

The global vision or world-wide communal consciousness we have mentioned already is a vision especially enjoyed by the more egalitarian societies. It may be that the literal vision of human problems that is supplied by the mass media will in fact be one of the most significant instruments in transforming societies into an egalitarian nature.

In any case, in egalitarian societies, "justice" has apparently become the most overarching concept and ideal, even more so than "peace" or "freedom." For this reason, racial and sexual discrimination has appeared most repugnant to citizens of such societies. We have become aware that even religious leaders, however, can be influenced to uphold unjust laws when their own material interests are at stake.

Yet in all fairness to religion, civil protests for justice have usually been more supported by religious leaders and religious groups than by politicians or individuals or groups of nonreligious character. What this means is that despite how some have ridiculed religious institutions for conserving, for simply following tradition, for even trying to upset the status quo—which has often been true—religion has directly or indirectly also shaped the most telling critiques of racial and sexual bigotry. Probably the reason for this, especially on the level of individual lay protestors, is that religion has been the most unlikely sphere in which one's ideals could be corrupted. There appeared little personal reward (other than simply the knowledge that one was trying to stand for the right) for participation in a civil rights march or demonstration, just as there was little personal reward to Buddhist monks who turned themselves into flaming torches to protest the Vietnam war.

This is not to say that we have arrived. There is still evidence of racial and sexual discrimination deeply within the structures of the most religious and most "Christian" parts of the U.S. culture. We still have had no black or woman as president. Poverty experienced by blacks and other minorities has not been seriously addressed for years. Many doors open in our society to whites and males are still closed to blacks and women. All one has to do is look at the highest positions in corporations, in law firms, and so on to realize that "ultimate concern" or religion, with its global consciousness, has a long way to go toward achieving justice even in our own country. In intellectual circles, we are just now beginning to realize how ethnically circumscribed have been not simply our hierarchical values schemes but even our theories of knowledge.

RELIGION AND RELIGIONS

What does the future hold for the relationship of any particular religion with other religions, or the relationship between our definition of religion as "ultimate concern" and the many different religions? No one can be sure.

What we can be sure of is that, as we suggested in an earlier part of this book, even the category and definitions of religion are Western and of fairly recent vintage. This fact should suggest that the issue of what belongs within this category of "religion" is not closed. We may be only in the beginning stages of systematically defining "religion" (or whatever we elect to call it) on the basis of real facts rather than imagined stereotypes.

Whether any definition will prove over the long haul to be sufficient in scope while not reductionistic is still not clear. But new studies are suggesting that even the hard historical data of the religions which we have been looking at for several decades must be seen in a much larger historical and sociological context.[8] We are not yet able to gain consensus that important ideas in one religion have their rather close-fitting parallels in other religions. There may be the equivalent of Christian "faith" in other religions—in a very generic sense. Or there may not be. If the latter is true, it would be inaccurate as well as inappropriate to refer to people belonging to other religions as "anonymous Christians." It may be that the implicit trust inherent in the idea of faith in its more general sense in Christianity and Judaism has counterparts in other religions. Or it may be that the differences are actually so great, that the mere idea of "trust" or "decision to trust," if illuminative for "religious" parallels, remains insufficient to distinguish religious faith from any other kind of faith. It may be that important concepts such as "incarnation," "soul," "spirit," "life," "salvation," "suffering," "death," and so on can serve for genuine dialogue or interchange of ideas between the various religions. But they must not be "leveled down" to the lowest common denominator, nor must one refuse to see common elements simply because one wants to retain superiority for his or her religion.

The future study of religions among intellectuals will not likely assume the superiority of one religion over the others, since they will reject such an assumption as not being objective. The dogmatic approach, which was concerned with the superiority of one religion, did emphasize the absoluteness which the true religious experience is conceded by many to take. That is, it understood the finality of a final revelation, or the absoluteness of the religious experience. So it dictated that one had to be closed to any other religion. For to seriously consider another was to doubt one's own experience, and doubt was taken to dislodge one from salvation or the Ultimate. But many scholars have considered doubt and examination as essentials to the pursuit of truth and have therefore abandoned this *a priori* exclusivistic posture.

On the other hand, if scholars are truly open to the actual data of various religions' practices as well as ideals, they cannot assume that one or more religions will not be superior to the others. Understanding and appreciation must precede judgment. And it will likely be so among the scholars.

But we cannot be sure that such an open or tolerant view will be adopted by the masses of humanity. That is, we cannot be sure that the

---

[8]Two of the more illuminating recent studies from a rather Christian viewpoint are Wilfred Cantwell Smith, *Towards a World Theology: Faith and the Comparative History of Religion* (Philadelphia: Westminster, 1981), and Hans Kung, *Christianity and the World Religions: Paths of Dialogue with Islam, Hinduism, and Buddhism* (Garden City, N.Y.: Doubleday, 1986). Of more substantial dialogue is the series being published by Paragon House Pub. of New York under the title of "New ERA books" (New ERA designating "New Ecumenical Research").

majority of people belonging to any particular religion will sincerely even want to understand and appreciate others' religions enough to study them. There seems to be no indication that people who belong to a particular religion are as a whole more receptive to other religions then they used to be. The majority remain almost totally uncritical of their own religion. And the less self-critical the religious movement, the more accelerated seems to be its growth.

What this points to is that perhaps the greatest issues in the area of the relationship of a particular religion to other religions will be: (1) the issue of whether growth of the particular community is deemed more important than truth, or truth is sought regardless of how it may affect growth; (2) how to bridge the gap between the intellectual understandings of religion or any specific religion and the common lay understandings; and (3) the degree of validity religion can have for those who have little understanding of even the single religion to which they belong, and little desire to learn more. History suggests that none of these issues is new.

CONCLUSION

This book has tried to introduce the student to the phenomenon of "religion" and, as a part of the process, to suggest some of the tension that grew in the West as culture appeared to shift basic paradigms. There is no easy answer for either what has occurred or for what should occur. And certainly we can make no claims on knowing the direction this important phenomenon will take in the future. But the first step to understanding religion is to realize, as Tillich suggested, that it is the substance of a culture, as culture is the particular form it takes.

The focus and scope of this book has, by design, been very narrow. But by such a brief introduction, perhaps the student will be encouraged to pick up the challenge to continue to search for the answers to the great questions which have been raised, and thus become a more responsible world citizen.

Index